James Dvorscak
1977

EVERLASTING LIFE AFTER DEATH

Everlasting Life
After Death

E. J. FORTMAN, S.J.

ALBA · HOUSE NEW · YORK

SOCIETY OF ST. PAUL, 2187 VICTORY BLVD., STATEN ISLAND, NEW YORK 10314

ACKNOWLEDGMENTS

Raymond E. Brown, S.S., Joseph A. Fitzmyer, S.J., Roland E. Murphy, O.Carm., THE JEROME BIBLICAL COMMENTARY,© 1968. Reprinted by permission of Prentice-Hall, Inc., Englewood Cliffs, N. J.

Ladislaus Boros, THE MYSTERY OF DEATH,© 1965 by Burns and Oates, Ltd. Reprinted with permission by Seabury Press, New York.

Karl Rahner, THEOLOGY OF DEATH and THE COMING OF HIS KINGDOM (Sacramentum Mundi). Reprinted with permission of Verlag Herder KG, Freiburg i Br.

Library of Congress Cataloging in Publication Data

Fortman, Edmund J   1901-
     Everlasting life after death.

     Bibliography: p.
     1. Future life. I. Title.
     BT902.F67   236'.2   76-41186
     ISBN 0-8189-0333-3

Imprimi Potest:
Daniel L. Flaherty, S.J.
Provincial, Chicago Province

Nihil Obstat:
Daniel V. Flynn, J.C.D.
Censor Librorum

Imprimatur:
✠ James P. Mahoney, D.D.
Vicar General, Archdiocese of New York
August 16, 1976

*Designed, printed and bound in the United States of
America by the Fathers and Brothers of the Society of St. Paul,
2187 Victory Boulevard, Staten Island, New York, 10314,
as part of their communications apostolate.*

1 2 3 4 5 6 7 8 9 (Current Printing: first digit).

DEDICATION

The author extends his deepest gratitude to all at Jesuit Retreat House, and especially to Rev. Patrick J. Boyle, S.J., for giving him the opportunity to finish this book.

FOREWORD

Today there seems to be a growing disbelief in life after death. Yet down the centuries men have been fascinated by the thought of a life after death. Would they survive death and be the same persons? Would they remember what had happened in their earthly lives? Would they be with and recognize and communicate with other people? Would they go on learning and loving, growing and living a really human life? Or would death be the end of everything?

If we can judge by the history of religions, most men have had some belief in some sort of survival of death. There is solid evidence of this belief in an afterlife in Paleolithic, Mesolithic, Neolithic times, as well as in ancient Greece, India, China, Assyria, Babylonia, Persia, Egypt, Rome. Men in every part of the world have professed belief in life after death.

But in our Western world in recent times belief in an afterlife has declined considerably. Surveys made by *Lumen Vitae* from 1947 to 1968 in Great Britain, Sweden, France, Netherlands, Finland, Norway, show that belief in a hereafter is decreasing everywhere. In every one of these countries there are more people who believe in God than in the hereafter. Everywhere in the U.S. belief in God is more general than belief in the hereafter. And in Eastern U.S. belief in a hereafter is rarer than in the rest of the country. Disbelief now touches deeply every country, age, profession, even the clergy and every religious denomination. "What is striking at the present time," says Dr. Aldwinckle, "is the degree to which thinkers who claim to be Christian have capitulated to this modern mood and seek to interpret the Gospel in purely 'this-worldly' terms." Schubert Ogden has written: "But what I must refuse to accept, precisely as a Christian theologian, is that belief in our subjective existence after death is in some way a necessary article of Christian belief."[1]

Why this growing disbelief in an afterlife? Is it due to the climate of rationalism and scepticism that has spread over the world since the eighteenth century? Is it due to the scientists and psychologists who claim they have proved that there is nothing in man that can survive death, nothing that capacitates him for continued personal existence and activity after death? Is it due to biblical critics who reject the traditional doctrine of an afterlife because it involves an excessively literal interpretation of biblical language and is built on a mythical view of the world as a three-storied universe, a view that is totally unacceptable today? Is it due to the fact that dogmas are a large part of the traditional doctrine of an afterlife, the dogmas of purgatory, hell, heaven, parousia, resurrection, judgment, and contemporary men find dogmas opposed to their conviction that all truths are relative and contingent? Is it due to the fact that many contemporary men find the doctrine of a predestining God who is responsible for a disembodied afterlife in purgatory, hell, heaven, utterly unattractive? Is it due to the theologians of hope who talk so much about man's future on this earth that they leave the impression that that is the only hope he has? Is it due to the fact that so many men today are so absorbed in securing the basic necessities for survival in this life that they have no interest in another life after death?

All of these factors and many others may well share the responsibility for man's growing disbelief in an afterlife. And so a book about life after death seems to be a very timely undertaking. But rather foolhardy also. For scientists today often bluntly reject such a life after death as impossible. Philosophers often ignore it. Scripture scholars and theologians quarrel over it. Christians themselves are strongly divided about it, many rejecting a temporary purgatory, very many rejecting an eternal hell, some even rejecting any kind of life after death at all. We are living in a period of widespread, intense and radical criticism of just about everything, God and Church and Scripture and Man and State.

That is why it might seem foolhardy to write about life after death today. Might it not be much better to wait until some of the dust of this devastating criticism settles a bit?

To wait for this to happen might mean a long, long wait. And the matter is too serious. For it is a matter of life and death, of death and life. If there is a life after death, and if there is a connection between a man's life before death and his life after death, then it is important to say this today and to say it again and again. And to back this up with as much evidence as possible. To some extent other writers have already done this in different ways and different degrees of conviction. But there is room for another effort. An effort by one who is not a scientific or philosophical sceptic or monist, by one who is not a disinterested observer nor a radical demythologiser, but by one who is a Christian theologian and a strong believer in life after death for all men. There is room for an effort to establish the reality of life after death as solidly as possible and to present this reality as attractively as possible.

My starting point will be the traditional Catholic doctrine of life after death and my aim will be to study and evaluate this against the background of today's biblical, theological, historical, scientific thinking. The basic Catholic doctrine of life after death has been this: (1) there is life after death in a disembodied condition for every human being until the general resurrection, and this involves a particular judgment at death, a temporary purgatory for some, a permanent hell and heaven and probably a permanent limbo; (2) at the Parousia of Christ there will be a general resurrection of all men, a general judgment of all men, followed by everlasting life for all men either in heaven or in hell.

In the study and evaluation of this traditional doctrine there are five basic questions: (1) will men actually have life after death? (2) if a man lives on after the death of his body, does he live on in virtue of a naturally immortal soul? (3) what connection is there between a man's life before death and his life after death? (4) does a man have life immediately after death and does this life continue in an interim state that perdures until the general judgment and what kind of life is this? (5) does a man go on living endlessly after the general resurrection and what kind of life does he have in this final state? To deal with these five basic questions the book is divided into five Parts: I. The Mystery of Life after Death: does every man actually have life after death? II. The Mystery of Man: if a man lives on after the death of his body, does he live on in virtue of a naturally immortal soul? III. The Mystery of Death: what happens to a man in death and what connection is there between a man's death and his life after death? IV. The Mystery of the Interim State: is there an interim state of existence and activity for all men which involves a particular judgment, a purgatory, a limbo, a hell, a heaven? V. The Mystery of the Final State: is there a final state of everlasting personal existence and activity for all men, which involves a parousia, a general resurrection and judgment, a new creation with a new heaven and a new earth?

For evidence of this afterlife we turn to the History of Religions and its record of after-life beliefs, to Spiritualism and its purported communications from the departed, and to Reincarnationism and its purported multiple reincarnations of every man. We look to Psychology and Parapsychology to see if they give us indications or evidence of man's destiny to and capacity for life after death. But most of all we look to the witness of Sacred Scripture in the sacred writings of the Old Testament and of the New Testament, and to the witness of the Church in the writings of the early Fathers and in the ecumenical Creeds and Councils.

Sacred Scripture is our most important source of evidence for life after death. For obviously God knows whether there is such a life after death for all men, and if He has chosen to reveal this to men, we can expect to find this revelation or hints of it in the Old Testament and the New Testament, which are the Word of God consigned to writing under the inspiration of the Holy Spirit. But Sacred Scripture is not our only source of evidence. It is not altogether self-sufficient, it is not always 'sui interpres,' it is not "norma normans non normata," as some theologians mistakenly contend. It is not a book that has dropped full blown from heaven. In a sense it is a book "of the Church," for the Church "defines the Bible as the Word of God and determines the canon of the sacred books."[2] It is a book transmitted by the

Church and needing at times to be interpreted by that Church. "Consequently, it is not from Sacred Scripture alone that the Church draws her certainty about everything which has been revealed. Therefore, both sacred tradition and Sacred Scripture are to be accepted and venerated" for they "form one sacred deposit of the Word of God, which is committed to the Church."[3] "The task of authentically interpreting the Word of God . . . has been entrusted exclusively to the living teaching office of the Church, whose authority is exercised in the name of Jesus Christ. This teaching office is not above the Word of God, but serves it, teaching only what has been handed on, and explaining it faithfully by divine commission and with the help of the Holy Spirit" (ibid).

So we look to the Church also, to the living teaching office of the Church, for evidence of life after death. We study the early Christian Fathers and writers, to learn how they read and understood the biblical witness to life after death. Even when they disagree in their interpretations they still offer us valuable evidence for they help us to see how one view gradually gained wider and wider acceptance until it became common and perhaps defined doctrine, under the guidance of the Holy Spirit. Then we turn to the early Christian Creeds that profess the faith of the universal Church, and to the early Christian councils, especially the ecumenical, dogmatic, councils that define for the universal Church what is to be believed by the universal Church.

Today there is a growing tendency among some theologians to down-grade ecumenical councils. To question their "ecumenicity" on the score of lack of universal representation, as if numerical universality were required for the ecumenicity and functional and obligational universality were not enough. I don't share this view. There is also a growing tendency to question the infallibility of these conciliar definitions on the grounds that the day of "absolutes" is over and so there is no absolute truth and we are free to reject any and every dogmatic statement or definition of council or pope. I do not share this view, for it is an excessively reactionary view that hopefully will gradually achieve greater objectivity. For an ecumenical council is still one of the most highly qualified witnesses of the Word of God that we can find. We may perhaps have to reconsider and update some of its words and concepts, its biblical and patristic foundations, but the basic affirmation of these conciliar definitions so carefully worked out with the assistance of the Holy Spirit will always remain true.

In this growing tendency to down-grade ecumenical councils there is, of course, a corresponding tendency to down-grade "dogmas" on the part of some of our more "modern" theologians, on the score of the historicity of these "dogmas." In this it is interesting to note what B. J. F. Lonergan, S.J., wrote in his *Method in Theology:* "The permanence of the meaning of dogmas was taught in the constitution, *Dei Filius* (DS 3020, 3043). Hence there is ever to be retained that meaning of the sacred dogmas that once was declared by the Church.... The meaning of the dogma is not apart from a verbal formulation, for it is a meaning declared by the Church. However, the permanence attaches to the meaning and not to the formula ... What God has revealed and the Church has infallibly declared, is true. What is true, is permanent: the meaning it possessed in its own context can never be denied truthfully.... The dogmas are permanent in their meaning because they are not just data but expressions of truths, and, indeed, of truths that, were they not revealed by God, could not be known by man. Once they are revealed and believed, they can be better and better understood.... Nor is this opposed to the historicity of the dogmas. For dogmas are statements. Statements have meaning only within their contexts.... What permanently is true, is the meaning of the dogma in the context in which it was defined."[4]

Today some historians also seem intent on down-grading papal and conciliar infallibility. Brien Tierney maintains that "in reality there is no convincing evidence that papal infallibility formed any part of the theological or canonical tradition of the Church before the thirteenth century. The doctrine was invented in the first place by a few dissident Franciscans, because it suited their convenience to invent it. Eventually, after much initial reluctance, it was accepted by the papacy because it suited the convenience of the popes to accept it." And Francis Oakley "calls for a general council to renounce the claim of infallibility for any particular papal or conciliar decrees." Then he adds that "even if this were to happen it must be remembered that no particular pronouncements would be infallible, even one that denied its own infallibility."[5]

Tierney is well aware that an historian cannot do the theologian's work but it seems that to some extent he is trying to do just that, and doing it not very well. He seems to think that if the doctrine of papal infallibility was not explicitly enunciated before the thirteenth century, it simply was non-existent before the thirteenth century but was invented in the thirteenth century. However, many doctrines existed implicitly long before they were explicitly developed and defined: they were present implicitly in either Scripture or tradition or both. The dogma of the triune God was not explicitly enunciated in Sacred Scripture, nor was it explicitly enunciated in any of the early ecumenical councils. It was not explicitly and definitively enunciated until the time of the "Athanasian Creed" or of Lateran IV. And yet the "raw material" for this dogma was already present in the New Testament, and the Holy Spirit in His own way and in His own time worked quietly in and on the Church's magisterium until it brought forth explicitly and formally and definitively our dogma of the triune God.

The same thing holds true for papal infallibility, as the First Vatican Council noted when it declared that "this Holy See has always held that the supreme power of teaching is also included in this apostolic primacy which the Roman Pontiff, as the successor of St. Peter . . . holds over the whole Church" (DS 3065). And also when it declared that "the Roman Pontiffs . . . sometimes calling together ecumenical councils or sounding out the mind of the Church throughout the world, sometimes through regional councils, or sometimes by using other helps which divine Providence supplied, have, with the help of God, defined to be held such matters as .they had found consonant with the Holy Scripture and with the apostolic tradition" (DS 3069). Was papal infallibility not also implied when the Council of Florence defined that "the Roman Pontiff is the true vicar of Christ, the head of the whole Church, the father and teacher of all Christians" (DS 1307)? Or when the Second Council of Lyons declared that "just as the holy Roman Church is bound more than all the others to defend the truth of faith, so, if there arise any questions concerning the faith, they must be decided by its judgment" (DS 861)? Or when the Fathers of the Council of Chalcedon accepted the Tome of Pope Leo as an accurate expression of traditional teaching? Was papal infallibility not implied in the Formula of Pope St. Hormisdas, which later councils accepted? Or in the teaching of St. Augustine and St. Peter Chrysologus? Or in the sermons of Pope St. Leo? Or in the ancient rule that was widely accepted in the early Church, to the effect that "the Roman Pontiff without a council can condemn heresies and define doctrinal points, but without the Pope neither can there be an ecumenical council nor can churches declare anything definitively?"[6]

Some theologians are declaring that papal infallibility is not necessary, as if that proved it was non-existent. But in manualist theology not even "ecumenical councils are absolutely necessary,"[7] although very useful. Are our seven Sacraments absolutely necessary? Yet they do exist and they are very useful, and they were not clearly described and defined for a long time.

Hans Küng wants to replace "papal infallibility" by "ecclesial indefectibility," on the grounds that there is no adequate biblical or historical basis for the dogma of papal infallibility, but that the notion of indefectibility is more adequately grounded in Scripture and tradition. Thus the Church, despite its mistakes (its fallibility), still communicates the Gospel without fail (its indefectibility) and thus remains in God's truth. This view of his has proved very attractive to some of our modern theologians but is it theologically solid enough to replace the traditional doctrine of infallibility? Definitely not, in my opinion.

For Hans Küng does not (and cannot) tell us how the Church determines what is the core of the Gospel, what is its central message, what is God's truth that she must communicate without fail if she is to be indefectible. But if she is to communicate God's truth indefectibly, then she must be able to say (infallibly) that this is God's truth, this is not God's truth. She must be able to say (infallibly) that Christ is true God and that Arius is wrong when he says Christ is not true God. Scripture is not adequately *"sui interpres"* nor *"norma normans non normata."* If Christ wanted His Church to be an indefectible interpreter and transmitter of His Gospel of salvation, must there not be an infallible magisterium in His Church to guarantee indefectible transmission of this Gospel? If the Holy Spirit is going to make the Church of Christ indefectible in communicating the salvific Gospel of Christ, must He not also make her infallible in determining what this salvific Gospel is, infallible in determining what is God's truth and what is not? And where would we expect the Holy Spirit to give His 'infallibilizing' assistance more fully than to the council or pope that claims—rightly—to speak for the universal Church and to the universal Church? Indefectibility without infallibility is hardly more than a chimera.

It is quite understandable how these historians and theologians, captivated by the spirit of critical inquiry that is in the air everywhere today, are drawn to question the origins and development, the biblical and historical foundations of traditional doctrines and dogmas. That is their right. But in the process they should not rashly downgrade the methods and results of the past. They should not be so captivated by their modern methods and principles as to give these the absolute value they seem intent on taking away from traditional methods and doctrines. They should remember that their methods and conclusions must be submitted to the test of time and of critical evaluation before they can have more than transitory value. The traditional methods and doctrines have undergone a long testing and they have stood up rather well.

That is why we chose to use them as our starting point. No one so far, in our estimate, has produced enough evidence to eliminate them. And so the traditional doctrines of conciliar and papal infallibility are still "in possession." Will they always be? We think they will.

Notes for Introduction

1. R. Aldwinckle, **Death In the Secular City,** (Grand Rapids, W. B. Eerdmans, 1947), pp. 19, 20, 42.

2. J. L. McKenzie, S.J., **Dictionary of the Bible,** (Milwaukee, Bruce, 1965), p. 96.

3. Vatican II, **Dogmatic Constitution on Divine Revelation,** nos. 9, 10; W. M. Abbott, S.J., **The Documents of Vatican II,** (New York, America Press, 1966), pp. 117-118.

4. **Method in Theology,** (New York, Herder and Herder, 1972), pp. 320-325.

5. "Historical Problems with Papal Infallibility", **Theology Digest,** Summer, 1972, 153ff.

6. Cf. Socrates, **Hist. Eccl.,** 2, 15, 17; Sozomenus, **Hist. Eccl.** 6, 22, 52.

7. J. M. Herve, **Manuale Theologiae Dogmaticae,** v. I, Parisiis, Apud Berche et Pagis, ed., 1957, p. 485.

CONTENTS

PART FIVE
THE MYSTERY OF THE FINAL STATE

PART I
The Mystery of Life after Death

Chapter 1
Is There Life After Death?

One of the oldest questions—and one of the most important and paradoxical—that a man has ever asked is this: will I go on living after I have died? Will there be for me a life after death? Many men in the past have answered Yes, and so do many men today. Many men in the past have answered *No*, and so do many men today.

But men have not always understood "life after death" in the same way. For life after death is capable of very different meanings. Life after death might mean: I will have the same kind of life after death that I have now. It might mean I will go on existing but only in the mind of God. Or absorbed into God so that I lose my personal identity and distinct personality. It might mean that I go on existing but in a state of sleep. Or in a state of restless wandering. Or in a ghostlike state of suspended animation.

What we are intent on here, however, is this: Do *I* go on living and acting after I have died? Do *I*, the person that I am now, go on consciously living and acting, after the death of my body? After death do *I* go on living and acting, in a way that is still human, though very different, perhaps, from the human way in which I live and act now? This is the question that interests us here. This is the question that is very important.

To find an answer to this question we might be content to study the teaching of Scripture and of the Church. But since disbelief in life after death seems to be growing rather rapidly, and since people have so many different concepts of life after death, it seems better not to start but to finish our study of life after death with the teaching of Scripture and of the Church. So we first turn to the history of religions to find out what religious people down the centuries have believed about life after death. Since we live in an empirical age, we face up to the question: is there any empirical or quasi-empirical evidence for life after death? And since Spiritualists, Reincarnationists and others to some extent claim there is empirical or quasi-empirical evidence for life after death, we study their claims and the evidence they present to back up their claims. Finally we turn to God and ask what He has said about life after death through Sacred Scripture and the Magisterium of His Church.

THE HISTORY OF RELIGIONS

The history of religions clearly indicates that men of all times and cultures believed in some kind of survival after death. There is evidence of this belief in Paleolithic, Mesolithic, Neolithic times, as well as in ancient Greece, India, Egypt, China and among men in every part of the world.

In Homeric Greece men believed in an afterlife that was not very happy for most of them. At death a man's soul became his "double," and if not properly separated from the body by ritual burning of the body it wandered near the tomb, restless and unhappy. When it was properly separated it went to Erebus, a gloomy underworld, the abode of King Hades, and there it had an existence that was barely worthy of the name, unconscious or at most half-conscious, capable of no real action or passion but only of feeble complaints. Some privileged men, demigods or heroes, were transported while still living far away "beyond the western wave" to the Elysian fields where they enjoyed a blessedly happy and immortal life like that of the gods.[1]

Among the Orphic sects of Greece, it seems, there were two ways for men to achieve immortal divine life. One was the way of mystical union with the god Dionysus, which a few Mystae attained by an orgiastic ecstasy. The other was by transmigration of souls and their reincarnation in one body after another until they were fully purified: then they were set free from the cycle of birth and death and enjoyed a life of delight and an eternity of unbroken blessedness. This blessed immortality, devoid of all embodiment, has been regarded by some scholars as the origin of the doctrine of the discarnate soul and of all western monasticism, asceticism, and mysticism.[2]

In the classical period of Greece Plato taught the immortality of the human soul, and tried to demonstrate this immortality by a psychological analysis of the nature of the soul. Since the very essence of the soul as principle of life was to be alive, it could not be thought of as dying. Since it was simple and non-composite it must be immortal, for what is non-composite is indispersible and indissoluble. Since the soul is a self-moved mover it is indestructible, for there is nothing outside it that could initiate the process of its destruction.[3] When the soul is set free by death it contemplates the eternal Ideas and when it is reincarnated it brings with it "reminiscences," the incomplete and obscure memories of the Truth.[4]

In India we find a belief in survival after death from earliest times on down to the present. In the Vedic hymns this is not connected with the doctrine of reincarnation, but from the Upanishads on, reincarnation is found in most every Indian religious sect, Buddhism, Jainism, Sikhism and all forms of Hinduism. The central doctrine of the Upanishads is that of a supreme divine soul called Brahma which is immanent in the world. Man goes through one reincarnation after another according to the law of Karma, with the nature of his successive incarnations determined by the nature of his deeds in his previous lives. Salvation and escape from Karma in the Upanishads lies in the ultimate identity of the empirical soul with the absolute soul, of the human self with the universal principle or Brahma, which entails loss of the individual's personality.

Belief in survival was an outstanding characteristic of the religion of ancient Egypt. Man's spirit lives on in the vault or tombs in which his mortal remains are placed. Ancient Egyptians early came to believe in a less gloomy life outside the earth for those who had well served the gods. In the Fifth Dynasty the right to entry into a solar paradise was given by ritual lustrations. To obtain a place in the abode of the sun or of Osiris one had to undergo a judgment and emerge successfully. The wicked are condemned to horrible tortures: the just will enjoy a blissful life in heaven. Some Egyptians even came to believe that heaven gave the righteous an intimate union with God, in the land of Osiris among the stars.[5]

The ancient Iranians (Persians) believed in a new life in the world beyond. Zarathustra (Zoroaster), the Iranian prophet, declared that at the crossing of a colossal bridge of the Requiter, souls will be judged one by one and achieve their eternal destiny. According to the Avesta those who can cross the bridge go to paradise, those who cannot fall into hell. The Avesta also teaches the resurrection of the dead, a last judgment and a transfiguration of the earth in a far distant future. But when the world comes to an end under a torrential rain of molten metals, hell and its inmates will disappear for ever and the space of hell will become an earthly paradise of perpetual delights.

The oldest of the Chinese religions believed in survival and the existence of a heaven not very different from earth. Man's lower soul, which controls his vegetative functions, ceases to exist soon after death. The higher soul survives and attains happiness in proportion to its world-knowledge and well-being. The Chinese openly profess a kind of scepticism about heaven and hell. There is some survival, they say, but its duration depends on the importance of the deceased's social rank.[6]

Does this universal belief in an afterlife give us an apodictic proof of such an after life? Does the fact that most people everywhere at all times believed in some sort of life after death, prove that there is such a life? No. Most people everywhere at all times also believed that the sun circles the earth, but it does not. And yet, this universal belief in an afterlife is a fact that demands an explanation. The simplest and best explanation is that there is an afterlife and men knew this either "intuitively," or "inferentially" or by "revelation" from God. Many other explanations have been offered but they simply do not explain this universal belief.

SPIRITUALISM

Spiritualism teaches that man enjoys a continuous life after death. It maintains that this has been demonstrated by communications from and with those who live in the spirit world.

If we look for the antecedents of modern Spiritualism, the earliest seem to lie in necromancy, an evocation of the spirits of the departed for the purpose of divination. This seems to have been practiced in all ages and rather universally, especially in India, Chaldea, Egypt, China, Persia. Rome knew it and Greek Oracles constantly invoked necromancers. It was known in the Old Testament and strongly prohibited under threat of severe punishment (1 Sm 28:3-25). Some of the prominent features of modern Spiritualism seem to be found in the ancient practices of necromancy such as communication through the *medium* of a specially 'sensitive' person in somnambulistic sleep accompanied at times by apparent levitation and elongation.

Modern Spiritualism began in the little village of Hydesville, New York, in 1848, with the Fox Sisters, Margaretta and Katie (15 and 12 years old). When raps were heard the girls challenged the raps and were answered sound for sound, so the account goes. It was soon discovered that these were signals. The signals declared that a murdered man was buried in the cellar and gave the name. The information was found to be true: so the story goes. But some Buffalo doctors made experiments which satisfied them that the Fox girls made the raps with their knee-joints or toes, yet the girls were not deterred. When an older sister, Leah, came on the scene, the rappings were now said to proceed from various spirit personalities through the medium of the Fox sisters. Soon the Fox sisters went to Rochester, then to Buffalo to exhibit their powers—for a consideration. According to one account Margaret became a Catholic, the sisters quarreled, there was a public confession of fraud followed later by a formal recantation of this confession, and still later the sisters became inebriates and moral wrecks.[7]

In spite of these dubious beginnings, Spiritualism marched on and grew rapidly, with Spiritualists maintaining that it was possible to enter into contact with the dead by the help of mediums and the instrumentality of table rapping. During the seances of 'physical' mediums, such as D. D. Home, Henry Slade, Eusapia Paladino, tables apparently rose 'telekinetically' from the ground, musical instruments played under wire cages and impressions of heads and limbs appeared in paraffin-wax. The great mediums, such as the American, Mrs. Piper or the Englishwoman, Mrs. Leonard achieved their best results in trance. Dead persons frequently seemed to communicate by means of such mediums and to give demonstrably correct information about their lives and accurate information about lost objects.[8]

The National Spiritualists' Association of America says that Spiritualism "is the science, philosophy and Religion of continuous life, based upon the demonstrated fact of communication, by means of mediumship, with those who live in the spirit world."[9] It teaches that death works no miracles, that it is a new birth into a spiritual body, the counterpart of the physical which is gifted with new powers. Neither punishment nor reward is meted out. There is no unchangeable bliss, no eternal damnation, no hell with brimstone and flames of fire, no devils, no last judgment, no vicarious atonement, no resurrection of the physical body. Individuality, character, memory undergo no change. The main principle of the new life is the progression of the fittest. The rapidity of progress is in proportion to the mental and moral faculties acquired in earth life. Higher and higher spheres correspond to the state of progress. Communion with the higher intelligences is open but of God the spirits know no more than we do. Christ was a great Teacher who descended to set an example. The communion of spirit with spirit is said to be by thought-reading and sympathy, and to be perfect between those whose beings are in harmony with each other. The infinite cosmos becomes a field where the highest developments of intellect may range in the acquisition of boundless knowledge. Two very fantastic but interesting descriptions of the Spiritualist afterlife are offered by Anthony Borgia and Hans Holzer.[10]

As a religion Spiritualism is obviously unacceptable for it involves an implicit negation of the Triune God, of Christ as

Savior of mankind, of Christ's Church and its teaching about an eternal life of heaven and hell. It seems to be a sorry attempt to construct a natural religion out of purported "communications" from "over there."

But if we summarily reject Spiritualism as a religion, this need not mean that we automatically reject all Spiritualist phenomena and alleged communications with the departed.

Prof. Ducasse presents the famous "Watseka Wonder" case, which he considers "as impressive a case as any on record," and the "communications received by the late Prof. J. H. Hyslop, purportedly from his deceased father, through the famous Boston medium, Mrs. Piper."[11] Prof. Hansel studies Eusapia Palladino, "the greatest medium of all time," Margaret Crandon, "the most famous of all American mediums," Mrs. Piper, "perhaps the most closely studied of all mental mediums" and Mrs. Leonard who "baffled psychical researchers for some forty years."[12] Dr. Gardner Murphy offers "evidence from three types of paranormal events: (1) spontaneous telepathic and clairvoyant events happening to ordinary persons, in which there is a suggestion of postmortem action or commerce of the deceased with the living; (2) mediumistic phenomena; (3) the complex technical developments which carry the mediumistic studies to the challenging, perhaps insoluble complexities known as "cross correspondences." In the course of this he indicates the development of the famous Mrs. Piper's mediumship and the amazing "cross-correspondences between her communications and those of the Verral automatists" and studies the "Lethe Case" and the "Ear of Dionysius."[13]

What are we to think of these mediums and their purported communications from "over there"? Three investigators have given three very different estimates of them. Alson J. Smith rates four of these mediums very highly, Mrs. Piper, Mrs. Soule, Mrs. Leonard and Mrs. Garrett. According to him the phenomena that they produced were subjected to all sorts of analysis, from infra-red rays to the probings of psychoanalysis and handwriting experts. The findings were always in their favor. No imputation of fraud was ever brought against them.[14]

Prof. Hansel rated Spiritualist mediums very, very differently.

The Fox sisters, he concluded, were merely tricksters, Eusapia Palladino's act was fraudulent, and so was Margery Crandon's. "On all those occasions when professional magicians were present, the mediums were completely exposed." "The later period of Mrs. Piper's career as a medium produced results that can only be regarded as farcical. The band of spirits who took over control seemed bent on communicating rubbish." The communications of Feda, Mrs. Leonard's control over there, were characterized "by ambivalent platitudes and evasion. Although packed with allusions and generalities, there was never anything as definite as a simple statement of name, address and date of birth."[15]

Dr. Gardner Murphy wrote: "there is the patent fact that in the case of many apparitions, in the case of some dreams, and in the case of a great many mediumistic performances . . . the *initiative*, the directing force, the plan, the purpose of the communication, seems pretty plainly to come from no living individual, however fragmentary, dissociated, or subconscious the vehicle appears to be . . . There seems to be a will to communicate. It appears to be autonomous, self-contained, completely and humanly purposive. The intent is didactic, clear, sure of itself, and shows initiative . . . It is the autonomy, the purposiveness, the cogency, above all the individuality of the source of these messages that cannot be by-passed. Struggle though I may as a psychologist for forty-five years to find a 'naturalistic' and 'normal' way of handling this material, I cannot do this even when using all the information we have about human chicanery and all we have about the far-flung telepathic and clairvoyant abilities of some gifted sensitives. The case looks like communication with the deceased . . . To me the evidence cannot be by-passed, nor on the other hand can conviction be achieved . . . But if this means that in a serious philosophical argument I would plead the anti-survival case, the conclusion is erroneous. I linger because I cannot cross the stream. We need far more evidence: we need new perspective; perhaps we need more courageous minds."[16]

In these purported communications with the deceased what

moved Dr. Murphy most was "a will to communicate. It appears to be autonomous, self-contained, completely and humanly purposive . . . and shows initiative." There is another case on record, a "classic," that shows most remarkably this "will to communicate," this "initiative" from *over there*.

This is the case of *"Patience Worth,"* "without doubt the most productive and talented ghost writer of her genre on record."[17] This case started on a July evening of 1913 in St. Louis, with Pearl Lenore Curran, the wife of John Curran, the State immigration commissioner. She and her mother, Mrs. Mary Pollard and Mrs. Edwin Hutchings were toying with a ouija board. They had played with the board before with no results. This time the pointer suddenly began to move and spelled out: "Many moons ago I lived. Again I come—Patience Worth my name." Further messages seemed to indicate that she lived in 1649 in England, emigrated to Massachusetts Colony, lived on Cape Cod and was killed during an Indian massacre about 1675.

In the course of the twenty-four years (1913-1937) that Patience "visited" Mrs. Curran, she dictated seven full-length books, thousands of poems, innumerable epigrams and aphorisms and thousands of pages of repartee. Prof. Roland G. Usher said of one of her books, *The Sorry Tale:* "unquestionably this is the greatest story ever penned of the life and times of Christ since the Gospels were finished."[18] The 1918 edition of W. S. Braithwaite's Anthology . . . of American poetry listed ten poems by Amy Lowell, five by Edna St. Vincent Millay and eighty-eight by Patience Worth. On Thanksgiving Day, Nov. 25, 1937, came the final communication from Patience. That day Mrs. Curran caught cold and developed pneumonia. She died in a Los Angeles hospital on Dec. 3, 1937.

C. S. Yost, editor of the *St. Louis Globe Democrat's* editorial page from 1915 till his death in 1941, was very favorably impressed by Patience Worth and wrote a series of articles about her, and a book called: *Patience Worth: A Psychic Mystery*, that produced widespread interest and reaction. Perhaps the most valuable account of Patience Worth is to be found in a book entitled *Singer In The Shadows*, by Irving Litvag of Washington University in St. Louis, and it is from this book that this section is largely derived. Much material about Patience is to be found in the morgue of the *St. Louis Globe Democrat* and in the Washington University Library. The Missouri Historical Society archives have more than twenty volumes about Patience.

Patience Worth was widely pondered and studied, rejected by some, accepted by others. Caspar Yost strongly doubted that she was merely a role assumed by Mrs. Curran. For there was no ceremony about her sittings, no dimmed lights, no compelled silences. She did not go into a trance. She even talked to other people while the board was in operation and made no apparent effort at mental concentration.

In the April, 1916 issue of the *A.S.P.R. Journal*, James H. Hyslop, former professor of Logic and Ethics at Columbia University and then Director of the American Society for Psychical Research, vigorously denounced the Patience Worth case and all those involved in it. He implied that fraud was involved and profit was the motive. Charles E. Cory, Chairman of the Department of Philosophy at Washington University, made a three year investigation of the case and concluded that Patience Worth was a subconscious personality of Mrs. John Curran. Prof. Otto Heller, another Washington University professor, wrote a report on the case in 1937. In this he indicated doubts about Mrs. Curran's honesty but admitted that he was completely baffled by the case. He found no collusion or fraud and insisted that none of the non-spiritualistic theories that had been advanced to explain the mystery had a leg to stand on. He was baffled by the "immense discrepancy between what Patience knows and what Mrs. Curran had learned." The authenticity of the historic background of her narratives and the accuracy of all details he found beyond question. He declared that "on its mechanical side the performance was scarcely short of miraculous, for Mrs. Curran with no text whatever before her had no difficulty in carrying on for two or three hours at a stretch . . . that stunning five-thousand word description of the Crucifixion in *The Sorry Tale* came out of a single session. And Patience Worth's dictations were finished literary compositions . . . and told consistently in the quaint idiom of a bygone century"[19] (Litvag, loc. cit. 282).

G. N. M. Tyrrell found it unplausible to suppose that the knowledge shown in these automatic productions was ever acquired by the normal consciousness of Mrs. Curran. If Patience Worth was a secondary personality she was a most unusual one, he felt, for in Mrs. Curran's automatism . . . she is consciously present during the whole of it. Patience Worth does not supplant the normal Mrs. Curran, nor does she seem to be an abstraction from her: "if secondary personalities of the type of Patience Worth are possible . . . they form an alternative to the discarnate theory, but scarcely a less marvellous alternative."[20]

Dr. Walter Franklin Prince made the most detailed examination of the facts of the Patience Worth Case in 1926 and published his findings in 1927 as *The Case of Patience Worth* (reissued in 1964 by University Books). He was convinced that Mrs. Curran "is a person of veracity . . . Every facility for examination was given me and every question answered." He ruled out the possibility of fraud. He declared: "I know of no proof that a secondary personality, subliminal or alternating, can show ability so tremendously in advance of that of the primary or normal consciousness, and ability which is sustained and perpetual . . . if a person is dissociated in a pathological and continuing extent, the fact is supposed . . . to be signalized by various symptoms . . . of hysteria. . . . But careful interrogation of Mrs. Curran and those who have known her, brings out no testimony by which this state at any period can be identified . . . no secondary personality ever manifested extraordinary talent in a field where the primary or conscious personality had not shown aptitude, or made earnest endeavor."[21]

Irving Litvag, the author of the most recent book on Patience Worth, could not accept the spirit-hypothesis and found weighty obstacles to the theory of subconscious personality. But he concluded: "I still lean slightly in the direction of the theory that Patience is a product of Mrs. Curran's subconscious, yet I readily

admit that this leaning stems more from my own temperament
and value system rather than from any strong weight of evidence
supporting this position."[22]

What are we to think? What or who is Patience Worth?
A secondary personality of Mrs. Curran or a discarnate spirit
"over there"? Many investigators have decided she is a product
of Mrs. Curran's subconscious, a secondary personality of Mrs.
Curran. But against this view there is the "immense discrepancy"
between what Patience knows and what Mrs. Curran had learned
(her schooling ended with the eighth grade, she had never been
to England or to the Holy Land nor read much of anything).
There is Dr. Prince's declaration: "no secondary personality ever
manifested extraordinary talent in a field where the primary or
conscious personality had not shown aptitude, or made earnest
endeavor." There was no evidence of pathological dissociation,
no sign of hysteria on the part of Mrs. Curran. If input and
output are in strict proportion, then it seems impossible to derive
Patience's extraordinary intellectual competence and literary skill
from the very ordinary intellectual competence and personality
of Mrs. Curran. There is no indication, no evidence that Mrs.
Curran did or could obtain by extrasensory perception the immense amount of historically accurate information she put forth,
or that "stunning five-thousand word description of the Crucifixion in *The Sorry Tale* that came out of a single session." The
simplest and the most satisfactory answer is that Patience Worth
was a discarnate spirit "over there." For the initiative, the directing force, the plan, the purpose of the communication came from
"over there." "Over there" there was a will to communicate,
autonomous, self-contained, completely and humanly purposive.
The case looks like communication with the deceased Patience
Worth.

What shall we conclude? Are there communications from the
departed that give solid evidence of life after death? It seems
very probable that there are. Dr. Gardner Murphy wrote: "the
case looks like communication with the deceased." It does. Prof.
Ducasse gives much the same balanced answer: "considering the

quantity of evidence we get over the mediumistic 'telephone'. . .
the *quality* of that evidence . . . and the *diversity* of kinds of it
we get . . . the conclusion . . . is, I believe, the same as that which
. . . was finally reached by Mrs. Sidgwick and Lord Balfour, by
Sir Oliver Lodge, Prof. Hyslop, Dr. Hodgson and a number of
other persons who like them were thoroughly familiar with the
evidence on record; who were gifted with keenly critical minds;
who had originally been sceptical of the reality or even possibility of survival; and who were also fully acquainted with the
evidence for the reality of telepathy and of clairvoyance, and
with the claims that had been made for the telepathy-clairvoyant
interpretation of the evidence, as against the survival interpretation of it. Their conclusion was essentially that the balance of
the evidence so far obtained is on the side of reality of survival
and, in the best cases, of survival not merely of memories of life
on earth, but of survival also of the most significant capacities of
the human mind, and of continuing exercise of these."[23] Thus
these "communications from over there," while they do not give
us empirical or quasi-empirical *proof* of life after death, do seem
to offer us a solid *probability* that there is manifest life after
death. Much more investigation and study will be needed to try
to determine more accurately just what "communications" can
be explained by psychology and parapsychology, and which
cannot, so that we can have better criteria for determining which
"communications" really come from "over there" and which
come from "over here."

If we conclude that some of these "communications" really
do come from "over there," we are faced with a theological
problem. According to traditional Catholic doctrine those who
have died are now living a temporary afterlife in purgatory or
an eternal afterlife in heaven or hell. Where are these departed
"over-there-communicators"? If Catholic doctrine allows us
only to say they must be either in purgatory or heaven or hell,
then it can seem more likely that they are "in purgatory" or in a
purgatorial condition. If Catholic doctrine allows us to think
that some of the departed are "somewhere else" than in purgatory,

heaven or hell, then it is possible and perhaps probable that that is where they are. It would hardly seem likely that they would be in heaven or hell. But here we can only speculate and wonder.

REINCARNATION

One of the oldest views of life after death is that of the Reincarnationists, according to whom each soul after death is given a new body and goes through a series of successive deaths and rebirths until it is finally perfectly purified. Over the centuries this view has taken various forms. No traces of this doctrine have been found among primitive Persians, Chinese, Egyptians, Indians, or Greeks of the oldest period. But about the 6th century B.C. we find it in Greece and in India. It became a characteristic tenet of Hindus and Buddhists down to the present time. In the West Teutons, Celtic peoples and several savage tribes of the West Indies professed this belief in reincarnation. More or less elaborate doctrines of transmigration have been widespread in the world, in Asia, Africa, Australia, Oceania, among North and South American Indians and in parts of Europe. In this century the idea of reincarnation has captivated many minds. Theosophy, Anthroposophy, the Spiritism of the school of Allan Kardec, the *Occultism* of Papus, Messianism, are now promoting the doctrine with great vigor.[24]

Ancient Greece

Reincarnation first appeared in ancient Greece about the 6th century B.C., and was probably a native development. It owes its scientific form there to Plato. According to him "human souls were originally created by the Demiurge out of Existence, Sameness, and Difference, and placed each upon a separate star from which they were shown the nature of the universe and the laws of destiny. All of them are, at various times, incarnated as humans. They die, are judged, experience punishments or rewards for their deeds in life, and after 1000 years are again incarnated. They choose their own new bodies, and this choice is of crucial importance, but it is governed partly by the necessity of their own nature. A soul that has kept itself free from bodily taint for three lives is released completely from the cycle of births; most souls live ten earthly lives—spread over 10,000 years—and then they rise again to the region of the gods and a vision of the Truth."[25]

Ancient India

From the Upanishads on reincarnation is found in most every Indian sect, Buddhism, Jainism, Sikhism, and all forms of Hinduism. The Brahmanism of the Upanishads has as its central doctrine that of a supreme divine soul called Brahma, which is immanent in the world and the object of hope is "union with this Absolute, resulting in perfect immortality, supreme freedom and ecstatic bliss." Sometimes a personal immortality is meant, sometimes impersonal absorption in the divine Transcendent. This state of bliss is commonly called Mukti or Moksa or release from Samsara, the cycle of rebirth. Upanishad thinkers forged the old idea of retribution into the inflexible law of Karma, according to which every deed leaves traces on the doer, and bears a harvest of joy or sorrow for the doer to reap. Karma dispositions or residual propensities of previous births are carried by causal bodies which determine circumstances of every birth. On coming into contact with causal bodies, souls which are eternal pure spirits set out on their samsara voyage; they acquire in addition subtle bodies which are the subject of experiences, and gross bodies such as we see. When the gross body falls off, one dies. But as long as the other two bodies remain attached to it, the soul must repeatedly come to birth till, through this discipline of samsara and the knowledge of Brahman, all Karma is consumed and overcome. It may take thousands and thousands of births and deaths before the liberating discernment should dawn upon the soul.[26]

Is there any escape from Karma? Yes. (1) The earliest Indian way of salvation is that of the Vedanta theology of the Upanishads, consisting in the mystical realization of the identity of the human soul with God. One loses one's personality in the great Impersonal and after that one cannot be born into any more bodies. (2) For Gautama, the founder of Buddhism, the way of escape lies in the extinction of desire. Since it is desire for life and its sham delights that causes rebirth, it is the extinction of desire that frees from rebirth and leads to Nirvana. But when Gautama was asked by his disciples whether Nirvana meant total extinction or only complete unconsciousness, he refused to answer.[27] Does Buddha exist after death? "He cannot be said to exist, he cannot be said not to exist, he cannot be said both to exist and not to exist, he cannot be said neither to exist nor not exist."[28]

For millions of Hindus and Buddhists reincarnation is a part of their faith, taught by their Sacred Books and their most respected teachers, handed down through long centuries, and devoutly accepted as part of their life and hope. There is a beauty in Buddhism and in the supreme bliss it offers in final salvation but this is so very, very remote. This supreme bliss is not like the Christian view of heavenly bliss. It does not involve union with the triune God of love, nor does it talk about the union between the members of a blessed community in this final state of man. But in its final state there is no suffering but ineffable peace in the realm of eternity. Yet all this is so terrifyingly remote and demands so many reincarnations before it can be achieved. This is its fatal flaw.

Modern India

Swami Abhedananda offers a modern defence of reincarnation. It is a doctrine, he maintains, that is unreservedly accepted by the vast majority of mankind today as it was in the past. Nor can any other theory such as the One Birth theory or the Theory of Hereditary Transmission explain why children who die young should come into existence and pass away without getting an opportunity to learn anything. The One Birth theory of Judaism, Christianity, Mahomedanism and Zoroastrianism is utterly unreasonable in holding that human souls are created out of nothing at the time of the birth of their bodies and continue to exist throughout an eternity of suffering or joy because of the few deeds they performed during the short period of their earthly existence. If the omnipotent, personal God created human souls out of nothing, could He not make all souls equally good and happy? Why would He arrange that one man is born with good tendencies and another with evil ones, that one is born intelligent and another idiotic? Could such a God be called just and merciful? Science, he adds, has disproved the theory of the creation of the universe out of nothing by the action of some supernatural power. The choice must be between reincarnation and resurrection, and the evidence strongly favors reincarnation. Reincarnation based on evolution is a scientific theory but resurrection based on creation is not.[29]

The futility of this argumentation should be apparent. It builds on an immature concept of "modern science," whose nature and limitations are never defined, but which nonetheless becomes the yardstick for measuring the truth and reality of everything. It asserts that this science has disproved the theory of creation of the universe out of nothing, something that neither this science nor any science has done or ever can do. It prides itself on accepting "evolution" instead of "creation," apparently unaware that there is no incompatibility between creationism and evolutionism if these are properly understood, and that quite a few Catholics hold both. It maintains that reincarnation is scientific but resurrection is not, obviously unaware that real science has nothing to say about either reincarnation or resurrection. It assumes but never proves that the soul has been existing from the beginningless past and will exist throughout eternity, something that "modern science" utterly rejects.

Theosophy

This is a modern form of reincarnation that was initiated in 1875 in New York City by Helena Petrovna Blavatsky, H. S. Olcott and W. Q. Judge. For Mme. Blavatsky man has a septenary constitution and consists of spirit, spiritual soul, human soul or mind, animal soul, vitality, astral body and physical body. Of these the first three are immortal, the others mortal. The astral body is a shadowy duplicate of the physical body, formed before birth but equally mortal. Death involves a rebirth that liberates the human spirit from the physical body to enjoy astral life, which will in turn be followed by forgetfulness and rebirth. The astral world is not the true heaven, but an emotional world that is the true home of grosser men and animals. Heaven or the mental world is achieved only after repeated incarnations. It is the true home of intelligence and the soul.

At the Adyar Temple in India, Mme. Blavatsky claimed that she had received direct written communications from two long-dead Tibetan Mahatmas. But in 1885 investigation by the London Society for Psychic Research stamped the entire process as a deliberate fraud without, however, dimming Mme. Blavatsky's reputation. After Mme. Blavatsky's death, Mrs. Besant became her successor as leader of the Theosophical Society. When four Theosophists were ordained in 1913-14 to the priesthood of the Old Catholic Church by Bishop Arnold Matthew, a Mr. Lead-beater was interested and was himself ordained in 1916 as bishop of the Old Catholic Church for Australia.[30]

Dr. Leadbeater tries to combine Gnostic, evolutionary and Christian elements in his theosophy. Man is a soul and has several bodies as vehicles and instruments in various worlds. Death is the laying aside of the physical body. The ego continues to live in his astral body until the force has become exhausted which has been generated by the emotions and passions of his earth-life. Then the second death occurs, the astral body falls away and a man finds himself in the mental body and the lower mental world. There he remains until the thought forces generated during his physical and astral lives have worn themselves out. Then he drops the third vehicle and remains once more an ego in his own world, inhabiting his causal body. The astral life corresponds to the Christian purgatory, the lower mental life to its Heaven. Hell does not exist. A man's real life covers millions of years. Each of such lives is a day at school. If he is an apt pupil his school life is comparatively short. In this school no one ever fails; every one must go on to the end. Man is divine in origin and has a long, double evolution behind him, that of the soul within and that of the outer form, and all according to the great law of cause and effect. There are perfected men and it is possible to come into touch with them and to be taught by them. The world is under the control of a perfectly organized hierarchy, so that final failure is impossible. In the Absolute and Infinite there are innumerable universes: in each universe countless solar systems, each with its solar Deity, the Logos, "God." Out of Himself He has called this mighty system into being. We who are in it are evolving fragments of His life; from Him we all have come; into Him we shall return. Why has He done this? God is Love and will become still more perfect Love when we through the slow process of evolution reach His own level and return His love. His manifestation is ever three-fold, and so all religions have imaged Him as a Trinity.

Such a fantastic religion represents a vivid imagination run wild. It can offer no proof. Could a God of love, of true personal system of cause and effect, of physical, astral, mental and causal love, possibly be the source of such an incredible hierarchical bodies, of evolution of body and soul through millions of years, and all this in the name of justice and love and perfection for each tiny spark of the Infinite? Our Triune God is replaced by an infinitely remote Gnostic Absolute of emanations who deals with His innumerable universes and countless solar systems through an innumerable number of hierarchically organized intermediaries. Gone is the God who so loved the world as to send His only Son to redeem and help us to achieve eternal and perfect union with the Father, Son and Holy Spirit and thus share in their everlasting happiness and unimaginable joy throughout eternity—and all this after one short earthly life.

Reincarnationists have offered many arguments to prove there is reincarnation. The Rt. Rev. I. S. Cooper maintains that without reincarnation the one life on earth is purposeless in millions of cases. And only the reincarnation theory can explain the enigmas of heredity, the mental and moral differences of people, the problem of evil, the rise and fall of nations, the reappearance of the characteristics of earlier races, the propensity to vice or virtue, to genius and infant precocity and sudden friendships. Obviously these arguments do not prove reincarnation is a fact, for reincarnation is not the only nor is it the best explanation of the phenomena mentioned. Reincarnationists often adduce *"déjà-vu"* (already seen) experiences as evidence that the persons who have these experiences have lived before and seen these scenes in that previous life. Psychologists generally reject the reincarnationist explanation and think that the "scene" or one very like it was seen or dreamed by that person earlier in life, or recognized only subconsciously, and thus left its impress on his memory, until the later encounter with that same "scene" or one very like it triggered the "déjà-vu" reaction.

Virtual memory of past lives is seen by some reincarnationists in the fact that persons are born with special talents, sympathies, antipathies, tendencies to virtue or vice. But the genetic inheritance of these persons and their early environment offer a more scientific explanation.

Hypnotic regression has been urged by reincarnationists as another way of "proving" an earlier life. By appropriate commands a hypnotist regresses the consciousness of a hypnotized subject to a time earlier than the birth or conception of his body. The most famous case of such hypnotic regression is that of "Bridey Murphy." In 1952 Ruth Simmons (Virginia Tighe), a young housewife living in Pueblo, Colorado, was hypnotically regressed by Morey Bernstein beyond the time of her birth and then she began to speak of a lifetime in Ireland in the 19th century. In succeeding sessions the story unfolded coherently and consistently and the hypnotized woman used words of which she was ignorant in her waking state, words which were correct for that time and place. But the Bridey Murphy story was attacked on all sides, by some as "the work of the devil," by others as the product of suggestion and coincidence. The *Chicago American* in May, 1965 mounted the most devastating criticism, claiming that Ruth Simmons as a girl in Chicago had excelled in dramatics, often recited monologues in Irish brogue and had played with the children of a neighbor named Bridey Murphy Corkell. Prof. Ducasse, however, after a careful study of the case and its documentation, was not convinced that the reincarnation hypothesis had been disproved. On the other hand, it can hardly be maintained that this case offers convincing evidence that Ruth Simmons was the reincarnation of a 19th century Bridey Murphy.[31]

One of the most scientific studies of purported cases of reincarnation is that of Ian Stevenson, M.D.[32] His study includes seven cases suggestive of reincarnation in India, three in Ceylon, two in Brazil, seven in Southeast Alaska, one in Lebanon. Though he is not at all satisfied with the method of study he used, it seems easily superior to those of other previous studies. After presenting his twenty cases with their documentation, he considered alternative explanations to that of reincarnation. He ruled out fraud, cryptomnesia, extrasensory perception and personation. Possession or reincarnation, he concludes, seemed to be the only adequate explanations of these cases, and "the conformity of the apparent memories of many of the cases to the psychological 'law' that recognition exceeds recall favors somewhat the reincarnation over the possession hypothesis." Do these cases "prove" reincarnation? Obviously not, for as Dr. Stevenson himself points out, they could be explained in terms of possession as well as in terms of reincarnation. But some of the cases, he declares, definitely require a *survivalist* explanation. In his estimate, then, there is evidence for life after death, either in terms of a discarnate "possessing" spirit or of a reincarnated soul or spirit. Is it perhaps at least possible that the doctrine of reincarnation, which is said to number about 700 million adherents, may be more than just wishful thinking?

The Bible and the Church

Some reincarnationists have maintained that neither the Bible nor the Church has condemned reincarnation. Edgar Cayce once said: "I can read reincarnation into the Bible—and you can read it right out again."[33] He read it into the Bible (Pr 8:22-31, Ws 8:19-20, Rm 9:11-14, Jb 1:20-21, Ml 4:5, Mt 16:13; 17:10; Lk 9:7-8, Jn 9:1-3). And modern Scripture scholars in their exegesis of these texts read reincarnation right out again. Long ago St. Augustine said, "It is only heretical perversity that may detect

an affirmation of reincarnation in the words of Holy Scripture."
But has the Bible *explicitly* condemned reincarnation? Not explicitly, perhaps, but implicitly and indirectly it has. For the
New Testament clearly affirms that men can in the span of a
single physical life win an eternal life of happiness that is not the
result of natural evolutionary causes and processes, but is brought
about only by God in and through Christ's salvific life, death and
resurrection to eternal life. And this eternal life, we are told by
Paul and John, begins in our physical life through the action of
the indwelling Spirit of Christ and continues eternally after our
single earthly life has come to an end.

Has the *Church explicitly* condemned the doctrine of reincarnation? It seems not. At times in the past it was thought that she
had—in the fifth Ecumenical Council in 553, in declaring: "If
anyone asserts the fabulous pre-existence of souls and shall assert
the monstrous restoration which follows it, let him be anathema."[34] Recent investigations, however, have shown that neither
this anathematism (first of a series of fifteen Origenist propositions in Cayce 281-284) nor one somewhat like it (first in a series
of nine propositions in DS 403-411) (Denzinger-Schönmetzer,
Enchiridion Symbolorum, Definitionum et Declarationum, Herder, Freiburg i.B, 1963, ed. XXXII) was the work of this Council
itself (J. Alberigo et al., *Conciliorum Oecumenicorum Decreta,
ed. altera*, Herder, Friburgi, 1962, 82). Hence this Council did
not solemnly condemn the Origenist theory of the pre-existence
and ultimate restoration of souls. It might be added, that even if
it had, it need not thereby have necessarily condemned every
doctrine of reincarnation.

But it seems that the Church has *implicitly* rejected this doctrine of reincarnation in its solemn teaching that soon after death
the souls of those who die in charity go either to purgatory or
to heaven while the souls of those who die in mortal sin go to·
hell (DS 856-8), and that those who go to heaven or hell go
there eternally (DS 76), that those who go to heaven enjoy
eternally the uninterrupted and beatific vision of the Triune God
(DS 1000-1001). For implicit in all these definitions is a belief

in one birth, one earthly life, one resurrection for all men with an eternity of reward or punishment according to the way they have lived and died in this one earthly life. (Could this teaching be restricted to those who die *after* Christ, so that these defini- tions apply only to them, and thus reincarnation might have taken place before Christ? This is extremely improbable).

CLINICAL DEATH REPORTS

Recently Dr. Elizabeth Kübler-Ross, an authority in the field of death and dying, offered some very interesting testimony to life after death. The Swiss-born psychiatrist is a former assistant professor of psychiatry at the University of Chicago. She says she is not a religious person but "bases her conviction about life after death on interviews with hundreds of men and women who were declared legally dead and then were revived."[35] "When questioned about their experiences while they were 'dead,' most of the patients said they were floating a few feet above their bodies, watching the resuscitation efforts. They could accurately describe the scene, the details of what was said, and the comings and goings of the rescuers and observers" (ibid). "When people die," she said, "from small children to aged adults, among both religious and non-religious, there is a common denominator. Three things happen: First, there is an experience of floating out of the body. The dying person perceives what is happening to his or her corpse . . . The second experience . . . is a feeling of peace and wholeness. Third is being met by someone who is already dead."[36] She once believed that death was the end of everything. Now she does not: "Now I'm certain that it is not." Later she believed there was life after death. "Now," she says, "I do not just believe it. I *know* there is life after death." We might add that the third point she mentioned, "being met by someone who is already dead," is especially interesting, because Anthony Borgia[37] has that same point in his description of Robert Hugh Benson's "journey over there," where he was met by a former priest-colleague.

We have been looking for evidence of life after death, and hopefully for empirical or quasi-empirical evidence. Obviously we have not found a great deal. Reincarnation offered us little or no solid evidence of a reincarnationist afterlife. Spiritualism offered us considerably more evidence, enough perhaps to furnish a solid probability of an afterlife on the part of some of the departed. But not enough to give us real certainty that all men live on after death somewhere over there, and live on in such a way that they not only exist but are intellectually alive and active. Dr. Kübler-Ross's testimony is very interesting, and hopefully will be further developed, but it is hardly convincing at present. For it is far from clear that the reports come from those who have been really dead and "over there." It seems very possible that those reporting have been merely in a trance or semi-trance state in which they were remembering or regrouping things they had heard or been taught in their past, or have merely had a "journey out of the body" of the kind we will describe in a later chapter.

So if we want certainty in this matter we must turn to the only one who can give us certainty, to the one who knows definitively whether man does live on after the death of his body, and this is God. Where can we expect God to tell us this? In Sacred Scripture, which is the word of God, and in the authentic magisterium of the Church He has established to interpret and define His biblical revelation.

<h2 style="text-align:center">SACRED SCRIPTURE</h2>

If any books can give certainty about the existence and nature of human life after death, it is these books that have "been written under the influence of the Holy Spirit (and) have God as their author" (DS 3006). And "since everything asserted by the inspired authors or sacred writers must be held to be asserted by the Holy Spirit, it follows that the books of Scripture must be acknowledged as teaching firmly, faithfully and without error that truth which God wanted put into the sacred writings for the sake of our salvation."[38]

Old Testament

Most scholars find no hope of survival expressed by the earliest writers of the Old Testament, no hope of rêal life after death. For as those writers understood human nature, there was in it no principle of survival. They envisioned the human person as an animated body and conceived of no other form of human life.[39]

For them men die and go to Sheol (cf. Is 14), a dim and shadowy underworld, a land of silence and forgetfulness, where they are in a state of utter inactivity and cut off from all relation with Yahweh.[40] They do not really "live" there because without their bodies their 'souls' cannot express themselves.[41] But the Old Testament did not view death as an absolute end to all life, as a total annihilation, because in Sheol men lived some kind of ghostlike afterlife, in a state of suspended animation, devoid of power and vitality (Ec 6:6; Jb 3:13-19; Is 14:10 etc.).

After long years, however, a vague hope of an afterlife for the just began to manifest itself in the Old Testament, based on the thought that if these had lived and died in communion with Yahweh, the author of life, then Yahweh would not let them die forever. There is perhaps a hint of this hope in Ps 49:15: "But God will ransom my soul from the power of Sheol, for he will receive me" (JBC 77:172). When this hope is finally expressed it takes the form of the resurrection of the body, the form that was consistent with traditional Israelite thought.[42]

It finds its first clear expression in Dn 12:2-3: "Many of those who sleep in the dust of the earth shall awake, some to everlasting life, and some to shame and everlasting contempt." The new life of the just, it seems, will be a transfigured existence unlike the life of the present world, for "those who are wise shall shine like the brightness of the firmament; and those who turn many to righteousness, like the stars for ever and ever." Here we meet a resurrection not only of the righteous but also of the wicked. And if "many" in the text should mean "all," then all men will rise.

The Second Book of Maccabees gives another expression of this belief in a resurrected afterlife: "the King of the world will raise us up, since it is for his laws that we die, to live again for ever . . . Ours is the better choice, to meet death at men's hands, yet relying on God's promise that we shall be raised up by him; whereas for you there can be no resurrection, no new life. . . . Our brothers already, after enduring their brief pain, now drink of ever-flowing life, by virtue of God's covenant, while you, by God's judgment, will have to pay the just penalty for your arrogance" (2 M 7:9).

And further on this book gives us the only Old Testament text that seems to indicate an intermediate state where the souls of the dead are believed to be purified and assisted in the process by the prayers of the living: "Next, the valiant Judas . . . took a collection . . . and sent it to Jerusalem to have a sacrifice offered for sin, an altogether fine and noble action, in which he took full account of the resurrection. For if he had not expected the fallen to rise again it would have been superfluous and foolish to pray for the dead . . . This was why he had this atonement sacrifice offered for the dead so that they might be released from their sin" (2 M 12:42-45). Here the author clearly attributes to Judas a belief in the resurrection of the just. "He sees Judas' action as evidence that those who die piously can be delivered from unexpiated sins that impede their attainment of a joyful resurrection. This doctrine thus vaguely formulated, contains the essence of what would become (with further precisions) the Christian theologians' teaching on purgatory" (JBC 27:82).

But it is in the Book of Wisdom that belief in a life after death stands out most clearly, in "the first and only instance in the Old Testament where future life with God is categorically and clearly affirmed as man's real destiny" (JBC 34:6). Here the writer tells us that God did not make death but that death came into the world through the devil's envy. For God created man for immortality and the man who practices virtue is assured of immortality: "Death was not God's doing" (1:13); "God did make man imperishable, he made him in the image of his own nature; it was the devil's envy that brought death into the world" (2:23-24); "But the souls of the virtuous are in the hands of God, no torment shall ever touch them" (3:1); "If they experienced punishment as men see it, their hope was rich with immortality"

(3:4); "they are in peace" (3:3); "the virtuous live forever, their recompense is with the Lord, the Most High takes care of them. So shall they receive the royal crown of splendor, the diadem of beauty from the hand of the Lord" (5:15-17).

Clearly here the writer affirms immortality for the virtuous, some kind of everlasting life. He may have been influenced by the Greek concept of the soul's immortality, but the immortality he teaches is not based on man's nature but on his relationship with God. He does not mention a resurrection of the body though this may be implied in chapters 3-5. Nor does he say what will be the state of the virtuous immediately after death. He merely says: "the souls of the virtuous are in the hand of God." Some have suggested that he, like Enoch, places them in Sheol with the souls of the wicked until the Judgment, when they will be brought out to be with God. But Sheol would hardly seem to be the place in which the virtuous would find peace. They are "with God and the saints," i.e., the angels, and at the last judgment they will receive further glory.

Thus in these *late* books of the Old Testament we find a clear witness to a belief in an afterlife, at least for the virtuous. Daniel and Two Maccabees envision this in the form of a resurrection of the body but Wisdom does not. This resurrection will take place, it seems, at the Last Judgment, but what will be the precise state and condition of the virtuous before the Last Judgment is not indicated here: they will be "in peace" and "in the hand of God."

New Testament

The New Testament tells us much more clearly that there will be an afterlife for men. And for all men, not just the virtuous, but also the wicked. And an everlasting afterlife that will be very different for the virtuous and the wicked, according to the kind of life they have lived on earth, according to the love or indifference they have shown for one another (Mt 25:31-46). It tells us of this afterlife especially in its teaching about heaven and hell, resurrection and judgment and eternal life. It is true that it wraps this teaching in very vivid apocalyptic and eschatological imagery, but underlying this imagery we see an un-wavering belief in a life after death for all men. In later chapters we shall consider heaven and hell, resurrection and judgment and eternal life individually and at much greater length. Now we merely touch on some of the salient points of this New Testament teaching that should sufficiently indicate its belief in an afterlife for all men.

A *heaven* in the life to come is affirmed both by the Synoptics and by Paul. In heaven the Christian will find his reward (Mt 5:12) and his treasure (Mt 6:20; Col 1:5). The Christian is a citizen of heaven (Ph 3:20), where God will build a home for him (2 Cor 5:1-5). Those who rise with Christ are taken with Him into heaven (1 Th 4:16f) and there endowed with a heavenly body.

A *hell* for the wicked is affirmed by the Synoptics. There Gehenna is mentioned eleven times. It is a place of fire (Mt. 5:22; 18:9), where the fire is unquenchable (Mk 9:43). It is a pit into which people are cast (Mt 5:29f; Mk 9:45; Lk 12:5). Sinners are punished in fire which is eternal (Mt 18:8), prepared for the devil and his angels (Mt 25:41).

A *resurrection* of the Christian is stressed in the New Testament, but a general resurrection of all seems indicated clearly enough in some passages (Jn 5:28-30; 2 Cor 5:10). The resurrection of Jesus is the principle of the resurrection of the Christian to the eternal life of glory. The Father who raised Jesus will also raise the Christian (2 Cor 4:14). Those who die with Christ will live with him (2 Tm 2:11).

A *general judgment* is indicated in many passages of the New Testament, especially in the Synoptics. There we find Jesus speaking about the judgment of individuals (Mt 7:2, 22-23; 12:36), of reward (Mt 6:4, 6, 18), of condemnation (Mt 5:22; Mk 12:40). The Mathean tableau (25:31-46) put the finishing touches to the Old Testament glimpses of the universalism of judgment.

Eternal life is affirmed in the Synoptics, in Paul and John. In the Synoptics Jesus teaches men to strive for eternal life (Lk 14:16-24; Mt 22:10-14; Mk 14:25). Paul says eternal life is the product of holiness (Rm 6:22), comes through faith and hope (1 Tm 1:16; Tt 1:2; 3:7), and is given by God to those who persevere in good deeds (Rm 2:7). This eternal life is the life of the world to come, but it begins here at baptism as a new life of the Spirit (Rm 6:4). John tells us that man obtains eternal life through faith in Jesus (Jn 3:15, 36; 20:31) and by keeping the commandments of God (Jn 12:50), and he retains this life by fraternal love (1 Jn 3:14f.). This life is fully and definitively received in the resurrection (Jn 5:25-29), but it is already had here initially by those who believe in Christ (Jn 5:24) and by those who eat his flesh and drink his blood (Jn 6:56ff.).

In later chapters we shall indicate more precisely how these passages are interpreted today, but in themselves they indicate clearly enough that the New Testament taught that there will be a life after death for all men.

CHURCH'S TEACHING

The biblical belief in a life after death has been solemnly affirmed in a dogmatic creed, and defined both by a General Council and by Pope Benedict XII. They have defined not only that there is life after death, but that justified and purified souls of adults and the souls of baptized children, soon after death are in heaven and possess eternal life even before they take up their bodies again and before the general judgment, while the souls of those who die in actual mortal sin go down into hell soon after their death and there suffer the pains of hell but on the Day of Judgment (they) will appear with their bodies before the tribunal of Christ.

Under the rubric of *Lyons II*, a general and reunion council held in 1274, there is listed the "Profession of Faith of the Emperor Michael Palaeologus," a profession of faith which had been "proposed in 1267 by Clement IV to Michael Palaeologus (and) the emperor, the clergy, and the people had to make this profession of faith to re-enter the Catholic Church." "The Emperor in the East subscribed to this creed through his ambassadors at Lyons in 1274."[43] This creed reads: "We believe in the resurrec-

tion of the body which we now have and in life everlasting"
(DS 854). It goes on to say: "The souls of those who have not
committed any sin at all after they received holy baptism and the
souls of those who have committed sin but have been cleansed,
either while they were in the body or afterwards . . . are promptly taken up into heaven. The souls of those who die in mortal
sin or with only original sin soon go down into hell, but there
receive different punishments. . . . On the Day of Judgment all
men appear before the judgment seat of Christ with their bodies,
to give an account of their deeds" (DS 856-859). This latter part
is repeated almost verbatim by another general and reunion
council, that of Florence, in its Decree for the Greeks (DS 1304-
1306). There is no doubt, then, that these councils were concerned with a profession of faith and with a dogmatic decree
that were meant to indicate clearly that life after death is a
dogma of the Catholic faith.

In *Benedictus Deus*, the Constitution he issued in 1336, Pope
Benedict XII declared: "By this constitution which is to remain
in force forever, we with our apostolic authority, make the following definition: In the usual providence of God the souls of
all the saints . . . holy apostles, martyrs, confessors, virgins and
others of the faithful who died after receiving holy baptism of
Christ—provided they had no need of purification at the time of
death—all these souls, soon after their death . . . are in heaven
and the celestial paradise with Christ, joined to the company of
the holy angels—even before these souls take up their bodies
again and before the general judgment . . . and they see the divine
essence with an intuitive and even face-to-face vision . . . and
those who see the divine essence in this way take great joy from
it and because of this vision and enjoyment are truly blessed and
possess life and eternal rest . . . and this same vision and enjoyment remain continuously without any interruption or abolition
of the vision and enjoyment and will remain up till the final judgment and from then on forever. Moreover, we define that . . . the
souls of those who die in actual mortal sin go down into hell soon
after their death, and there suffer the pains of hell. . ." (DS
1000-1002).

That Benedict XII meant to define the existence and to some extent the nature of life after death seems very clear, in spite of the fact that some of our modern theologians do not seem to consider this a papal definition. For DS 1000-1002 says *ad occasionem hs. definitionis "ex cathedra."* Further before he defined it Benedict XII had asked for serious discussion by theologians of this matter that had a solid biblical and patristic foundation. Obviously he was dealing with the message of the Gospel, for life after death, the beatific vision and eternal life are substantial parts of the doctrine of salvation. He clearly meant to define it when he declared *"hac in perpetuum valitura Constitutione auctoritate Apostolica diffinimus."* For a long time this has been accepted as a papal definition of a dogma of the faith. And that it is and remains until it is validly, not wishfully, dislodged.

The *Fifth Lateran Council,* a general council held from 1512-1517, made certain solemn declarations about the human soul and its immortality: "With the approval of this Sacred Council, we condemn and reject all those who claim that the intellectual soul is mortal or that there is a single soul for all men. We condemn those who raise doubts about this matter. For the soul is not only truly, of its own nature, and essentially the form of the human body, as is stated in the canon of our predecessor Pope Clement V of happy memory and published in the (general) Council of Vienna, but also it is immortal and, corresponding to the number of bodies into which it is infused, is capable of being multiplied in individuals, is actually multiplied and must be multiplied" (DS 1440).

Perhaps it should be pointed out that what the Council defined was simply that the intellectual soul is immortal, not that it is naturally immortal, and not that it lives on in a completely disembodied state until the resurrection of the dead. But although the Council Fathers did not define these last two points, it is quite probable that they did subscribe or would have subscribed to them.

And so as far as these documents are concerned, the soul's *natural* immortality and its *disembodied* life after death, are open to question and study. Later on these documents will be studied in greater detail in the light of recent conciliar criticism and questioning, so as to determine more precisely just what they basically and essentially affirm about life after death and the immortality of the soul. But even now it seems quite evident that these dogmatic documents solemnly declare an unwavering belief in life after death and in an immortal human soul.

Vatican II was not a dogmatic council in intent, but its teaching is in complete agreement with the dogmatic doctrine presented above. Thus it declares: "When we have finished the one and only course of our earthly life we may merit to enter into the marriage feast with Him and to be numbered among the blessed. Before we reign with the glorious Christ, all of us will be made manifest 'before the tribunal of Christ' . . . At the end of the world, 'they who have done good shall come forth unto resurrection of life; but who have done evil unto resurrection of judgment' (Jn 5:29). Some have finished with this life and are being purified. Others are in glory, beholding 'clearly God Himself Triune and One, as He is.' After they have been received into their heavenly home and are present to the Lord, through Him and with Him and in Him, they do not cease to intercede with the Father for us. . . . When Christ shall appear and the glorious resurrection of the dead takes place, the splendor of God will brighten the heavenly city."[44]

And in *Gaudium et Spes* we read: "Though made of body and soul, man is one. . . . He discerns his own proper destiny beneath the eyes of God. Thus, when man recognizes in himself a spiritual and immortal soul, he is not being mocked by a deceptive fantasy springing from mere physical or social influences. On the contrary he is getting to the depths of the very truth of the matter. . . . Man rebels against death because he bears in himself an eternal seed which cannot be reduced to sheer matter. . . . The Church has been taught by divine revelation and herself firmly teaches that man has been created by God for a blissful purpose beyond the reach of earthly misery. . . . God has called man . . . so that with his entire being he might be joined to Him in an endless sharing of divine life beyond all corruption" (No. 14, 18).

CONCLUSION

History of Religions indicates that men of all times and cultures believed in some kind of human survival after death. Some Spiritualist "communications" seem to offer a solid probability that there is conscious and intelligent human life after death "over there somewhere." While the Reincarnationist "arguments" for reincarnation are not convincing, some of the purported cases of reincarnation seem to require a "survivalist explanation" but they by no means "prove" that any or all men are reincarnated after death. And while the Church does not seem to have explicitly and solemnly condemned Reincarnationism, it does seem to have implicitly rejected this doctrine in its solemn teachings about the afterlife of men in purgatory, hell and heaven. Vatican II seems to have gone on record against this doctrine when it declared: "When we have finished the one and only course of our earthly life we may merit to enter into the marriage feast with Him and to be numbered among the blessed." When we turned to Sacred Scripture we found in some of the late books of the Old Testament a clear witness to a belief in an afterlife at least for the virtuous. In the New Testament we found a clear witness to a belief in an afterlife for all men, that will be endless and very different for the good and the wicked. And the Church's Magisterium solemnly affirmed and defined this biblical belief in life after death in the dogmatic pronouncements of General Councils and of Pope Benedict XII. And Vatican II clearly expressed its complete agreement with this biblical and magisterial teaching about life after death.

Notes for Chapter 1

1. John Baillie, **And the Life Everlasting,** (Oxford Univ. Press., 1934, 1956), pp. 1-86.

2. Alain Hus, **Greek and Roman Religion,** (New York, Hawthorn Books, 1962), pp. 46-57.

3. J. Baillie, **loc. cit.**

4. A. Hus, J. Baillie, **loc. cit.**

5. M. and L. Becque, **Life after Death,** (New York, Hawthorn Books, 1960), pp. 43-50.

6. Becque, **loc. cit.**

7. Nandor Fodor, **Encyclopedia of Psychic Science,** (New York, University Books), p. 361; J. Liljencrants, **Spiritism and Religion,** (New York, Devin-Adair, 1918).

8. H. Bender, "Parapsychology". **Sacramentum Mundi,** 5, (New York, Herder and Herder, 1969), pp. 153ff.

9. N. Fodor, **loc. cit.,** p. 360.

10. A. Borgia, **Life In the World Unseen,** (London, 1958); H. Holzer, **Life after Death,** (London, Sidgwick & Jackson, 1971), pp. 57ff.

11. C. J. Ducasse, **The Belief in a Life after Death,** (Springfield, Ill., Charles C. Thomas, 1961), pp. 171-182.

12. C.E.M. Hansel, **ESP: A Scientific Evaluation,** (New York, Charles Scribner's Sons, 1966), pp. 209-229.

13. G. Murphy, **Challenge of Psychical Research,** (New York, Harper & Bros., 1961), pp. 185-209, 214-269.

14. A. J. Smith, **Immortality,** (New York, Prentice-Hall, 1954).

15. Hansel, **loc. cit.,** p. 228.

16. **Loc. cit.,** pp. 271-273.

17. A. Spragget, **The Unexplained,** (New York, New American Library, 1967), pp. 19-23; Irving Litvag, **Singer In the Shadows,** (New York, The Macmillan Co., 1972); S. Ralph Harlow, **A Life after Death,** (New York, Doubleday & Co., 1961), pp. 98-110; A.J. Smith, **Immortality,** (New York, Prentice-Hall, 1954), pp. 71-76.

18. Litvag, **loc. cit.,** p. 159.

19. **Ibid.,** p. 282.

20. **Ibid.,** pp. 283-284.

21. **Ibid.,** p. 274.

22. **Ibid.,** p. 297.

23. **Loc. cit.,** p. 203.

24. Cf. P. Siwek, **Experimental Psychology,** (New York, Joseph Wagner, 1958); John Baillie, **loc. cit.,** pp. 114-118; T. Berry, **Religions of India,** (Milwaukee, Bruce, 1971), pp. 141ff.

25. H. S. Long, "Transmigration", **New Catholic Encyclopedia,** (New York, McGraw Hill, 1966), v. XIV, pp. 257-259.
26. Samuel Rayan, S.J., "The Eschatological Hope of Hinduism", **The Problem of Eschatology,** v. 41, **Concilium** series.
27. Baillie, **loc. cit.**
28. Berry, **loc. cit.,** pp. 141ff.
29. **Reincarnation,** (Calcutta, 6th ed., 1951).
30. R. K. MacMaster, "Theosophy", **New Catholic Encyclopedia,** v. XIV, pp. 74-75.
31. Cf. Morey Bernstein, **The Search for Bridey Murphy,** (Doubleday); Gina Cerminara, **The World Within,** (New York, W. Sloane Associates, 1957), pp. 11-23; J. Head and S. L. Cranston, **Reincarnation, An East-West Anthology,** (Wheaton, 1968), pp. 300-301; Ducasse, **op. cit.,** pp. 276-299.
32. **Twenty Cases Suggestive of Reincarnation,** (New York, American Society for Psychical Research, 1966).
33. N. Langley, **Edgar Cayce on Reincarnation,** (New York, Castle Books, 1967), p. 169.
34. Cayce, **loc. cit.,** p. 281.
35. **Chicago Tribune,** Oct. 16, 1975, pp. 1, 23.
36. **Our Sunday Visitor,** Sept. 14, 1975, p. 3.
37. **Op. cit.**
38. W. M. Abbott, S.J., ed., **The Documents of Vatican II,** (New York, Guild Press, 1966), **Dei Verbum,** no. 11, p. 119.
39. **The Jerome Biblical Commentary,** (Englewood Cliffs, Prentice-Hall, 1968), pp. 168-178.
40. J. L. McKenzie, S.J., **Dictionary of the Bible,** (Milwaukee, Bruce, 1965), pp. 800-801.
41. X. Leon-Dufer, S.J., ed., **Dictionary of Biblical Theology,** (New York, Desclee Co., 1967), p. 496.
42. Cf. M. Dahood, **The Psalms,** Anchor Bible.
43. J. F. Clarkson, S.J., et al., **The Church Teaches,** (St. Louis, B. Herder Book Co., 1955), pp. 6, 72.
44. Abbott, **loc. cit., Lumen Gentium,** nos. 48-51, pp. 80-85.

Chapter 2
Is Man Naturally Immortal?

There is life after death for every man. That is what we have found. Every man is destined to live on after the death of his body. That is what we have found. But then a question quickly arises. Is this destiny to life after death written into man's very nature? Is every man by his very nature destined for and capable of life after death? Or is every man by his nature destined for death and incapable of life after death?

If he is by his very nature destined to die and yet lives on after the death of his body, this would seem to involve a special arrangement on God's part. Such that every man's life after death, his immortality, would not be a natural immortality but a gift-immortality, a special destination and capacitation produced by God Himself at death.

While such a gift-immortality is, of course, quite possible, it hardly seems likely that God would make every man mortal by his very nature, and then make him immortal by a special gift. God might make the *good* immortal in this way, by a gift-immortality that would reward their good earthly life. But it hardly seems likely that God would also make the *wicked* immortal in this way, by a gift-immortality, so that He could punish them after death for their earthly life of wickedness.

Hence if *every* man is destined to have life after death, as we have found, it would seem much more likely that God would write this destiny into every man's nature and make him capable by his very nature of life after death. How? By building into every man a principle of life after death, a principle that would destine and capacitate him for life after death. And this is what traditional Christian doctrine has maintained, that every man is destined and capacitated for life after death by his very nature, in virtue of a naturally immortal soul that is an essential principle of every man.

And so we are confronted with the Mystery of Man. And we are faced with the basic question: *What is man?*

WHAT IS MAN?

This is a question that has fascinated and baffled men down the centuries. Is man just an animal? Or is he much, much more than a mere animal? Like animals he sees and hears and tastes and smells and touches. Like them he lives and is capable of nutrition, growth, reproduction, local motion. But unlike them he thinks and reasons and talks and develops languages and symbols to communicate his thoughts. He builds tiny mud huts, great palaces, mighty Cathedrals, the Colosseum of Rome, the Parthenon of Athens. He produces haunting Christmas carols, glorious Gregorian chant, magnificent operas and symphonies. His masterpieces of painting and sculpture in the great galleries of the world are breathtaking. He develops a mighty mathematics that enables him to travel to the moon and back. He reaches out toward the ends of the cosmos with his light and radio telescopes. He sends man-made satellites to measure and photograph Mars and Venus and Jupiter and Saturn and send back to planet earth their measurements and their pictures. He sends his voice and his image by radio and television to the ends of the earth and far beyond. By his chemical and physical science he explores the very depths of matter and harnesses its energy by nuclear fission and fusion. By his biological and psychological science he delves ever more deeply into the intricacies of human life with the aim of developing a man who will be better and better, more long-lived, maybe even immortal.

Man is no tiny creature. Can he, then, in essence be no different from other animals? Must he not be essentially different from animals who live only a few years and then die forever? Can he have only material powers, limited by the limits of time and space? Must he not also have immaterial powers that transcend time and space limits? Is he just a mortal body? Or must he not also be an immortal soul? A person? Destined by God to live and love and be happy with God forever? These are questions that have intrigued man throughout man's history and always will. For man has always been a "mystery" to man, and very likely always will be to pilgrim man. But the basic question still is:

What is Man? Plato thought man is really only his soul, a soul that is not truly and essentially united to this body, a spiritual soul that is set free from this body to go on living and living. The Old Testament presents man as a creature made in the image and likeness of God. Man is responsible for his own acts and becomes a sinner but with hope of salvation. He is mortal. He does not simply "have" a soul and body: rather he "is" soul and body, an animated body. The New Testament tells us that before the coming of Christ man was under the dominion of sin, sinful and mortal. But by incorporation in Christ he receives a new life, enjoys the freedom of a child of God and the hope of salvation. He is called to love his neighbor and will stand acquitted or condemned by his response to this calling. Interpreting this teaching of Sacred Scripture the Church solemnly affirmed that man is a creature of God in both soul and body, but still a substantial unity in which a rational and intellectual and immortal soul is essentially the "form of the body" (DS 360, 800, 1440, 3002-3, 3224).

In the light of all this Christian theology has generally viewed man as a composite being, made up of body and soul. His soul is created from nothing and is immaterial, incorruptible, immortal, gifted with intelligence and free will. Thus by its very nature man's soul is capable of life after the death of its body.

Today, however, there is a strong drift away from the traditional view of man as a body-soul composite by scientists, biblicists, theologians. They find it too dualistic and too hard, if not impossible, to reconcile with the findings of modern science and modern biblical scholarship. Man is a unitary being, they insist. "Man is an essentially unitary being," Karl Rahner writes, "substantially one, and not the final addition of two beings, which could be thought of, at least, as originally existing in themselves" (*Sacramentum Mundi* 4, 415ff). John Shea strongly echoes this anti-dualistic trend. "This dualistic view of man," he writes, "so long the ally of Christian faith, does not correspond with either modern or biblical anthropology. Modern science envisages man as a psychomatic unity. The physical and spiritual aspects of any human life interrelate so closely and overlap so extensively that the only valid viewpoint is a holistic one. The spiritual and physical aspects can be distinguished but never separated. In other words, the 'soul' is not a detachable part of human nature, capable of independent activity and existence. The biblical view of man closely parallels the modern. . . . According to both modern and biblical understanding man is not a dichotomy, a meshing of parts. He is a 'unitary actuality' and cannot ever be satisfactorily disassembled. So today if Christian hope for a future life is to be realistically symbolized, it should not be imagined as an independent separated soul which at a future date will be united to a resurrected body but as the emergence of the whole man into the fullness of life."[1]

What is to be said of this widespread anti-dualistic trend? That seems to consider modern scientists and biblicists as the final arbiters of truth, whose modern dogmas should replace the traditional but antiquated ecclesial dogmas? And whose monistic view of man should replace the traditional Christian view of man? Is there solid evidence for the contention that we should accept this monistic view of man and reject every kind of dualistic view of man? Or is it just possible that we must take a view of man that is both monistic and dualistic, a view that still requires an immaterial and naturally immortal human soul? It seems very important to look carefully at modern scientific and biblical evidence for "monistic" man, and to try to determine its value.

Science

Many, if not most, modern scientists and psychologists seem to be materialistic monists, for whom all reality is matter or ulti-

mately reducible to matter. Just as in the older and more established sciences, so too in modern American psychology, the only
fundamental principles dealt with seem to be *physical*. For anything to be accepted as "real," it must be explicable by physical
law, measurable by scientific methods.

A dualism that posits two kinds of reality, one physical, one
psychic, one material, one immaterial, is considered incompatible
with the findings of modern science. *Monism*, writes Corliss
Lamont, is "the verdict of science." The connection between
man's mind and body is "so exceedingly intimate that it becomes
inconceivable how one could function properly without the other
. . . Man is a unified whole of mind-body or personality-body
so closely and completely integrated that dividing him up into
two separate parts more or less independent becomes impermissi-
ble and unintelligible." Dualism is "unnecessary . . . the complex-
ity of the cerebral cortex, together with the intricate structure
of the rest of the nervous system and the mechanism of speech,
makes any explanation of thought and consciousness in other
than naturalistic terms wholly unnecessary."[2]

Gardner Murphy, a distinguished psychologist, declared that
"difficulties which were already serious three centuries ago, as
the physiology of the brain began to be understood, have become
more and more serious, and the intimate unity of psychological
and physiological processes known to us through anatomy,
physiology, psychopathology, even bio-chemistry and histology,
makes the concept of an independent soul recede more and more
into the land of the utterly incredible and unimaginable."[3]

To many these and similar monistic arguments seem cogent
but they really are not, for they involve bad logic, fallacious
inference. The proponents of these arguments argue from an
intimate connection between mind and body, from an intimate
unity of physiological and psychological processes to their basic
identity. This is bad logic, to say the least. From their intimate
unity they conclude to their indistinction and inseparability.
This again is bad logic. Not too long ago scientists thought that
the intimate unity of subatomic particles proved their inseparability. Now they know better since they have managed to sepa-

rate many of them. Now they realize that the most intimate union of elements is quite compatible with their real separability. They should realize that an intimate union of mind and body, an intimate union of physiological and psychological processes does not prove their inseparability.

Psychologists can show and have shown that man is a most intimate psychosomatic unity, a deeply unitary being in which physiological and psychological processes are so closely connected as to rule out an independent soul of the kind that Plato or Descartes posited. But they have not shown and cannot show that there is in man no non-material reality, no non-physical reality, no "meta-empirical principle of being in the one man," call it "soul" or "spirit" or whatever you prefer, "which cannot be adequately described by the concepts and methods of natural science," and which can after the death of its "body" go on existing and acting personally and intelligently. But it is one thing to say that science and psychology cannot prove that there is not any non-material element in man. It is quite another thing to say that we can prove that there is in man such a non-material element, an immaterial soul, an immaterial soul that is naturally immortal. Can we prove this? We think we can prove this, with at least high probability from psychology and parapsychology and with certainty from biblical revelation and from ecclesial interpretation of this revelation. First we turn to:

Psychology

To look to psychology for evidence of an immaterial, naturally immortal soul in man can appear rather foolhardy. For among psychologists today the term "soul" is in rather wide disrepute and it is rarely used by them. Many regard it merely as a relic of an outmoded essentialism or of a primitive dualism that implies that man is not a unitary being but the addition or composition of two independent beings. They want to be existentialists, not essentialists, monists, not dualists and so they stress man's existence, not his essence, his unity and not his duality. Instead of talking of a "soul" some prefer to talk of a primordial ego, of mind, of consciousness, of spirit, of a self-embodying spirit, of a meta-empirical principle, of person. So that "the term soul itself seems to be ignored by contemporary philosophers and to be used primarily in theological and moral circles."[4] It may help to look at this "soul's" history.

In its long history the term soul has been variously described and defined. Aristotle at first accepted from Plato the "myth of the soul as a divine—immaterial—sojourner on earth—imprisoned in a body," but later he viewed the soul as "an entelechy or form, inseparable from its body, or at any rate certain parts of it."[5] In the Old Testament our English word "soul" translates the Hebrew *nepesh*, whose basic meaning seems to be self or person, the self as person, as the conscious subject of action and passion. The Greek concept of soul (psyche) appears only in Wisdom.[6] In the New Testament the Greek psyche is used, and this is translated in English by soul. It still means "the totality of the self as a living and conscious subject," much as it did in the Old Testament. St. Augustine was "the first of the Latin Fathers to have a clear concept of soul as a spiritual substance intimately united to the body . . . the soul is a completely immaterial substance."[7] For Thomas Aquinas, likewise, man's soul is immaterial, spiritual in its essence, an immaterial intellectual substance that is the form of the body. And it is this view of the soul as an immaterial, intellectual, immortal form of the human body that has been 'canonized' by the Church's solemn magisterium. With Descartes we reach an extreme dualism of soul and body, in which "the soul, located in the pineal gland, is an immaterial, unextended being interacting with the body through the medium of the brain and nervous system."[8] For Kant the soul is still an immaterial, spiritual, immortal animator of the human body, but with "Nominalism and the rise of empirical and mathematical science" the concept of soul is gradually emptied "of its original meaning as substantial form of living beings."[9] Can such an immaterial soul, that is physically and mentally invisible, be shown to exist—inferentially? Over the years various arguments have been advanced.

Long ago *Origen* said, "Let those who think the mind and

soul is a body tell me, if this were so, how it could receive and understand reasonings which are difficult and subtle, and contemplate and know things invisible and incorporeal."[10] *St. Thomas* wrote, "If anyone does not wish to say that the intellectual soul is the form of the body, let him find a theory whereby the act of understanding is the action of this man, for everyone knows by experience that *he* understands."[11]

Prof. Aldwinckle offers an interesting argument based on the reality of the 'I' of personal identity. "It is assumed by many today," he says, "that 'science' teaches that man is no more than his body." But he is much more. For "every knowing or cognizing subject is in some degree self-conscious, aware of being the self-same being throughout different experiences." "Self-consciousness, awareness of self-identity, memory, freedom, acts of moral obligation" are "empirical facts" which "no established empirical evidence from the sciences compels us to deny." Though this enduring 'I', which is somehow more than just a series of experiences, is denied by Buddhists, Hume and his followers, yet the "reality of the 'I' or 'self' is obvious to anyone who introspects, who looks into his own self-consciousness, into his own experience of self-awareness. This 'I' of personal identity cannot be reduced to or explained solely by changes in the physical body, however closely it is linked to that body in our present existence." If there is no such enduring 'I', how can I speak of my freedom and responsibility? How can I experience shame, guilt, moral approval or disapproval in regard to acts done years ago? This enduring 'I' must be an enduring entity which is more than a sequence of psychological states rooted ultimately in physical changes. And if there is such an enduring 'I' there must be in our makeup a non-material element, whether we call it mind, soul, spirit, or self, else our experience is incoherent.[12] This non-material element is or is ultimately rooted in what has traditionally been called an '*immaterial soul*.'

J. Bobik recently offered two arguments. The first is simple. If human soul means 'source of thought activity,' then there are human souls if there are things that think. But there are things that think (I think and I recognize that others think). Hence there are human souls. The other is more complicated. In the realm of physical changes (and of sensitive activity) in man, the forms received in his knowing experiences (e.g. this image, this taste) are individual forms because what receives them is individual matter. But in another of man's knowing experiences, in his act of understanding, he receives a form that is not an individual form (e.g. humanity, rationality, animality). Hence in man what receives this non-individual (or absolute) form, is not individual matter, is not the power of some bodily organ (else this material organ would individualize the form received). Therefore this receptive (and effective) power in man is an *immaterial* power, and ultimately an *immaterial soul*.[13]

These arguments are mainly based on the presence in man of immaterial activities and immaterial forms. They may be stated a bit differently for further clarity. In man there are both material activities (walking, tasting . . .) and immaterial activities (e.g. reasoning, judging, understanding). These must have a proportionate principle (else they would not be). This proportionate principle must be proximately both material (i.e. body) and immaterial (i.e. mind) but ultimately it must be *immaterial*. Why? Because what is material cannot principiate what is above it (what is immaterial) but what is immaterial can principiate what is below it (what is material), as is obvious in the case of God. Therefore in man the ultimate principle of all his human activities must be immaterial, must be an immaterial soul or spirit. The argument may be put in still another way. In his knowing experiences man receives both material forms (spatial images, e.g. of this tree) and immaterial forms (non-spatial ideas, e.g. of truth, justice, beauty). But to receive a material form the recipient must be material, to receive an immaterial form the recipient must be immaterial. Hence to receive both forms man must proximately be both material (body) and immaterial (mind), but ultimately an immaterial soul or spirit.

These arguments, though they may not apodictically demonstrate the immateriality of the human soul, yet do furnish solid reasons for saying that it is at least highly probable that man must have and so does have an immaterial soul as the ultimate principle of his human activities.

A Naturally Immortal Soul is even more widely controverted than an immaterial soul. A human soul is finite by its very nature. It is not eternal. Only God is eternal. What could make such a finite thing incapable of dying and capable of living forever? If the human soul is essentially the form of its body, how could it go on existing without its body? What could it do without a body? And so on and on run the objections to a naturally immortal soul. Long ago Justin and Tatian, it seems, maintained that the human soul was not immortal by nature but could become immortal if it lived according to God's law.

Can we "prove" that there is in man a naturally immortal soul? The Scholastics generally maintained that we could, though a few of them said we could prove this only with probability, not with certainty.[14] Recently Ignace Lepp wrote that "it is impossible to prove the immortality of the soul scientifically."[15] Yet according to J. E. Royce "the doctrine that the human soul is immortal and will continue to exist after man's death and the dissolution of his body is one of the cornerstones of Christian *philosophy* and *theology*" (*New Catholic Encyclopedia*, 13; 464). And immortality "does not mean . . . continued existence in the memory of mankind or as a symbol . . . it does not mean absorption into the eternal existence of God or transmigration into another being. Immortality means actual continued existence in one's own identity" (ibid 466). And *natural* immortality means that the soul's immortality is due to its own nature, to the very nature God has given it, so that the God who has destined man to everlasting life gives him a soul that can and will live an everlasting life.

Many arguments have been advanced over the years to 'prove' the natural immortality of the human soul. Plato argued from the simplicity and spirituality of the soul and its likeness to the divine. Tertullian argued from the simplicity of the soul, Lactantius from the moral order, Augustine from the indestructibility of truth, Gregory of Nyssa from the simplicity of the soul and the immateriality of its intellectual operations, Thomas Aquinas from the spirituality and the substantiality of the soul. More recently C. Boyer argued from the spirituality of the soul, from man's natural desire of living always, from the immaterial objects of man's intellect, from the necessity of a moral sanction in an afterlife.

J. E. Royce presents briefly but well two of these arguments, one from the nature of the soul, the other from moral sanctions. "Of its nature," he points out, "the human soul is incorruptible. Being simple, it lacks any spatial or constitutive parts into which it can break up. Being spiritual, at the death of the body it is not subject to corruption incidental to any intrinsic dependence on matter, for its spiritual operations of intellection and volition show it to have only extrinsic dependence on matter. The only way it could cease to exist is by annihilation, the failure of God as First Cause to conserve it in being. But for God to annihilate what he has made immortal by nature would be inconsistent and unreasonable, a contradiction of His own design. Such an imperfection is impossible to God" (loc. cit., p. 466). In his argument from moral sanctions he writes: "One may infer the logical necessity of a life after death from the fact that people generally experience moral obligation and a sense of responsibility.... Yet one sees people trying to do what they think right, and receiving no reward in this life. Others, who commit crime, go unpunished; and still others are punished unjustly for crimes they did not commit. Moral values, a sense of obligation, and of responsibility find no adequate sanction in this life. Unless there is a life after death in which wrongs will be righted and people receive what they deserve, the whole notion of obligation seems irrational.... A sanction that is not everlasting is not adequate ultimately . . . Only immortality provides adequate sanction" (ibid).

I. Lepp has added an interesting argument for the soul's immortality based on evolution. "For millions of years," he wrote, "the immense and complex process of evolution on our planet seems to have tended toward the emergence of spirit. It is inconceivable that this long preparation could end in pure and simple nothingness. The spirit's survival beyond corporeal disintegration thus appears to be fundamentally demanded by evolutionary creation. . . . The law which demands that man dies as an individual also demands that he subsist as a person. . . . What essentially constitutes man is his spiritual soul and this, therefore, is what will survive. If we do not survive our empirical death as persons, then the whole long process of evolution is inexplicable and absurd. . . . It seems to me in keeping with the known laws of evolution to suppose that when the life of the body ceases, the spirit is re-energized and capable of attaining a new level of evolution" (loc. cit., pp. 167, 168).

What is to be said of these arguments? Do they strictly demonstrate that man has a naturally immortal soul? Probably not. But if someone approaches them with an open mind and good will they can strongly point him in this direction and gradually lead him to realize that God has destined him for everlasting life and given him an immaterial soul as ultimate principle of personal identity and activity, an enduring immaterial entity which is capable of everlasting life and which God will never annihilate.

Parapsychology

Philosophical psychology has given us solid evidence that there is in man more than his body, that there is in man an immaterial and naturally immortal soul as ultimate principle of personal identity and activity which is capable of everlasting life. So there is in man an enduring immaterial entity that is capable of life after the death of its body. But capable of what kind of life after death? Prof. Ducasse views the human mind as a system of three interrelated dispositions or capacities, which he calls "psycho-psychical, psycho-physical, and physico-psychical, according, respectively, as the cause-event and the effect-event entering in the description of a given capacity are, both of them, psychical events; or, the cause-event psychical but the effect-event physical; or the cause-event physical but the effect-event psychical". He concludes that "if a mind continues to function after the death of its body, its functioning would not then normally include exercise either of its physico-psychical or of its psycho-physical capacities" (op. cit., pp. 54, 55). But he thinks that if physical events came into the ambit of a discarnate mind, the mind's activity would be *paranormal* and of the kind that parapsychology calls "clairvoyant" or "psycho-kinetic". So we turn to parapsychology to see if it can offer us any evidence to back up the psychological evidence for an immaterial and naturally immortal soul and also give us some indication of what kind of life and activity this immaterial soul as ultimate principle of personal identity and activity might exercise after the death of its body.

To turn to parapsychology may seem a rather surprising procedure. For today parapsychology is in much the same disrepute that psychology was not long ago. Prof. Hansel, one of the most uncompromising opponents of parapsychology, wrote not long ago: "the whole body of scientific knowledge compels us to assume that such things as telepathy and clairvoyance are impossible, and that the psychic phenomena do not correspond to the basic requirements of all natural science."[16] And H. J. Muller, a Nobel laureate, "ranked the adherents of parapsychology among the lunatic fringe of wishful thinkers."[17] Why are some scientists so opposed to parapsychology? The simplest answer seems to be that they are materialistic monists who dogmatically maintain that phenomena which do not admit of a materialistic, a physical explanation, cannot be genuine occurrences. Parapsychology deserves better treatment than this, for graduate work in parapsychology has been done at Harvard, Yale, Columbia, Duke, St. Joseph's College, Oxford, Cambridge, Utrecht. Intensive research is being carried on today in the area of parapsychology in the Iron Curtain countries.[18] Recently Andrija Puharich, a neurologist, wrote an interesting book called *Beyond Telepathy*[19] as a pioneering attempt to rationalize "the anatomy and dynamics of the mind". He starts from "examples of telepathy, clairvoyance, the action of mind at a distance, and most remarkable of all—the personality freeing itself of the body and traveling at will across the reaches of time and space", and then "analyzes the biological, physiological and psychological conditions leading to the control of *psi plasma*". . . which, he maintains, "can exist independently of the physical body" (ibid xiv).

What is parapsychology? It is the study of what are called paranormal or psychic events. Five such paranormal phenomena stand out: (1) *telepathy* (communication between minds independently of the channels of sense and notwithstanding distance and intervening material obstacles [Ducasse, op. cit., p. 140]); (2) *clairvoyance* (perception of objects or scenes or forms distant in space or time and not at the time accessible to the organs of sense [ibid]; (3) *precognition* (advance knowledge of a future occurrence which cannot be inferred in any normal way and which does not take place in consequence of the advance knowledge (Hans Bender, "Parapsychology," *Sacramentum Mundi 5*, 154); (4) *psychokinesis* (the influence of mind on matter, of psychological processes such as will upon physical events without utilization of the nervous and muscular systems (Murphy, op. cit., 156); (5) *out-of-the-body experiences* (supernormal excursions beyond the physical body (Murphy, op. cit., 287; Ducasse, op. cit., 141). Is there any evidence that such paranormal phenomena actually occur?

Many cases of *spontaneous* telepathy, clairvoyance, precognition, psychokinesis have been described by Gardner Murphy, Nandor Fodor (*Encyclopedia of Psychic Science*), Alois Wiesinger, O.C.S.O. (*Occult Phenomena: In the Light of Theology*), Richard Woods, O.P. (*The Occult Revolution*), S. Ostrander and L. Schroeder. Spontaneous cases of out-of-the-body experiences are presented by R. A. Monroe (*Journeys Out of The Body*), Nandor Fodor (op. cit.), Allen Spragget (*The Unexplained*). One of the most famous cases of spontaneous clairvoyance is that of Emanuel Swedenborg (1688-1772). At Gothenburg in 1756 Swedenborg had a clairvoyant vision of a devastating fire which was raging in Stockholm, some 300 miles away. He reported this vision and it was found to agree fully with the account of the fire that a courier brought up from Stockholm a few days later.[20] Do such cases of spontaneous paranormal phenomena give us solid evidence that man has paranormal powers? Many (most?) of the cases do not: they are too open to the charge of fraud, or delusion or wishful thinking. But some derive from very reliable witnesses and their authenticity seems unimpeachable. The clairvoyant vision of Swedenborg was investigated by Immanuel Kant and found by him to be authentic. It seems beyond doubt that *some* of these spontaneous cases do give *solid evidence* for the existence in man of paranormal powers, of extra-sensory mental abilities.

Most investigators in psychology and parapsychology, however, prefer experimental to spontaneous evidence and are committed to a maximal use of the experimental method. Is there any experimental or quasi-experimental evidence for these paranormal phenomena? Louisa E. Rhine, the wife of J. B. Rhine, the noted statistical experimenter at Duke University, wrote that "the record shows that it has been possible by indirect procedures to secure reliable results . . . ESP was established, and with much effort extending over several years and involving many subjects and various experimenters, the types of psi phenomena (telepathy, clairvoyance and prerecognition) were separated and psychokinesis too was established. This means that a new potential reach of mind was shown, a reach not bound by physical limitations. Such a mental ability operating without the physical limitations which restrain perception by the senses shows an aspect of man that is different in *order* from that of the physical universe."[21]

Has ESP been established? J. B. and Louisa Rhine thought so, and Hans Bender declared that the results of the Rhine experiments "have been confirmed by many investigators using constantly improved methods."[22] Prof. C. E. M. Hansel maintains that ESP has not been established. In his book, *ESP*, he wrote that he singled out the "conclusive experiments" (Pearce-Pratt, Pratt-Woodruff, Soal-Goldney, Telepathic Welsh Schoolboys) that had been made in recent years in the matter of ESP and subjected them to a very critical examination. He concluded, "it cannot be stated categorically that trickery was responsible for the results of these experiments, but so long as the possibility is present, the experiments cannot be regarded as satisfying the aims of their originators or as supplying conclusive evidence for ESP; other explanations than ESP can account for their results."[23]

What is to be said of Prof. Hansel's investigations? They were thoroughgoing in their intent and their execution, and devastating in their conclusions. But (1) Prof. Hansel can hardly be considered an 'ideal' investigator, for he started with the assumption that "such things as telepathy and clairvoyance are impossible"; (2) had he not been so intent on 'disestablishing' ESP, he should have noted that some of the experiments *did* offer strong, if not conclusive evidence of ESP; (3) he might have eliminated the 'possibility of trickery' by repeating some of the experiments himself, or by using an "acceptable model for research made available by the investigators of the U.S. Air Force Research Laboratories."[24]

Besides these parapsychological experiments in the U.S. and Great Britain, some notable experiments have been made in the Iron Curtain countries and they add strong, perhaps conclusive evidence of the existence of paranormal powers in some men and women, notably Karl Nikolaiev, Josefka, Vanga Dimitrova, Nelya Mikhailova.

In the Moscow-Siberia Telepathy Test (1966) Karl Nikolaiev, the receiver, was at Novosibirsk, Siberia. In Moscow, about 1860 miles away, Yuri Kamensky, the transmitter, only knew there would be six objects to send telepathically to Nikolaiev, each would be brought to him separately by the committee and he would have ten minutes to transmit per object. Dr. Kogan reported in the scientific journal, *Radio Technology*, that Nikolaiev satisfactorily received half of the telepathic images and successfully zeroed in on thought from Moscow not once, but six times. In March 1967, Nikolaiev was in Leningrad hoping to pick up telepathic messages from Kamensky in Moscow. Nikolaiev was in a soundproof, isolated room, wired to a lab full of monitoring machines. He had no idea when the telepathic messages from Kamensky would come. . . . Isolated in a chamber in Moscow, Kamensky began his telepathic transmission. Abruptly, three seconds later in Leningrad Nikolaiev's brain waves changed "drastically." Apparently the Soviets had caught the moment when telepathy lights up in the brain. It was a few seconds before

Nikolaiev was consciously aware of receiving . . . the image of a cigarette box that Kamensky had transmitted.[25]

Milan Ryzl, a research associate of the Duke parapsychology Laboratory and the only communist ever to receive the McDougall Award for distinguished work in ESP, had a girl called Josefka run through 250 ESP cards. She scored 121 hits, whereas chance expectation would be 50. Vanga Dimitrova, the Bulgarian oracle, a state-employed psychic, is famed for her clairvoyant and prophetic powers. She is expert at psychically giving people information about missing friends and relatives. But her uncanny ability to see even two decades into the future is the most unusual part of her psychic talent. She predicted the days on which her husband and her father would die, and they died on the exact days Vanga had specified. Research seems to show, according to these authors, that 80% of what she predicted is right, and that is not a poor score in prerecognition. Nelya Mikhailova is outstanding for her psychokinetic powers. The Mendeleyev Institute of Metrology studied her and stated in *Moscow Pravda* that she had moved aluminum pipes and matches under the strictest test conditions, including observation on closed-circuit television. Soviet scientists reported that by her PK (psycho-kinetic) power she had moved and stopped the pendulum of a wall clock, moved plastic vases, water pitchers weighing a pound, and an assortment of dishes, cups and glasses—and all without touching the objects. Watching scientists and reporters found "no hidden threads, magnets, or other gimmicks."

Uri Geller, an Israeli ex-paratrooper, seems to have manifested psychokinetic powers just as great as Nelya's. Under strictly controlled laboratory conditions at the University of London in June 1974, by intense concentration alone, he increased the number of counts per second of a Geiger counter to 200 times the normal rate, shattered tightly sealed crystals, moved a compass needle 40 degrees. In a television broadcast over the British Broadcasting Corporation network in Nov. 1973, he demonstrated the bending of keys and the starting of broken watches. "Within minutes, the BBC switchboard was clogged with phone calls from listeners reporting that knives, spoons and keys were bending in their homes, and that watches and clocks that had not run for years were ticking away." But Geller has also failed time and again at critical moments, to his great embarrassment.[26]

What is to be said of these reported phenomena? Do they give solid evidence of paranormal powers? They have been variously evaluated. The book, *Psychic Discoveries Behind the Iron Curtain*, received very negative reviews in JASPR (v. 65, pp. 88, 495). Prof. Hansel, of course, says the phenomena that he investigated give no conclusive evidence, but Cyril Burt pointed out that Prof. Hansel's judgment was based on "assumptions that are no longer valid" (*Parapsychology Today*, pp. 215-16). According to Sir Cyril himself, "(1) there is strong experimental evidence to show that under certain conditions . . . something that for convenience may be called telepathy does in fact occur between two or more persons; (2) there is similar evidence, not so extensive, in favor of what is termed clairvoyance; (3) evidence drawn from so-called 'spontaneous experiences,' partly confirmed by experimental results, suggests the possibility of something very like precognition; (4) similar evidence, though far more meager, suggests the possibility of retrocognition . . . (5) there is some slight experimental evidence, not as yet very convincing, in favor of psychokinesis."

Some of the ESP claims of Dr. Rhine and other experimenters Gardner Murphy does not rate very highly. Much of the data they offer he finds it hard to accept. For they mix a considerable amount of psychological and philosophical speculation with large masses of more or less authenticated materials. And they deal with events that do not readily fit into the time-space-motion-energy system of our modern physical science. But he apparently gives their claims about psychokinesis a higher rating. Granted that many of the psychokinesis experiments are only rough-and-ready affairs conducted with very little proper control, he yet finds that independent experimental work does tend to support Dr. Rhine's conclusions. And he declares, "I do not say the conclusions are established. . . . I say that the thoughtful modern reader can no longer slam the door on psychokinesis" (op. cit.,

p. 182). Out-of-the-body experiences appear to him to be real and "consonant with a modern conception of the unity of the living system in which mental phenomena, such as a tendency to undergo bilocation . . . are experiences not very far from the known terrain of general psychology" (ibid., p. 287). He adds something that is very significant: "what has been implied here about paranormal cognition (including experimental telepathy, clairvoyance and precognition) applies almost in full force to PK likewise and indeed in all likelihood to every type of paranormal process. We are dealing with a *basic dualism* in human nature between a normal and a paranormal process, at least with a practical *functional dualism,* in the sense that we must strenuously exclude every possibility of normal physical action upon external objects or events if we are to include our observed phenomena as PK" (op. cit., p. 277).

There seems little doubt that there are authentic cases of telepathy, clairvoyance, precognition, psychokinesis, out-of-the-body experiences. The paranormal phenomena and events that we have studied—and the many, many others that we have not studied— seem to force us to this conclusion. Hence there are in some men at least paranormal powers that under appropriate conditions can bring about such paranormal phenomena and events. And if such paranormal powers are found in some men, it seems logical to conclude that they are latent in all men, for all men are basically alike.

Do these paranormal powers *prove* the existence in man of an immaterial soul? Perhaps not. But they do point very strongly in that direction. For they imply that there is a basic functional dualism between normal and paranormal functioning and processes. And this functional dualism strongly points to a basic dualism in man's very nature, a dualism of matter and of spirit, of body and of soul. So that man is existentially and functionally an incarnate spirit, and embodied soul. Thus man is an existential unit who has (or is) a material body and an immaterial soul with immaterial as well as material powers.

Do these paranormal powers further indicate that this immaterial soul is also naturally immortal? They definitely seem to.

For if I have such paranormal powers through which I can function outside my body and at a distance from my body without the mediation of my body's sensory or muscular apparatus, they would seem to indicate that I, or my immaterial soul as the ultimate principle of my personal identity and activity, could after the death of my body go on functioning without this body at all, and thus be naturally immortal.

Would these paranormal powers and activities also indicate something of the nature of my life after death? They would and they do. They strongly indicate that in my life after death I will have telepathic powers, clairvoyant powers, precognitive (and retrocognitive) powers, psychokinetic powers, as well as the power of trans-temporal and trans-spatial journeyings in which I will be able to *see, hear, touch* material events and embodied persons. A man, then, need not fear that if he goes into an afterlife, even into a disembodied afterlife, this afterlife will be one of inactivity. Rather he can expect not only to continue some (much?) of the mental activity he has in his earthly life but in addition to exercise regularly mental powers that are now merely paranormal.

Now we leave parapsychology much as we left psychology, grateful for the light they have shed on the mystery of man but wishing they had given us much more light and much, much more certainty.

Sacred Scripture

If psychology and parapsychology have not furnished us with complete certainty that man has an immaterial and naturally immortal soul, this need not be too surprising. For man is a mystery. And human intuitive and reflective powers are not adequate to reach the depths of a mystery. But God has made this mysterious man. And if He has given him an immaterial and naturally immortal soul, perhaps He will tell us or give us leads that we can follow. Has He told us in Sacred Scripture that He has given man an immaterial and immortal soul?

Old Testament

Some Scripture scholars today seem strongly inclined to say *No*. As they read about biblical man in the Old Testament they do not find God telling them he is a dualist man composed of body and soul. Rather he is a monistic man. It was *Greek* psychology, they say, that was dualist and divided man into body and soul. Hebrew psychology conceived man as a unitary being to whom such dualism did not apply. Thus the *Jerome Biblical Commentary* declares: "the Hebrews did not conceive of man as constituted of a material body and a spiritual soul" (34:12; 77:16). And again: "man in the Old Testament is conceived of as a unity and not as a composite of different principles" (77:66). And so these scholars see Old Testament biblical man as a strictly unitary being and not as a body-soul composite. But their simplistic view of Old Testament biblical man is rather surprising. For even if the Old Testament man is a unitary being, why should this Old Testament view of man be viewed as normative for us today? If these same scholars insist that the Old Testament is not to be viewed as teaching science in Genesis and elsewhere, why should they accept it as teaching psychology? If Old Testament writers show little awareness of an afterlife for man, why should one be so quick to accept their views of man in this life? If Old Testament writers view man as a unitary being, must this mean that he is in no way dualistic? Could it not mean that he is not dualistic in the Platonic or Cartesian sense, but dualistic perhaps in some other sense? And could it not be, perhaps, that the Old Testament writers sometimes had a glimpse of a dualistic man with a material body and an immaterial soul?

Actually it does seem to give some slight indication of this, for as Prof. Barr has declared: "it is quite easy to show that in late Judaism the soul could be regarded as separate from the body" (Ws 3:1 and 2 Maccabees). "Nor is it self-evident," he adds, "that this is always due to Hellenistic influence. It may very well have been the result of tensions and problems within Judaism itself."[27] The Hebrew was not a materialist nor a behaviorist for even if he lacked an explicit distinction of body and soul, he did not lack the distinction of bodily and mental activity (cf. R. Aldwinckle, op. cit. 68ff). For as H. Wheeler Robinson has pointed out, "the unity of personality as conceived by the Hebrew, found its emotional expression chiefly under the name of nephesh, whilst the intellectual and volitional activity centered on the heart as its organ."[28] What is more, the Old Testament does not regard death as an absolute end to all life, as a total annihilation. For it does attest to survival of some kind after death, especially by its belief that all the dead go to Sheol, where they live some kind of ghostlike afterlife (Ec 6:6; Jb 3:13-19; Is 14:10). If there is some kind of afterlife (and this not from the 'spirit' which has gone back to God), and some kind of retention of identity in it, must there not be a principle of this afterlife and identity, a "ghostly" principle, or in a later terminology, an immaterial principle or soul?

It may even be argued that there is some slight indication of a naturally immortal soul in the Book of Wisdom, where we read that "the souls of the virtuous are in the hands of God . . . they are in peace . . . their hope was rich with immortality" (Ws 3:1ff). This immortality of Ws has been called the enduring life of the psyche. And J. P. Weisengoff adds that it seems likely that "the whole Book has as its basis the conviction that the soul survives after death," but "the immortality of which the author speaks is never the immortality which the soul has of its very nature."[29] Yet even if we grant that the author of Wisdom does not speak of a natural immortality, it seems possible to argue to an underlying naturally immortal soul. For if the virtuous persons before and after death are identical, there must be a vehicle or 'carrier' of this identity, and the only reasonable vehicle of such identity is a naturally immortal soul, but one that is then gifted with virtuous immortality, or with what will later on be called 'eternal life' or the 'beatific vision.'

New Testament

The New Testament offers much more solid, if inferential evidence, of the existence in man of an immaterial and naturally immortal soul. For in many ways and in many passages it indicates that there is a life after death for all men, as we showed more fully in the previous chapter. And if all men will have life after death we infer, and correctly we think, that all men have an immaterial and naturally immortal soul.

Most often, it is true, the New Testament speaks of an afterlife, an 'eternal' life for those who are good and holy. Thus in the Synoptic Gospels Jesus teaches men to strive for eternal life (Mt 19:16ff; Lk 14:16-24; Mk 14:25). Paul says eternal life is the product of holiness (Rm 6:22), comes through faith and hope (1 Tm 1:16 etc.) and is given by God to those who persevere in good deeds (Rm 2:7). Though this eternal life is the life of the world to come, it begins here, he points out, at baptism as a new life of the spirit (Rm 6:4). According to John this eternal life, which is obtained through faith in Jesus (Jn 3:15, 36;20:31) and by keeping the commandments of God (Jn 12:50), is already had here (Jn 5:24) but is fully and definitively received in the resurrection (Jn 5:25-29).

But the New Testament also says there will be life after death for the wicked, for "the rich man . . . also died and was buried . . . in Hades, being in torment" (Lk 16:19ff). And it declares that this afterlife for the wicked will be everlasting: "Depart from me, you cursed, into the eternal fire prepared for the devil and his angels. . . . And they will go away into eternal punishment, but the righteous into eternal life" (Mt 25:41, 46).

Obviously these passages, and others, do speak of an afterlife that is "eternal," that is "everlasting." Just as obviously they say nothing explicitly about an immaterial and immortal soul. But implicitly and inferentially they do. For the same person who lived before death lives on after death. Thus there must be a "carrier" of this personal identity and the only reasonable carrier of such personal identity into everlasting life is an immaterial and immortal soul. For if my personal identity goes on into everlasting life, so must my immaterial soul, and hence it must be immortal. And if this soul of mine is naturally immaterial, it is also naturally immortal. If God has destined all men to everlasting life, then He made them intrinsically capable of everlasting life. And this intrinsic capacity for everlasting life can not come from man's mortal body but only from his naturally immaterial and immortal soul.

The Church's Magisterium

Since Sacred Scripture has indicated that man has an immaterial and immortal soul, we can expect that the magisterium of the Church will echo and clarify these indications both in its solemn and in its ordinary magisterium. And this it has done. In its solemn magisterium it declared that "man . . . is composed of spirit and body" (DS 800), has one rational and intellectual soul (DS 657), and this soul is truly and by its own nature the form of the human body (DS 902) and immortal (DS 1440). In its ordinary magisterium it teaches both that man is substantially one in origin, being and final destiny (DS 3896, 685, 2851) but also made up of a material body and a spiritual soul, a soul whose spirituality and immortality can be proved (DS 2766, 2812). This soul is the vital principle in man (DS 2833). In a schema prepared for Vatican I the theologians of that Council declared: "This . . . soul, created from nothing, immaterial, incorruptible, immortal, and gifted with intelligence and free will . . . is essentially different from the human body but is truly, of its own nature and essentially the form of that body, so that together with the body it constitutes human nature truly and really one."[30]

Some interpreters have said that the definition of the soul's immortality (DS 1440) leaves open the question whether the soul is naturally immortal or only supernaturally so because of a special gift of God. If this definition is taken just as it stands, this is correct enough. But no definition should be taken in abstraction from other definitions of the Church. And in other definitions the Church has declared that after death the *wicked* go into a hell of *everlasting* punishment. Obviously then their souls must be immortal. Just as obviously their immortality would not be a 'supernatural immortality due to a special gift of God.' For it is inconceivable that God would make naturally mortal souls into supernaturally immortal souls just to capacitate them for everlasting punishment. So their souls and the souls of all men must be naturally immortal, to capacitate them intrinsically for the everlasting life to which God has destined them, either in heaven as God wishes, or in hell if they freely choose this.

It seems very clear, then, from the teaching of Sacred Scripture and of the Church's solemn and ordinary magisterium that although man is a unitary being he does consist of a material body and a naturally immaterial and immortal soul.

This soul, however, is not and is not meant to be an independent psychic entity, an independent being or substance in man, accidentally conjoined to his body. According to the Council of Vienna it is in itself and essentially the form of a human body, and hence not an immaterial soul that is related to the human body in the way of Platonic or Cartesian dualism. But if the human soul is *essentially* the form of my body, another question is being raised today. Will my soul after the death of my body somehow need to be "re-embodied" in order to go on existing and acting?

Some Protestant theologians have been moving toward such a "re-embodiment" at death, such as J. M. Shaw and Russel Aldwinckle. Prof. Aldwinckle opts for an "embodied" afterlife for both the good and the wicked. Some Catholic theologians have been moving in this direction also. They seem to base their position mainly on the teaching that the human soul is *essentially* the form of the body, as the Council of Vienne and Thomas Aquinas have taught. If the soul's relation to the body belongs to its very essence, they argue, then it would seem impossible to have a human soul that was not to some extent informing a human body. It would seem to be impossible to have a "disembodied" soul. C. Cooney has written that for some modern thinkers, "man is a being who, while existing permanently within himself, bodies himself forth in a human organism—so that the human body is thus the product or form of a man's present powers of embodiment. Eventually with death, and ultimately with glory, greater powers of embodiment will be released—and ultimately a bodying forth in the likeness of the risen Lord."[31] Ladislas Boros shares this view of "re-embodiment" after death.

He seems to envision three embodiments, one in our pilgrim state, another in our interim state, still another in our final state. Immediately after death every man will receive (produce?) an interim embodiment, different from his pilgrim embodiment, which will enable his soul to go on existing in a way that is in harmony with the conditions of this new interim state of life and activity. At the general resurrection each man will receive his final embodiment which will fit him for the everlasting life of his final state. This view of a new embodiment of the soul after the death of its body has many interesting features and implications. We shall consider these later when we deal with the Interim State and ask what form life after death will take in this Interim State.

So we have looked at the Mystery of Man. We pondered the contention of many scientists and psychologists that in man there is nothing but matter and rejected it. We turned to psychology and to parapsychology for evidence that there is in man not only matter but also an immaterial and naturally immortal soul, and found evidence that gave us high probability, if not certainty of the existence of such a human soul. Then we turned to Sacred Scripture and to the Magisterium of the Church and derived from them evidential certainty of the existence in man of an immaterial and naturally immortal soul (or "spirit", if you prefer this term). In our First Part we showed that man will have life after death, that I, the person that I am now, will have a conscious and active life after death, since God has destined every man to a life after death. But then arose the question: is this destiny to life after death written in man's very nature? Is every man by his very nature destined for and capable of life after death? Or is every man by his nature destined for death, so that God at death will have to contravene this natural destiny He gave man and give him a new destiny and capacity for life after death? In Part II we showed that God wrote into every man's nature a destiny and a capacity for life after death by giving him an immaterial and naturally immortal soul.

We might close this Part II with some words of I. Lepp:

"the change effected by death concerns man's very essence. He is transported beyond the dimension of space and time which constitutes the very stuff of existence on earth. It is not empirical man who is immortal, but the spiritual principle in him. . . . There is in fact a very real continuity between what a man is in his spatiotemporal existence and what he will be in life after death."[32]

Notes for Chapter 2

1. **What a Modern Catholic Believes about Heaven and Hell,** (Chicago, Thomas More Press, 1972), pp. 47-48.

2. **The Illusion of Immortality,** (New York, Philosophical Library, 1950), pp. 114-118.

3. **Op. cit.,** pp. 271-272.

4. M. Gorman, **New Catholic Encyclopedia,** v. 13, p. 459.

5. **Anim.** 413a 4-5; cf. I.C. Brady, **New Catholic Encyclopedia,** v. 13, p. 459.

6. J. L. McKenzie, **loc. cit.,** pp. 837-839.

7. Brady, **loc. cit.**

8. Brady, **loc. cit.,** p. 457.

9. M. Gorman, **loc. cit.,** p. 459.

10. **De principiis,** 1. 1. 7, 126C.

11. ST 1a, 76; I. C. Brady, **New Catholic Encyclopedia,** v. 13, p. 456.

12. **Op. cit.,** chapter 5.

13. **New Catholic Encyclopedia,** v. 13, pp. 460-461.

14. Cf. C. Boyer, S.J., **Cursus Philosophiae II,** Parisiis (Desclee de Brouwer, 1936), p. 172.

15. **Death and Its Mysteries,** (New York, The Macmillan Co., 1968), p. 160.

16. Cf. J. B. Rhine and R. Brier, ed., **Parapsychology Today,** (New York, The Citadel Press, 1968), pp. 212-216.

17. Ducasse, **op. cit.,** pp. 146, 150, 151.

18. Cf. S. Ostrander and L. Schroeder, **Psychic Discoveries Behind the Iron Curtain,** (Bantam Books, 1971).

19. (Garden City, N.Y., Doubleday, Anchor Press, 1973).

20. Fodor, **op. cit.,** pp. 373, 46.

21. **Parapsychology Today,** pp. 260ff.

22. **Loc. cit.,** p. 157.

23. **Op. cit.,** p. 241.

24. Hansel, **op. cit.,** p. 233.

25. Ostrander and Schroeder, **op. cit.,** pp. 14-28.

26. J. G. Fuller, "Is He Charlatan or Miracle Worker?", **Reader's Digest,** Sept., 1975, pp. 79-83.

27. J. Barr, **Old and New in Interpretation,** (London, SCM Press, 1962), p. 52.

28. **The Christian Doctrine of Man,** (Edinburgh, T & T Clark, 1911), p. 26.

29. "Death and Immortality in the Book of Wisdom," **Catholic Biblical Quarterly,** no. 3, 1941, pp. 104-133.

30. J. F. Clarkson, S.J. et. al., **The Church Teaches,** (St. Louis, B. Herder Book Co., 1955), no. 348.

31. **Understanding the New Theology,** (Milwaukee, Bruce, 1969), pp. 14-15.

32. **Loc. cit.,** pp. 169-170.

PART III

The Mystery of Death

Chapter 3
Does Man's Death Determine His Afterlife?

Death has always fascinated men. And they have viewed it very differently. Augustine said, "of all things in the world only death is not uncertain." Karl Jaspers thought "death is something inconceivable, in fact really unthinkable." Aquinas said that "of all human evils, death is the worst" for by it man is "robbed of what is most lovable: life and being." Sartre declared that human freedom must be exercised in a world where God is dead and death for man is the final end. Epicurus wrote: "Death is nothing for us; for as long as we are, death is not here; and when death is here, we no longer are. Therefore it is nothing to the living or the dead." Cicero thought "the life of a philosopher is a perpetual meditation on death. . . . To philosophize is to learn how to die." Heidegger tells us "to gain a vivid realization of death as a constitutive part of life, not as a mere end of life. If it is taken into life in a personal way, it will effect a revolution in our behavior." Camus wrote: "because of death human existence has no meaning. All the crimes that men could commit are nothing in comparison with that fundamental crime which is death."[1] For many men, then, death is a mystery indeed.

Why should we study death now? We have just shown that there is life after death. Why not bypass death and simply consider this life that comes after death? There are many, many reasons for first studying death. Death is a mystery. A vital mystery. And there are many vital questions about it that need pondering. (1) Do all men die? Men take this for granted. But does God? Has God said all men die? (2) Why do men die? To most men the obvious answer is that death is a natural, a biological, an evolutionary necessity for man. He is made for death. He is a being-for-death. But what does God say? Does He say man's death is due to man's nature? Or to something else? (3) What is death? Is it something that happens to men, and happens differently to different men? Or is it something that man does, every man, no matter how different the time, the place, the manner of his death may be? If it is something that every man does, what is this? (4) Does this determine what kind of life after death every man will have? And determine this irrevocably and for all eternity?

If it does, then obviously death is a matter of vital significance, of vital significance for all eternity. Then as a man dies so he will live for all eternity. Then death is not just the end of a form of life, it is also the beginning of a new form of life that will never end. Death is a vital mystery that very much needs to be pondered.

DO ALL MEN DIE?

The answer seems to be a very simple affirmative. Everywhere we look we see graveyards and crematories. Everything we read takes every man's death for granted. Science tells us that men start dying at birth. They seem to be built for planned obsolescence. The Bible, too, says all men will die. In the Old Testament the Psalmist wrote: "As a mere breath every man stands . . . verily all men are but a breath." "No man can at all ransom himself . . . that he should continue to live forever, without seeing the pit." "Even wise men die; the fool and the brutish alike perish" (Ps 39:5, 11; 49:7-11). And in the New Testament we read: "Men are destined to die once and after that to be judged" (Heb 9:27); "Through one man sin came into the world and death followed sin, and so death spread to all men, because all men sinned" (Rm 5:12). And it is this passage from Romans that is stressed by the Council of Trent in its Decree on Original Sin (DS 1512). Karl Rahner adds that "this proposition . . . that all men will, in fact, die . . . as divinely revealed . . . embraces the entire conceivable human nature."[2]

Will science perhaps be able to extend man's life span indefinitely, by transplants, deep freezing or other as yet unknown techniques? Speaking scientifically this might seem possible, but hardly probable. But speaking biblically and conciliarly it seems we must say that no matter how far scientists may extend man's life span, every man will still at one time or another die.

Except perhaps Parousiac men, those who will be alive at the end of the world, at the Parousia (1 Cor 15:51-53; 1 Th 4:14-18). St. Ambrose and St. Augustine and others thought these would die and slumber a while before being summoned to the Last Judgment. St. John Chrysostom and St. Jerome and others taught that the just who were alive at the last day would be glorified without having died. Contemporary exegesis seems to think that the faithful living at the Parousia will not die but will be transformed instantly into glorified persons. The *Jerome Biblical Commentary* declares that in 1 Cor 15: 51-53 "the Apostle solemnly announces a mystery, a truth of God's revelation. The faithful living at the Parousia will not die . . . but will be transformed." And it adds, "the mystery announced here, that the just who are living at the Parousia will not die," is also found in 1 Th 4:15-17 (51:86).

What of men who may be living elsewhere in the universe than on planet earth? Of these we know nothing definite. But if they have not sinned, have not been subject to our law of death, and are justified, it is conjecturable that they might 'die' not in the way we do, by "break", but in the way that "Adam" would have died if he had not sinned, i.e. by "transformation".

WHY DO ALL MEN DIE?

The answer seems obvious. They die because they are by nature mortal and not immortal. They start dying at birth and sooner or later their constructive and conservative powers are no longer able to do their work. Then they deteriorate and yield to destructive processes. And so men die. Whether you regard this death as a biological *accident* or as a biological *necessity* or whether you ascribe it to some chemical or physical or physiological law or to some combination of these, makes little substantial difference. Basically the natural and obvious explanation is very simple. God made man mortal in nature and so he must die.

But did God make man mortal? The Book of Wisdom tells us that "God created man for immortality and made him the image of his own eternity, but through the devil's envy death came into the world" (2:23-24). Sirach writes that "sin began with a woman, and thanks to her we all must die" (25:24). In the famous passage of the epistle to the Romans we are told that "sin entered the world through one man, and through sin death, and death has spread through the whole human race because everyone has sinned" (5:12ff.). In 1 Cor 15:21f we are told that "death came through one man and in the same way the resurrection of the dead has come through one man. Just as all men die in Adam, so all men will be brought to life in Christ." Thus it would appear that death came into the world "through the devil's envy", through "a woman", "through one man", but basically through "sin" because "everyone has sinned". And so we have the doctrine that death is due to sin, is the punishment of sin, of "original sin", a doctrine that has a long tradition in the Church and has been regarded as a matter of faith.

Today, however, this traditional doctrine is being subjected to a great deal of study and criticism. There seems to be an ever-growing tendency to reject the historicity of Adam and to hold that St. Paul and the Council of Trent only assumed that historicity but did not teach or define it. Many theologians and biblical scholars reject the Adamic origin of original sin. Pier Schoonenberg, S.J. says that the notion of all men descending from one couple is a presupposition based on an antiquated picture. He prefers to understand original sin as "man's historical situation". Z. Alszeghy, S.J., and M. Flick, S.J., adopt an evolutionary view of mankind and find this incompatible with the classical theology of human origins which involved a state of original justice and strict monogenism. In their evolutionary perspective they prefer to consider original sin the "incapacity of mankind to reach that superior kind of existence to which it was originally destined".

In these newer views of human origins and of "original sin," is death still the result of, the punishment of sin, as it was in classical theology? A. Vanneste thinks we should no longer use original sin to explain the origin of suffering and death in the world. S. Trooster declares that "our present-day, evolutionist view of man . . . does not provide for a 'paradisal' existence of primeval man and so death should not be simply ascribed to the sin of such a primeval man." But he adds that "in spite of the fact that the account of paradise visualizes evil in this world as caused by sin, it does not point to the first parents alone as being guilty, but instead considers all of mankind and all men responsible for suffering and death by virtue of their solidarity-in-sin."[3]

George Dyer likewise opts for an evolutionary view of man. He thinks that mankind could gradually have evolved to a point where it was capable of free choice. Then a divine invitation for man's divinization was given to one man who acted for the race as a corporate personality. He rejected the invitation, became the first sinner, and the evolutionary process took a new path. Had man accepted the divine invitation, he would as a person have perfectly mastered his own nature, eliminated suffering and passed ultimately to his definitive perfection without experiencing death as we know it.[4]

This is an attractive opinion and it has the double merit of keeping the substance of the teaching of Scripture, tradition and Councils, and of putting it into the contemporary context of evolutionary man. It traces original sin to a primal fault which immediately affected the entire race but it does not demand a single sinning first couple, Adam and Eve. It implies that the human race in its present state suffers numerous hardships, ignorance, concupiscence, the inevitability of suffering and death, which do not seem to be explained sufficiently by the fact that man is composed of body and spirit. It fits well with God's destination of all men to eternal life with Him in beatific vision, love and joy, for it tells us that in God's original plan man was not to suffer and die as we do now, but was to pass to his definitive perfection without experiencing death as we know it now.

What would have been man's condition if the "man who acted for the race as a corporate personality" had not rejected the divine invitation but instead had accepted it? If we call this man "Adam" perhaps we can apply to him what theologians have said about Genesiac Adam before his fall: he would have been immortal not by virtue of his nature but by reason of a divine gift, whereby his body-soul unity would not have dissolved against his will. The end of man then would have been a "deathless death," a "pure active manifest completion from within." "He would surely have experienced an end to his life ... but this end ... a death without dying, would have been a pure, apparent and active consummation of the whole man by an inward movement, free of death in the proper sense, without suffering a violent dissolution of his actual bodily constitution through a power from without" (K. Rahner, op. cit., pp. 34-35).

The difference between death "before sin" and "after sin" has been described by some theologians through the distinction of death as "transformation" and death as "break." Before sin death would not have been a "break" but only a "transformation." There would have been rebirth to eternal life, but the passage from earthly to eternal life would have occurred in an entirely different manner, without rupture or suffering, without untimely break, decay of the body, disruption of all relationships. Death would have been the herald of happiness free of gloom and anguish. In the original state designed by God man would not have been separated from his body. His body would not have been delivered up to decay, and death would not have severed the relations between the living and the departed. While being reborn to eternal life, he would have transformed his corruptible form into a spiritual body. He personally would have re-created his body.[5] God had intended death to be the way of reaching our final state in full consciousness and freedom, and with the wealth of our experiences intact.

After sin death is a "break," with the body ending in 'corruption,' when the physico-chemical synthesis is exhausted. Often now death is a brutal break, a break with relatives and friends, with the deep pain of separation. Often death is caused from the "outside" by some accident. Often it seems to come too soon or too late, even in the most worn-out organism. Why did God permit this death as a "break"? Because of man's sin, it seems, because man wanted to go his own way. We can conjecture several reasons why God permitted this kind of death we know. In an evolutionary order this kind of death would be normal and "natural." When man rejected God's offer of death as "transformation" and chose isolation from God instead of communion with God, then man embarked on a way of life—like that of other organisms—that would end in death as a break. When the physico-chemical synthesis was exhausted the soul would no longer be able to quicken the body and must 'leave.' But this departure would be to the soul's advantage, for death would give it a chance to create a body that is truly its own and entirely subordinate to the spirit. This was God's intention, to give man a nature that would enable him, a created being, to acquire a creative power and skill to make him a person reborn from becoming to eternity.

But the death of the God-Man changed the meaning of death as a "break." For now man may remain united with God even up to the very instant of his departure from life. It is now possible for him to "die in the Lord." "Baptism makes Christian death possible. The Holy Eucharist continuously nourishes the life of the Christian in order that, through assimilation to Christ's death, his own life in his daily actions and sufferings may grow from within toward that consummation which achieves its full perfection in death. Extreme Unction (the Anointing of the Dying) is the consecration of the end of this life to the death of Christ.

All the sacraments implant in the mortal life of the Christian not only the Lord's death, but his eternal life as well" (K. Rahner, op. cit., pp. 78-79).

WHAT IS DEATH?

Traditionally death has been defined as the "separation of body and soul." And although this definition had little foundation in Sacred Scripture, it was widely accepted by the Church Fathers, by philosophers and theologians in the West. Many philosophical and theological syntheses built heavily on it and many Church doctrines and dogmas involved it. Today this definition is not in such repute everywhere. In his analysis of this classic definition Karl Rahner finds that it is important but inadequate. We must accept, he says, this "classical theological description of death" and admit that it "does, in fact, enunciate some very essential considerations about death . . . namely that the spiritual life-principle of man, the soul, assumes in death, as it were, a new and different relation to that which is usually called the body." But "even though this description be accepted as adequate for the biological passing of a man or of an animal, it fails completely to indicate the specifically human element in the death of man . . . It is absolutely silent . . . about one very important aspect of death, namely, that it is an event for man as a whole and as a spiritual person. . . . For it is *man* who dies. . . . But the fact that human death does contain this characteristic element of *final decision* is not at all indicated by the expression, "separation of body and soul" (op. cit., 16, 17, 18).

Here Karl Rahner touches on one of the most interesting developments in today's theology of death. For quite a few Catholic theologians today are viewing death as a "final fundamental option," as "personal self-fulfillment," as "an act that man interiorly performs," as "a transformation," as "man's first completely personal act," as "active Dying," as "*Final Decision.*"

But is death really a "final decision," is there in death a "final fundamental option" that determines every man's eternal destiny? Man's life on earth is a pilgrimage, we know, and this pilgrimage ends at death. And as a man dies, good or bad, in grace or in mortal sin, so will he be for all eternity. This is common Christian doctrine. But just what does it mean? If a man fell into a coma and never regained consciousness again, what moment of his life determined his eternal destiny? The moment he went into the coma, was the common answer. If he was in mortal sin at that moment, and never recovered consciousness, he had no opportunity for repentance and so would inevitably die in grave sin and go to hell.

Today another view is spreading rapidly. And in this view the man in the coma would have an opportunity to repent, even though to human measurements he never recovered consciousness. He would have an opportunity to make a final fundamental option, a final decision for or against God, an irrevocable decision that would determine his destiny for eternity. He would have this opportunity to make his final decision not before death nor after death but *in death*. In death every man would have the full consciousness and freedom, the full possession of the power and the lucidity needed to see his entire life and sum up all his previous decisions and *rectify* or *ratify* these decisions. In this moment he makes a final and irrevocable decision for or against God (K. Rahner) or for or against Christ (L. Boros), and thus completes and seals his whole spiritual life. Death is thus not a mere accident, suffered passively. It is an active consummation, man's highest act by which he disposes of the whole of his existence in a totally radical and effective way. Everyone will be for eternity exactly what he wants to be, what he finally chooses to be. Step by step during his adult life he makes his fundamental orientation toward self or toward others, toward love of self or love of others, toward Christ or against Him, toward God or against Him. Absolutely speaking he may still change his long-standing selfish orientation, but his deeply ingrained habits make a reversal extremely difficult.

Not just adults but infants, too, "would be able to make their decision in full liberty and knowledge at the moment of death . . . they, like all other human beings, awake in death to their full liberty and complete knowledge. In death they too are brought face to face with the essential dynamism of their spirit and also with the basis of the world, and in this confrontation meet their Redeemer. . . . In death the infant enters into full possession of its spirituality, i.e. into a state of adulthood that many adults themselves never reach during their lifetime. The result of this is that no one dies as an infant, though he may leave us in infancy."[6] Can we speculate about the final decision infants will make? If they died after receiving baptismal grace, it would seem certain that they would all opt for God. If they had not been baptized, it would seem probable that all of these would also opt for God, since in their life there was no sin or rejection of God that might be a reason for rejecting Him now.

Quite a few Catholic theologians today hold this theory in one form or another: Karl Rahner, L. Boros, R. Gleason, J. Pieper, A. Winklhofer, E. Mersch, R. Troisfontaines, P. Fannon, J. H. Wright, R. Nowell. Is there any proof for this theory?

There is no explicit foundation for the theory in Sacred Scripture or in the Fathers or in the General Councils or in the great theologians. L. Boros has made an interesting attempt to offer a philosophical and a Christological basis for the Hypothesis of a Final Decision, and his final conclusion is that: "Death is a sacramental situation. As the basic sacrament it is present and active in the inner structure of each individual sacrament, and these in their turn, are signs of grace stretching forward to life's supreme encounter with Christ—in death" (op. cit., p. 169).

Perhaps the best argument for this theory is drawn from a consideration of God's universal salvific will as it is expressed in 1 Timothy: "God our Savior, who desires all men to be saved and to come to the knowledge of the truth. For there is one God, and there is one mediator between God and men, the man Christ Jesus, who gave himself a ransom for all" (1 Tm 2:3-6). If God's universal salvific will means that God offers every man before death a real opportunity for personal salvation, then this theory applies that will as no other single theory has ever done in the past. If it means that every man has an opportunity before death to encounter Christ his Savior and accept or reject Him, then this theory applies that will. If it means that every man before death is offered grace of Christ sufficient to enable him to make a believing, trusting, loving acceptance of that Christ, then this theory verifies that. If it means that every man before death is offered an opportunity to determine in full lucidity and full freedom his eternal destiny with or without God, then this theory verifies that. And it is the only theory so far presented that makes God's sincerely salvific will effectively operative for every man before death, no matter what his condition as a pilgrim may be.

Many other arguments for this theory may be grouped under the heading of "fittingness" or "congruity." Thus it befits a God of love and mercy, it is argued, to grant all men a final moment of grace and free decision. It befits Christ who died for all men that all men should have an opportunity to encounter their Savior before death and accept or reject Him and His redemptive grace. It befits man's freedom and dignity that his pilgrim life should terminate by a fully free and conscious decision for or against the God who made him free. It befits man that he should not die as an animal does, passively, by an accident or chance or biological necessity, but actively by an act of his own that determines his eternal destiny.

These arguments obviously do not prove this theory. And the theory leaves many important questions unanswered. Must *all* men really make such a final fundamental option, even baptized infants and martyrs whose salvation seems so certain? Further, the theory aims at having every man die "humanly," but in this theory is it really a "man" who makes this final decision? Or just a "soul"? These questions, and many others, need to be answered, if this theory is to do all that it is meant to do. And of course it must be accepted by the Church before it can become something more than a mere theory. But it is an interesting and attractive theory, and it is valuable both in its main thrust and also for the insights it offers to a variety of theological and doctrinal topics. But it needs much more study, especially a great deal more theological study, for it seems improbable that reason or philosophy alone can offer it much solid support. It deserves the best efforts of theologians for it is concerned with a matter that is of vital importance and that has agitated the minds of men of all kinds, at least since the time of Christ. If Christ has made all men and redeemed all men, should not all men be given the opportunity for a salvific encounter with their Savior before they die? If God has called all men to an endless and happy life after death with Him, should not all men be given an opportunity before death of heeding or rejecting this call?

IS DEATH THE END OF MERIT, DEMERIT, CONVERSION?

The theory of death as final decision assumes that the decision each man makes in death is final and irrevocable. Is this assumption correct? Is death really the end of merit, demerit, conversion? Many non-Catholic theologians say it is not.

Dr. J. A. T. Robinson thinks it is both untrue to the New Testament and involves an inadequate idea of God to put such an "excessive" emphasis upon the moment of death. To make the moment of death the time of final judgment appears to him to be unjust, for few men and women, if any, are in such a spiritual condition at death as to merit either heaven or hell in the traditional sense. Could a loving God assign some of His children to eternal bliss and others to eternal separation from Himself on the basis of what seems to be an arbitrary moment of time, namely physical death?[7]

Prof. Aldwinckle believes that Dr. Robinson's point is well taken and he thinks that "God in His compassion has decided to leave the definitive act of final judgment until the parousia," so that "the final judgment, that is, the irrevocable acceptance or rejection of men by God, only takes place at the End. Until the parousia, no man's eternal future is finally and irrevocably settled. Before the End, all men still will have their chance to respond to God in Christ" (op. cit., p. 136, 137).

Theosophists and other Reincarnationists, Spiritualists, and various kinds of Universalists, likewise reject death as the moment of final irrevocable decision. God would be unjust, the Theosophists argue, to those who die after only short lives, for men are unable to reach perfection in a short life. But instead of putting off the final decision till the parousia, as Prof. Aldwinckle does, they want men to go on in endless reincarnations because they can always grow more perfect and can never reach absolute perfection.

If these positions are simply based on wishful thinking or on a purely subjective estimate of God, it is easy to brush them off. But if they are based on the teaching of Sacred Scripture, on a proper interpretation of these sacred writings, then they deserve careful consideration. Are they so based? Does Sacred Scripture say death is the end of human merit, demerit, conversion? Do the early patristic interpreters of Scripture say this? Do the general councils of the Church say or imply this? These are the questions that need an answer.

Sacred Scripture

Sacred Scripture nowhere says formally and explicitly that human death is the end of human merit, demerit, conversion. But it does say this equivalently and implicitly in many passages, where it says that reward, punishment and judgment will be according to works done before death, in the present earthly life. Such passages are found in the Old Testament, e.g. in Ps 62:12: "and you yourself repay man as his works (in this life) deserve." And in Pr 24:12: "He himself will repay a man as his deeds (in this life) deserve." Since the Old Testament was slow in reaching the concept of a life after death, these texts are of little value in that direction, but they do seem to see death as the end-point of merit, demerit, conversion.

The New Testament gives us a much clearer and stronger testimony, in a Synoptic Gospel, in the Pauline corpus and in John. In the parable of Dives and Lazarus we hear Father Abraham saying to the rich man who was in torment, in Hades: "between us and you a great gulf has been fixed, to stop anyone, if he wanted to, crossing from our side to yours, and to stop any crossing from your side to ours" (Lk 16:22ff). The Jerusalem Bible notes (121) that the "gulf" is a symbol: the destiny of saved and lost is "unalterable," and hence death, man's condition at death, determines whether he goes to Abraham's bosom or to the torment of Hades. Remove the imagery and the message seems clear: death is the end of merit, demerit, conversion.

Three passages in the Pauline corpus may be singled out. Rm 2:6 tells us, "he will render to every man according to his works." What works? Obviously works done in his earthly life, before death. In Ph 1:23 we read, "For me to live is Christ, and to die is gain." Why is death a gain? "Because it will unite him forever with Christ and will enable him to enter into eternal possession of true life."[8] In 2 Cor 5:6-10 we read: "we know that while we are at home in the body we are away from the Lord, for we walk by faith, not by sight. . . . So whether we are at home or away, we make it our aim to please him. For we must all appear before the judgment seat of Christ, so that each one may receive good or evil, according to what he has done in the body." What determines our future destiny? What we have done in the body, when we walk by faith, that is, before death. Thus again death is the end of merit, demerit, conversion, for when we appear before the judgment seat of Christ we shall receive either reward or punishment for the good or evil we have done during our earthly life.[9]

Two passages from the Johannine corpus may be noted. In Jn 5:28-29 we are told: "for the hour is coming when all who are in the tombs will hear his voice and come forth, those who have done good to the resurrection of life, and those who have done evil, to the resurrection of judgment." So again death is the cut-off point. "The just will rise to eternal life and the evil to damnation, each being judged according to his works" (JBC 63:85). What works? Obviously the works done in his earthly life, before death. Rv 2:10 tells us: "Be faithful unto death, and I will give you the crown of life." Death again is the cut-off point. Faithfulness unto death merits the crown of life, lack of this does not. Death is the end of merit, demerit, conversion.

If we turn to the early Christian writers we find a small minority view and a large majority view. For Origen and a few of his followers death is not the end of conversion. In his doctrine of the *apocatastasis* Origen taught that ultimately "all things are restored to their primeval order. All rational creatures will eventually be brought into subjection to God . . . not by force or necessity . . . but by discipline, persuasion and instruction."[10] But generally this view was rejected. Far and away the great majority of the early Christian interpreters of Scripture thought and taught that death was the end of merit, demerit, conversion. This was the teaching of Cyprian, Aphraates, Hilary, Basil, Chrysostom, Jerome, Fulgentius, Gregory the Great.[11] Clement of Rome spoke of St. Peter and St. Paul as having departed straight to "the holy place," finding there a great company of martyrs and saints "made perfect in charity" (Kelly, loc. cit., pp. 463-4). For 2 Clement "entrance into the kingdom is earned by good works and charity" (done before death). Justin "regards the kingdom of heaven as a prize to be obtained after death for virtuous conduct" (during this life). And so that teaching went on and on and became the common doctrine, the common belief, the common interpretation of the teaching of the sacred writers.

Doctrine of the Church

Does the Church teach authoritatively and definitively that death is the end of merit, demerit, conversion? Karl Rahner seems to say just this, when he writes that "a third proposition *of faith* . . . affirms that with bodily death man's state of pilgrimage comes to a definite end . . . his decision as a mortal spiritual person, reached during the time of his bodily life, is rendered final and unalterable" (op. cit., p. 35). Is he right?

Pope Vigilius (c. 543) may have approved this anti-Origenist canon taken from the edict of Justinian: "If anyone says or holds that the punishment of devils and wicked men is temporary and will eventually cease, that is to say, that devils or the ungodly will be completely restored to their original state: let him be anathema" (DS 411). Obviously this is not a definitive reply to our question, whatever minor value it may be given as a rejection of apocatastasis. In 1254 Pope Innocent IV wrote to the Bishop of Tusculum, declaring that "if anyone dies unrepentant in the state of mortal sin, he will undoubtedly be tormented forever in the fires of an everlasting hell" (DS 839). Here the Pope does say that one who "dies unrepentant in the state of mortal sin . . . will undoubtedly be tormented forever in the fires of an everlasting hell," and so for such a one death is the end of merit, demerit, conversion. But this is of course not definitive papal teaching, though it does clearly indicate the mind of the pope on this point. Two general councils, Lyons II and Florence, declared that "soon after death the wicked go to hell and the cleansed go to heaven" (DS 854, 1306, 1305). These were 'defining councils' and their intent seems clearly to have been to put forth a definitive declaration. And death, for these conciliar fathers, was obviously the cut-off point, so that those who die in (unrepented) mortal sin go to hell while those who are (cleansed) just go to heaven. But three points must be noted. (1) The councils do not say immediately after death, but "soon" after death. (2) They do not say explicitly that the wicked go to hell *eternally* (though presumably they meant this). (3) The Greek Church shared in and subscribed to the decisions of these two councils, while presumably still holding to its own doctrine that the intermediate state is *capable of change* for those who have died in grave sin, *if* they have not left this world in a condition of final impenitence.

In the light of these adnotations, if it is not a "proposition of faith," as K. Rahner says, that death is the end of man's state of pilgrimage, the end of merit, demerit, conversion, it is "at least theologically certain," as other theologians assert. Does this mean that "Universalism," the doctrine that ultimately all men will be saved, is not absolutely ruled out? If it is not absolutely ruled out by these definitions, it does seem to be absolutely ruled out by two other dogmatic declarations. For both the "Athanasian Creed" and the Fourth Lateran Council declare that at the Second Coming of Christ and the resurrection of the dead, the wicked will go into "everlasting fire," "perpetual punishment," while the good will go into "eternal life . . . eternal glory with Christ" (DS 76, 801). But we shall study this point more fully when we treat of hell later on.

If part of the "Mystery of Death" was: *why* is death the end of man's pilgrimage and the end of merit, demerit, conversion, then the theory of death as "final decision" has given us something of an answer. But to another part of the mystery of death: *how* is death concretely the end of merit, demerit, conversion, or how does God bring it about that in death and not before nor after death every man is enabled to make a fully free and eternally irrevocable decision for or against Christ—to this part of the mystery the answer is still far from clear. For the one who makes this "final decision" must still be in the pilgrim state, must still be the same human being he was before death, and yet he must be in a condition in which he has to some extent the powers of a "pure spirit," so that *he* can with fullest freedom, with fullest consciousness, with fullest knowledge of what is involved, make a final and irrevocable decision for or against God, for or against Christ. Here most of the mystery remains. Here much more study and reflection is needed.

CONCLUSION

To the question, will *all* men die, we answered *yes*, but we admitted there might be exceptions to this for parousiac men and for men living elsewhere than on planet earth and hence not subject to our law of death.

To the question: *why* do all men die, we answered "because man sinned." Had he not sinned, he would not have had to die, even though by his nature he was destined to die a bodily death (death by "break"). God would have "gifted" him with immortality. That is basically the traditional answer, and it still seems to be a matter of faith, notwithstanding some strong criticism of its biblical foundations. This traditional answer gives the only adequate explanation of what man has been and done down the centuries of his existence. For whether you explain this "sin of man" as the sin of Adam (as we have done traditionally), or as the sin of the evolutionary first sinner (as G. Dyer does very well), or as the sin of the world (as many other theologians do today), it is still the "sin of man" that offers the only adequate explanation of the radical distortions we find in historical man's relations to God, to his neighbor, to his world, from his long-ago beginnings down to the present.

This does not mean that God arbitrarily made death the punishment for man's sin. It merely means that by sinning man rejected God's gift of immortality and so reverted to his natural, biological necessity of dying. Had man not rejected God's gift of immortality by sinning, he would have passed from earthly life to eternal life with God, not by way of death as "break" (as we do today), but by way of death as "transformation." At the end of his early pilgrim life he would have been in union with God and would not have needed to make a final decision for God (or self). But when he sinned, he was no longer habitually (but freely) united with God throughout his earthly life. So then he had to decide freely for or against God (or Christ) and thus "death as break" became "death as final decision." And so in virtue of His universal salvific will God arranged that in death every man, whatever his condition, would have all the lucidity, consciousness, knowledge and freedom to make a final and irrevocable decision for or against God, to accept or reject God's invitation to eternal life with God, to choose eternal isolation in self or eternal communion with God.

But is death really the end of merit, demerit, conversion, the final moment for pilgrim man of salvation or perdition? So that the decision he makes in death is utterly free and personal and yet utterly final, irrevocable, eternal? This in many ways is the most important, the most vital question about death. And we found from our study of Scripture and the Church's magisterium that if it is not a "proposition of faith" it is at least theologically certain that death is the end of merit, demerit, conversion.

Dr. J. A. T. Robinson expressed strong opposition to this "excessive" emphasis on the moment of death. He said it was untrue to the New Testament, but it is not. For in the New Testament the time of decision is always the period before death, never the period after death. We will be judged, the New Testament says, by what we have done "in the body," not by what we will do "out of the body." Everywhere death is the cut-off point. Dr. Robinson says this heavy emphasis on death "involves an inadequate idea of God." But the idea of God that it involves is the idea of Jesus, of Paul, of John. Is their idea of God inadequate, and only Dr. Robinson's idea of God (whatever it may be) adequate? To make the moment of death the time of final judgment appears to Dr. Robinson to be unjust. But apparently it does not seem unjust to God, to the New Testament writers, to the Church's magisterium. Where is there any injustice if God's universal salvific will arranges that everyone will have in death the fullest freedom, lucidity, knowledge, to opt for or against God? Dr. Robinson considers physical death "an arbitrary moment of time." But is it? Physical death is the natural end of empirical and historical man. It is the end in terms of man's mortality. It is the end in virtue of man's free and sinful rejection of God's proferred immortality. Could a loving God, Dr. Robinson asks, assign some of His children to eternal bliss and others to eternal separation from Himself on the basis of physical death? Whether God *could* or could not do this we leave to Dr. Robinson. We are concerned with what He *does*. And He does not do this. He loves all His children so much that He gives them all a last opportunity in death to respond to His loving invitation to live with Him for all eternity. But since He has given them a tremendous power of freedom in keeping with the high dignity of man, He allows them also freely to reject His invitation in death. He will try to win their love, but He will not force them to accept Him and eternal life with Him. If they decide to choose self and isolation from God instead of God and eternal communion with Him, He will ratify their choice. They are not slaves. He has made them creatures of tremendous dignity and power. He made them able to make a free and eternal choice, and the choice they make in death He will ratify.

Dr. Robinson thinks the moment of physical death is too arbitrary a time. But what other "time" would be less arbitrary or more satisfactory? We are dealing with a pilgrim man who is an empirical and historical man. Why should pilgrim man not correspond to empirical and historical man? If each man's empirical life begins with the beginning of his earthly life, why should it not end with the end of his earthly life? What other "time" or period would be better for all men? We know so little of the afterlife. We are not sure there is "time" in it or what kind of "time." And if there is a "time for change," what would determine its duration? How much would be long enough for Dr. Robinson? And what would be the conditions that would make for change and further merit, demerit, conversion?

If we look at Dr. Aldwinckle's position, that men will have an opportunity for change and conversion until the parousia, but not after that, what is gained by this? If, as some scientists suggest, the parousia is billions of years away? Isn't it in some sense just as arbitrary a moment as the moment of physical death, to use Dr. Robinson's view of what is "arbitrary"? And where will these changelings be in this interim period? And what will they be doing? And how will their change be measured? And by what? And by whom?

The traditional view has a very solid biblical foundation and it has been ratified again and again by the Church's magisterium. It does leave a great deal of mystery surrounding man's death, but less than do the variant views. It is in possession and it should stay in possession until God in and through His Church changes it. It is a solidly grounded interpretation of divine revelation, too solidly grounded to be changed by wishful thinking or by making God over into the image and likeness we should like Him to have.

Notes for Chapter 3

1. Cf. J. Pieper, **Death and Immortality,** (New York: Herder and Herder, 1969).

2. **On the Theology of Death,** (New York, Herder and Herder, 1961), p. 14.

3. **Evolution and the Doctrine of Original Sin,** (Glen Rock, N.J., Newman, 1968), pp. 130, 133.

4. "Creation and Fall", **Chicago Studies,** v. 12, Fall, 1973, pp. 272-274.

5. Cf. Roger Troisfontaines, **I Do Not Die,** (New York, Desclee, 1963), pp. 196ff.

6. L. Boros, **The Mystery of Death,** (New York, Herder and Herder, 1965), pp. 109-110.

7. **In the End, God,** (London, Collins Fontana, 1968), p. 44.

8. K. Sullivan, **New Testament Reading Guide on Philippians,** (Collegeville, Liturgical Press, 1960), p. 15.

9. C. J. Peifer, O.S.B., **New Testament Reading Guide on Corinthians,** p. 85.

10. J.N.D. Kelly, **Early Christian Doctrines,** (London, Adam & Charles Black, 1965), 3rd ed., pp. 473-474.

11. J. M. Herve, **Manuale Theologiae Dogmaticae, IV,** p. 494.

PART IV

The Mystery of the Interim State

Chapter 4
Is There An Interim State?

We have seen that there is life after death. And in giving evidence for the existence of life after death, especially from the Church's magisterium, we noted that this magisterium assumes in its declarations that there is life *immediately* after death—in an interim state that extends to the General Resurrection at the end of the world. But since the matter is so important, and since there are scholars who say there is no real life immediately after death because they find nothing in the Scriptures about such an interim state, we now center our study on this Interim State. And we are particularly concerned to find out what Scripture and the early Christian Fathers and recent theologians say about such an interim state.

Does Sacred Scripture tell us much about an interim state? Does it even tell us anything at all? A noteworthy answer to these questions was given by B. M. Ahern, C.P., in an article published in the 1961-1962 Proceedings of the Catholic Theological Society of America. In this article he looked for evidence of an interim state in the Old Testament, in intertestamental literature and in the New Testament.

The Old Testament offered him no evidence that the Jews had produced a universally accepted eschatology. But it did indicate that in late Hebrew thought there was a vague awareness that in some mysterious way reward and punishment begin immediately after death, because the justice of God required this.

In the intertestamental period he found this thought and this awareness applied to Sheol. Sheol previously had been only the abode of the dead, with no distinction in reward and punish-

ment. Now Sheol "became instead a provisory stage where the
dead anticipate their future lot. One part of this resting place is
called Paradise, for there the just enjoy felicity, another part,
called Gehenna, is a place of punishment for the wicked."

In the New Testament it is of course Christ who concerns
him most of all, and Christ especially as Luke presents Him. He
thinks that Christ had made His own the Pharisee doctrine of
an interim period, and that Luke realized this and recorded it
in the parable of Dives and Lazarus (16:19). There Christ made
it clear that there is reward and punishment immediately after
death. Again it was Luke who recorded Jesus' word to the thief
on the cross, 'This day thou shalt be with me in paradise'
(23:43), to indicate that right after death the good thief (and
other righteous men) would enjoy life with Christ. And it is
Luke again, this time in the Book of Acts, who made it clear
that early Christian writers did have a concept of union with
Christ at death. For in his account of the death of Stephen we
read that "as they were stoning Stephen, he prayed, 'Lord Jesus,
receive my spirit' " (7:59). Here "there is no question of awakening only at the final resurrection. Even at the moment of death
Stephen lives in some way with Christ."

Is death important for Paul? Death and its immediate aftermath? When he studies Paul, B. M. Ahern finds that physical
death was not a matter of vital concern for Paul. Not that Paul
was entirely indifferent to death. For he spoke of it twice as
a blessing (Ph 1:21-23; 2 Cor 5:1-10). And he felt that it would
be "for him a true 'gain,' rendering definitive his baptismal death
with Christ and intensifying his baptismal life with Christ."
But it was not death that greatly concerned Paul. It was the
parousia of Christ and the resurrection of the individual: these
dominated Paul's thought and desires. For he believed that "no
matter what death may achieve in intensifying life with the
Lord it cannot match the full and rich consummation of the
parousia." For in his thought death "does not bring that full
life with God which only the *total* man can know." And "for
this resurrection is necessary, the resurrection of the individual
and the people of God. Even those who have died in Christ must

still await the 'redemption of the body' and the restoration of all things" (Rm 8:23).

Did Paul, then, make any advance beyond "the contributions of St. Luke" to the doctrine of an interim state? Very little. It would be "the task of later theology to illumine the interim period between death and final consummation." This it would do "by focusing the light of precise philosophy on the data of revelation to formulate a full thesis on the beatitude of the soul immediately after death" ("The Concept of Union with Christ After Death in Early Christian Thought," pp. 7-20).

Early Christian Writers

Early Christian writers in one way or another, explicitly or implicitly, taught that there was an interim state between death and the resurrection at the end of the world. But there was considerable hesitation about affirming that before the resurrection and final judgment anyone was admitted to the face-to-face vision of God. Yet these writers taught clearly enough that from the moment of death the good and wicked are separated from one another. According to Justin at death the souls of the good and wicked are given separate dwelling places, to await the day of the last judgment. For the just the interim state is one of natural blessedness, and only after the resurrection at the end of the world do they gain the glory of heaven. Tatian seemed to think that the souls of the wicked are not only separated from the body but are annihilated until the last day, whereas the souls of the good are separated from the body for a time but remain in existence. Irenaeus wrote: "If the Lord descended into the shadow of death where the souls of the deceased were, then arose in the body, and after His resurrection ascended into heaven, evidently the souls of Christians will also go to that invisible place which God has destined for them and will remain there until the resurrection. Then receiving their body and rising in their entirety, that is, bodily, as the Lord arose, they will arrive at the vision of God." Tertullian thought that all souls except those of the martyrs are consigned to the lower regions. There the good experience refreshment and consolation and the evil punishment and pain. But the martyrs are at once given entrance into paradise with Christ.

Many of the early Fathers—Tertullian, Origen, Cyprian, Ephraem, Ambrose, Augustine, Chrysostom—pointed out that it was a common practice to offer prayers and good works for departed souls, a practice that seems to indicate a belief in the existence of a state after death in which the souls of the just would be fully purified before entering heaven. St. Hilary of Poitiers used the parable of the rich man and Lazarus to warn sinners that hell would receive them at once at the moment of death, with no respite before their punishment began. While many writers affirmed the eternal duration of hell, some such as Origen, Gregory of Nyssa, Didymus the Blind, Evagrius and Ambrose did not. Many thought the blessed went to heaven right after death but many others thought there would be a delay on suspension of the vision of God until the last judgment.

Clearly then these early writers were not in full agreement about this interim state, even though in one way or another they taught there was such a state. Not one of them, however, seems to have thought of an immediate resurrection after death. Not one of them seems to have considered this interim state one of sleep. Instead it involved an annihilation of the wicked (Tatian), an interim detention of all but martyrs in lower regions (Tertullian), an immediate admission of martyrs into heaven (Tertullian) and of sinners into hell (Hilary), and an interim purification of some of the just for entry into heaven (Ephraem, Cyprian, Ambrose, Augustine).

If there was such disagreement among these early writers, perhaps we should expect similar disagreement among Protestant and Catholic theologians of our day.

Protestant Theologians

Some hold the traditional view that there is a conscious interval after death for the Christian during which his soul or spirit is destined to wait in an intermediate disembodied condition until a distant resurrection day when his body will be raised up and reunited with his soul or spirit. Others such as Oscar Cullmann, Helmut Thielike, J. Mackintosh Shaw and Russell Aldwinckle, hold somewhat different views. But they all agree that there is life after death, and immediately after death, and they generally base this contention on much the same passages from the Gospel of St. Luke and the writings of St. Paul. They are especially concerned with those who die "in Christ" and they hold that these live on "with Christ" somehow. There they retain their personal identity and enjoy a personal immortality that is due not to a naturally immortal soul but to the operation of the indwelling Spirit of Christ. About those who do not die "in Christ" they seem much less concerned and much less clear, perhaps because, as they say, the New Testament is less concerned and less clear about these. But to these also they seem to ascribe a life after death, which they find very hard to explain. To what is their afterlife due? To a naturally immortal soul? To say this, they think, would be to espouse a Hellenistic view that conflicts with biblical anthropology. To the working of the indwelling Spirit? Hardly, for the Spirit of Christ would hardly vivify those who did not die "in Christ." Thus they are left with several difficult problems, which will stand out more clearly as we look more closely at the various positions.

Oscar Cullmann holds that there is an interim state but that it is one of 'sleep.' Scripture, he contends, nowhere says the resurrection of the body takes place immediately after the individual's death, as Karl Barth maintained. It does say that the dead are still in time and in a condition of 'sleep.' They are still 'in time' for, while death is conquered (2 Tm 1:10), it will not be abolished until the End (1 Cor 15:26 Rv 20:14). For them there is another time-consciousness, that of sleep. Paul's most usual image for this interim state is, "they are asleep." They are waiting, but because of Easter (Mt 27:52) death for them has lost its horror and 'sting.' They are in union with Christ; they are "with Christ" and in special proximity to Christ because of the Holy Spirit. A man who lacks the fleshly body is nearer to Christ than he was before, if he has the Holy Spirit, because there is no fleshly body now to hinder the Holy Spirit's full development. This afterlife of the soul is not based on any natural immortality of the soul. It is not due to the natural essence of the soul but to the Holy Spirit. The inner man already transformed and made alive by the Holy Spirit before death, continues to live with Christ in this transformed state but in the condition of sleep. Those who die in Christ are already living in Christ due to a divine intervention through the Holy Spirit, who has already quickened the inner man in earthly life by His miraculous power.[1]

Helmut Thielicke takes a position that resembles Dr. Cullmann's and yet is quite different. Like Dr. Cullmann he insists that the interim state is not "to be understood as a form of immortality based on some energy potential in the soul, nor a state analogous to the resurrection. . . . Rather it is a state of Divesting and Waiting (2 Cor 5:4ff), or positively, a **state** of "being with Christ" (Ph 1:23) that indicates not immortality but at most indissoluble communion with Christ, personal fellowship with Christ. But what is with Christ is not my soul or some particular piece of me, but I, insofar as I am a participant in the fellowship of Christ. . . . The form in which "I" am to be with Christ (somatic or psychic, interimistic or in eternal continuity) is not a valid object of question or psychological analysis, for faith lives from the resources of its object. These statements . . . fit well into a context of total personhood and confirm rather than contest biblical anthropology.[2]

Helmut Thielicke may not consider "the form in which 'I' am to be with Christ" a valid object of question, but it really is if he means to maintain that an objectively real "I" lives on after death, so that the "I" here and the "I" there are personally identical, are the same person. And if he does not mean to maintain this, then all talk about life after death for "me" is nonsense. If "I" after death am only an object in the mind of Christ and have no other real existence, or if "I" die and another person replaces me after death, then this is not personal life after death for me and it is not what Paul desired and intended. If the identity of "me" after death with "me" before death, involves a continuity of some kind between "me" after death and "me" before death, as it seems obvious it must, then something of "me" that constitutes "me" must be the vehicle or bearer of this continuity. It is useless to appeal to "total personhood" and "biblical anthropology." For in any adequate explanation of total personhood or biblical anthropology the personal identity of "me" before death and of "me" after death, must be considered and either maintained or rejected. If "I" live in Christ here through the operation of the Holy Spirit and "I" continue to live after death through the operation of the same Holy Spirit, what this one same "I" is and what constitutes it are valid questions that must be considered. And Helmut Thielicke does not consider them. Perhaps he and Dr. Cullmann ought to consider the advisability of a *modern* doctrine of a naturally immortal soul.

J. M. Shaw offers an interesting view of life after death that seems to do away entirely with any interim state. Building largely on 2 Cor 5:1-10, Ph 3:21 and Col 2:12, he maintains an immediate resurrection at death of those who die in Christ. It is at death that the spirit of the believer assumes its spiritual resurrection body. There is thus no interval between death and entrance into a glorified embodied existence and the intermediate state of disembodied nakedness between death and resurrection vanishes. At death the believer or Christian become "clothed upon" with the spiritual and immortal body "which is the gift of the Spirit." This spiritual body in fact is already being gradually formed here and now under the influence of the life-creating Spirit of Christ. The Spirit is even now working a gradual transfiguration of our whole personality, and when this is complete it "shall transform the body of our humiliation into conformity with the body of Christ's glory" (Ph 3:21). What will be this future life of those who are in Christ at death? It will be a life of spiritually embodied existence, guaranteeing and safeguarding continued personal identity and mutual recognition in the life to come. It will be a life of development in character and service. It will be a life of varied reward and glory.

But what of those who are not in Christ at death? For these

J. M. Shaw finds much less guidance in the New Testament. So he concludes in the words of Dr. Charles that "to share in the resurrection according to the all but universal teaching of the New Testament, is a privilege of those only who are spiritually one with Christ and quickened by the Holy Spirit." The kind of resurrection set forth in the New Testament is a resurrection which is possible only to those who are in saving fellowship with God, since it is based on and grounded in faith-union with a risen, living Christ and Savior. If there is a resurrection of others, the matter is nowhere explicitly indicated by the New Testament writers.[3]

This view is interesting and attractive but it needs much more development to render it acceptable. Its biblical foundation is far from cogent. Neither the Fathers nor the great Scripture scholars and theologians and Church councils of the past, nor the faithful Christians down the centuries, seem to have thought there was any such immediate resurrection at death or that such a resurrection was implied in Scripture. They all looked forward to a general resurrection at the end of time, as their creeds professed. Dr. Shaw must somehow harmonize his view with that general resurrection. And he must consider that "spirit" of the believer that lives on in its spiritual resurrection body: what is it and how does it account for personal identity and personal continuity and immortality? He must give more thought to those who are not in Christ at death, for they would seem to be the majority of mankind. What happens to them at death? Do they cease to exist? Or live on in a "new embodiment"? If God created all men, sends Christ to redeem all men and wills all men to be saved, would He will a life-after-death for only a small minority of mankind?

Recently *Russell Aldwinckle* of McMaster University has given us a very important study of life after death in contemporary theology and philosophy, in his book, *Death In The Secular City*. In it he offers a measured criticism of the views of J. A. T. Robinson, Paul Tillich, I. T. Ramsey, Oscar Cullmann, Gordon Kaufman and others and a persuasive defense of the Christian doctrine of personal life after death. Personal immor-

tality in an "embodied" form seems to him to be a plain implication of the New Testament faith in God. And there must be,
he maintains, an intermediate state of existence after death which
continues until the parousia, since the final judgment of men is
not made until the parousia. Since the Catholic doctrine of purgatory is based on the assumption that the final judgment of men
coincides with the moment of death, he finds this doctrine unacceptable. But if there is a total and final repudiation of the
divine offer of salvation by some men, this must result in their
eternal separation from God.

Unbelievers as well as believers enter this intermediate state
at death, but the believers are Prof. Aldwinckle's major concern.
Believers are defined in terms of repentance, faith, loyalty to
Christ and some evidence of the fruits of the Spirit. But only
God knows who is such a true believer. Such true believers will
have an assurance that death cannot separate them from the love
of God in Christ and from fellowship with Christ. They will
have a conscious awareness of self and of Christ's presence
through the indwelling Spirit, and a joy that comes from being
in Christ and in His presence. They will be with Christ after
death, enjoying a full "embodied" existence but looking forward
to the ultimate consummation. Since personal continuity does
not demand the same identical physical body they have here,
their after-death embodiment will not be a literal resuscitation
of their present physical bodies. But they will have personal
immortality and identity and continuity in an "embodied" form
of some kind and will be in Christ not as a half-person but as a
full person. Since the final judgment does not take place till the
parousia the believer has the possibility of spiritual growth but
also the possibility of retrogression, of sin and failure. But he has
the humble certainty that the transforming grace of God in
Christ has made him such a man as cannot—morally and spiritually—deny the God in whose life he is rooted and anchored.
His, however, is a spiritual certainty, not a logical one, springing from trust in the Lord who can hold us up when we are in
danger of falling.

Does this interim embodiment mean the elimination of the

general resurrection at the End? No. The general resurrection still has purpose and importance. It stands for the entry of the believer into full communion with the whole body of the faithful at the End when Christ claims his whole people in the corporate reality of the kingdom, the communion of saints and of just men made perfect.

What of the unbelievers? They too, it seems, will have a conscious and embodied existence in the interim state. But they will be in a condition of spiritual groping and uncertainty and deprived of the joy which they would have if they were in Christ. They have a chance to change and become Christians for the grace of God will not cease to operate and thus they will be able to know the divine love and presence and to respond to it. Whether they will is difficult to say. If we take very seriously human freedom to reject divine love, it becomes very difficult to frame a dogma of universalism which would make the salvation of all men rigorously necessary. What if these unbelievers stubbornly persist in their rejection of divine love? God will have no choice but to reject them and permit them to pass out of existence—at the parousia.

It must be said to his credit that Prof. Aldwinckle has courageously faced many of the serious issues that a modern view of eschatology entails. He takes a solidly Protestant position and tries very hard to evaluate the evidence for and against it—that is, the biblical evidence. He gives little or no attention to evidence that can be drawn from the Fathers and the Church's liturgy and councils. He finds unacceptable the Catholic position on purgatory, on an everlasting hell, on a particular but final judgment of the individual at death that removes any further opportunity for a basic change of status. He does not accept Universalism though he seems to incline to it. He feels strongly that his stress on life after death is entirely compatible with a deep concern for improving conditions here on earth. But if I read him correctly, he ends up far from satisfied with the positions he has espoused. Could it be that he realizes he has perhaps conceded much too much to modern psychology and biblical exegesis and too little to the methods and conclusions of traditional Protestant theology?

If we take these four theologians together we find them all basing their afterlife doctrine mainly on Paul's teaching that those who believe and live "in Christ" here, will be "with Christ" hereafter. This is their strength. But when they draw such different conclusions from their basic biblical principle, we wonder whether their *sola scriptura* principle ought not to be supplemented by interpretations of the Fathers and of the Church's magisterium. This they do not do. This is a weakness. Further they say if I am a believer in Christ at death, I will be "with Christ after death." But they say little about what this may mean. What does it mean to be "with Christ" *there?* More than it means to us to be "with Christ" here? More than it meant to the Apostles to be "with Christ" in Palestine? What is this Christ? Where is He? How am I with Him there? How am I the same "I" that I was before death? Was I an embodied "soul" or "spirit"? Am I now that same "soul" or "spirit" (disembodied or newly embodied)? How am I the same "person" after death that I was before death? And what am I doing now? And what of the unbelievers, who do not die "in Christ"? Are they with the believers? Elsewhere? What are they doing that can bring about their conversion to the state of believers?

Obviously no one of us can answer these questions adequately. But modern man has a right to expect modern theologians to consider these questions and to offer at least some tentative answers. For if these modern theologians are quick to reject traditional positions because of the purported findings of modern biblicists and psychologists, they should also be quick to face up to the questions that this rejection raises. This these theologians do not do. This is another serious weakness.

Catholic Theologians. For centuries the Catholic position on life after death has been very clear-cut, for it was a matter of faith for Catholics everywhere. There were two stages in this life after death, an interim stage between the death of the individual and the general resurrection at the end of the world, and a final stage from the general resurrection on throughout eternity. Admittedly there was a great deal of mystery surrounding both stages, but the basic elements were clear for they had either been solemnly defined by the Church or had come to be accepted by theologians as theologically certain.

In this Catholic position death is the entry into the life after death. Every man must die as a punishment for sin. With death all possibility of merit, demerit, conversion, ceases. So a man's life after death is determined by the condition he is in when he dies. Though God sincerely wills all men to be saved, not all actually seem to be saved and reach heaven. Immediately after death there is a particular judgment for each individual, in which Christ tells him his fate and its justice. This is a final and irrevocable judgment and execution of the sentence, and it will not be reversed in the general judgment at the end of the world. The just, those who die in the grace of Christ, but burdened with temporal punishment due to sin and thus in need of purgation go to Purgatory until they are ready for entry into heaven. There they cannot help themselves but they can be helped by the suffrages of the faithful on earth. The souls of those who have not committed any sin at all after they received holy baptism, and the souls of those who have committed sin but have been cleansed either while they were in the body or afterwards in purgatorial punishment, are promptly taken up into heaven. The souls of those who die in mortal sin or with only original sin go down into hell but there receive different punishments. (The "hell" or "limbo" of unbaptized babies will be treated later on.) Christ is at the right hand of God the Father and from there He shall come to judge the living and the dead at the end of the world and then he will reward all, both the lost and the elect, according to their works. All the dead will rise again with the bodies they now have so that they may receive according to their works, whether good or bad: the wicked, a perpetual punishment with the devil; the good, eternal glory with Christ.

Substantially this is the Catholic doctrine of the afterlife according to the Creeds, the general Councils of II Lyons, IV Lateran, Florence, Trent, and of Pope Benedict XII. And substantially this is still the position of Catholic theologians. But some of them offer variant views on the interim state. We look at four of these.

A. Winklhofer adopts a strictly traditional position. "It is Catholic teaching," he writes, "that the souls of the dead go immediately after death into heaven, purgatory or hell. . . . Directly after death, without the least interval, death or life comes into effect according to the inner state of each individual and according to the way in which he has faced the redemptive mystery of death. He immediately reaches a final state."[4] For him it is the disembodied soul that goes into the intermediate state. Man has a soul that is endowed with natural immortality. At death it separates from the body and goes into a timeless and spaceless existence. It continues to live in a state of wakefulness, not of sleep, and retains an awareness of self and of personal identity and of real links with the cosmos. All the activities that proceed from man as compounded of body and soul cease with death and it is doubtful if the soul is able to perform even its essentially spiritual acts. Without an extraordinary divine intervention it cannot have a complete continuity of consciousness and fullness of self-consciousness. The soul is a substance so incomplete that apart from the body it is as a television set without an aerial or an eye without a lens. After death the person is the same but is constituted in a different way.

The difficulties of this traditional view stand out bluntly. "After death the person is the same but is constituted in a different way": what does this mean? *Essentially* the same person but differently constituted? Before this person was constituted by a body and a soul. Now there is only the soul. How can this disembodied soul be essentially the same person as the embodied soul? It is not enough to affirm that it is. Some explanation is needed, but not given. Was it perhaps the soul itself, even when embodied, that made me essentially this person? If this is what is meant, this should be clearly indicated and justified as much as possible. Again, it is easy to say the soul goes into a "timeless existence" but what does this mean? If the soul really goes on living, must it not have a succession of thoughts and volitions? Is this timeless existence? If the soul goes on living and acting till the parousia which is perhaps billions of years away, is this timeless existence? Much, much more explanation is needed. This is a serious weakness of the traditional view.

Pierre Benoit presents an intriguing Pauline view of the interim state. What is this state, he asks? A state of full spiritual activity for man's "separated" soul? A state of "sleep" for all its powers? Does biblical anthropology permit us to hold there is real life without the body? Would it not be better to regard the resurrection as taking place for each individual directly after death?

For his answers he looks mainly to St. Paul (2 Cor 5:1-10; Ph 3:20-21; Col 2:12; Ep 2:6). And he finds Paul confident that even without his body and in a state of "nakedness" he will already be "with the Lord." Paul is not very clear about this life with Christ outside the body, he thinks, but two things are certain: (1) Paul does not give up the traditional belief in the general resurrection; (2) and he grants that directly after death and before the general resurrection there is a life outside the body with the Lord, which is to be preferred to life in the body and to exile from him (2 Cor 5:6-8). But what does Paul mean by this life "with Christ" which the Christian will have outside his earthly body? Not the life of an "immortal soul" in the Platonist sense. But a new, supernatural, mysterious yet real life drawn from a "spirit" placed in man at baptism by the new creation and the indwelling of the Spirit of Christ (2 Cor 5, 5). Can't we admit, he asks, especially if we think in the anthropological categories of Semitic monism rather than those of Platonist dualism, that the spirit which gives life to the soul retains after the death of the earthly body a mysterious but vital link with the risen body of Christ and finds in him the source and means of supernatural and blissful activity? It is the very body of the risen Christ, already established in the glory of heaven, which is waiting to be joined fully and definitely with his chosen ones. This body of Christ which unites to itself all the bodies of Christians as its members, we have already mystically put on at baptism (Gal 3:27; Rm 13:14). This does not exempt us, he feels, from looking forward to the final resurrection of the body as the definitive redemption of the whole human being (Rm 8:25), but it enables us to conceive in the interval an already essential possession of heaven because it is in union with him who even now possesses this life to the full in the whole of his being, body and soul. Since we know that we are already united here below in the Holy Spirit with the body of the risen Christ, we are able to believe that directly after death we shall find in this uninterrupted union the source and means of our essential blessedness.[5]

This is a tantalizing view of an interim "life with Christ." A "spirit" has its embodiment in and from the body of the risen Christ: this is an unusual concept, to say the least. And it hardly seems to be the teaching of St. Paul. For if Paul teaches that the "spirit" has a new embodiment at death, this embodiment is the spirit's own embodiment and not that of the risen Christ. What is more, Pere Benoit leaves very important questions unanswered. What is this "spirit" and what is its function before and after my death? This "spirit" was not "I" before my death but was placed *in me* by the Holy Spirit. Is it my "soul," if I have a soul? And what am "I"? If I live in and from the risen body of Christ, what am I? What is this "I" that lived before death and lives after death? What is its relation to "spirit" and to "embodiment"? These questions need to be answered. They are not answered here.

Ladislas Boros opts for an interim state of *immediate* but *initial* resurrection at death, followed at the end of time by a final and complete resurrection in a transfigured universe. He builds his position largely on two basic points: (1) that the soul cannot exist without a body and (2) that the resurrection from the dead is somehow an eschatological event. We usually think, he says, of the death of a human being as the separation of soul and body. But man is one entity. If the soul by its very essence stands in relationship to matter, then the soul cannot exist without a body. Yet revelation emphasizes repeatedly that man's resurrection from the dead is an eschatological event and coincides with Christ's second coming at the Last Day. How shall we reconcile these two points, he asks? Karl Rahner, he points out, has suggested that in death the human soul does not become "non-corporeal" but enters into a *pancosmic* relationship and is present everywhere in the universe. But why stop at this half-way solution? The more radical solution would be to say that the resurrection takes place immediately at death and yet is an eschatological event. For the *risen* human being needs the transformed and transfigured universe as his dwelling place. The transformation at the end of time, therefore, would involve the final completion of the resurrection that has already occurred at death. Thus the soul is never without a body. Immortality and resurrection are in fact one and the same.[6]

This view has much in its favor. It does away with the difficult concept of a "separated soul" living and acting by itself after death. It fits better with the biblical view of man as one, as a unitary totality. It suggests an answer to the difficulty of continued personal identity after death and it applies to all men, not just to Christians. But this view also leaves important questions unanswered. If the "soul's relation to the body belongs to its very essence,"[7] and if "immortality and resurrection are one and the same," does this mean that this actual immortality is a "gift-immortality" or a "natural immortality"? Does the human soul at death lose all its former embodiment and acquire a new embodiment? If it acquires an entirely new embodiment, can I be the same person after death as before death? If I am the same person, it would seem that what really and essentially makes me a "person," an "ego" and what is the carrier of my personal identity, memory, personality, is merely my soul. What then happens to the concept of man as a single human being? If the soul retains something of its former embodiment, what is this and how is it retained? These questions need to be pondered and to be given at least tentative answers.

Gregory Baum offers a view of eschatology that stresses the present and final states of mankind but by-passes the interim state. For him the kingdom of God is the central biblical notion by which Christ announced man's glorious destiny. This kingdom is the rule of God's word in the history of man and men's entry into a new heaven and a new earth. At the end of time Jesus will return to establish the kingdom in glory. Unfortunately in our western culture there has been a certain spiritualization and privatization of God's promises which has made Christians concentrate on their personal future, and has equated the kingdom of God with heaven, with personal salvation and with the immortality of the soul. This must be changed. For today we do not like to make belief in personal survival after death something that weakens our yearning for God's coming into human history to deliver all people from the power of evil. The Christian doctrine of the resurrection of the body is the central affirmation that prevents the message of the kingdom from being understood in an exclusively spiritual and private manner: God's victory is not confined to the soul nor limited into individuals: what is affected is the whole of humanity. In the past we have been too concerned with our personal future: what will happen to me after I die? Today we prefer the original Christian perspective that saw the divine promises as referring to the new heaven and the new earth. Today we must be more conscious of the socio-political consequences of the message of the kingdom. Jesus Christ did not give us information about the world to come. Teachings about heaven, hell and purgatory are not information about a future world but a message about the present-as-well-as-the-future. They initiate us into a new consciousness. They mediate salvation and a new perspective.[8]

This view has some good points, but in general it offers a very unsatisfactory approach to eschatology, and it is not easy to see why it was included in "An American Catechism." If there has been an excessive spiritualization and privatization of God's promises, then we should do away with the excess. But in the process we should not try to do away with a man's proper concern for his personal future and his personal life immediately after death. Vatican II along with much modern psychology and theology has properly stressed the individual, the person, the dignity and responsibility of the person. If Christ did not give us all the information about the future that we might like to have, yet He did give us some, and so did St. Paul and the Fathers of the Church and the Councils of the Church and the great theologians. Why should we ignore this? If it was bad to give too much attention to our personal future, it is just as bad to give too little. If we have been too little conscious of the socio-political consequences of the message of the kingdom, then let us become more conscious of these consequences but not to the extent of ignoring man's personal future in the interim state. If it was wrong to equate the kingdom of God with heaven, with personal salvation, with the immortality of the soul, it is just as wrong to equate it only with the eternal life of the far, far future. Why is it so wrong to be properly concerned with our immediate afterlife? St. Paul was concerned with it. So was Christ on the cross when he said to the good thief, "this day you will be with me in paradise." So were some of the Gospel parables. If it is good to look to the far future when God will be victorious over all evil and we will have a new heaven and a new earth, then it is also good to be practical and to realize that for most Christians their immediate afterlife with Christ is now of more urgent concern than the full completion of God's kingdom in the remote, remote future.

Just like their Protestant confreres, then, these Catholic theologians have varying views about life after death, but they all agree that there is such a life. None of these theologians consider this life after death one of "sleep." Some see the interim state as one of "disembodied life," others as one of a "newly-embodied life," of one kind or another. Most stress the afterlife of the individual; one stresses the far-future life of the community. Most of them do little more than try to interpret the meager data of the parables of Jesus and writings of St. Paul. Like their Protestant confreres they are too little concerned with trying to explain the personal identity and continuity and activity of those in the interim state. This is regrettable. For unless modern man is given some—at least tentative—explanation of what he will be and do in the interim state, how can he have any real interest in this afterlife? It is not enough merely to tell him that if he lives and dies "in Christ," he will be "with Christ" forever. He wants to know what it will mean to be "with Christ" or "not to be with Christ." He would like to know how "being with Christ" will satisfy all his rational desires throughout eternity.

CONCLUSION

When we took up the question of an interim state we encountered another aspect of mystery. For some scholars declared that there is no life immediately after death, because Sacred Scripture says nothing of such a life. But we found that both Jesus in the Lukan Gospel and Paul in several of his epistles indicated quite clearly that there is life immediately after death. The early Church writers, too, generally taught that there is such an interim life, though they disagreed about its nature and extent. However, not one of them seems to have thought of an immediate resurrection after death or to have considered the interim state one of sleep. That there is life immediately after death the Church's solemn magisterium declared in its definitions about purgatory, hell and heaven.

When we studied certain modern Protestant theologians, we found that they all agreed that there is life after death, at least for those who die "in Christ." With those who do not "die in Christ," they seemed little concerned. Protestant traditionalists continued to explain life after death in terms of a naturally immortal soul that lives on in a disembodied condition until the general resurrection. But four modern theologians offered variant views.

For Oscar Cullmann those who "die in Christ" live on in a state of "sleep," but their afterlife is due not to a naturally immortal soul but to the Holy Spirit. His view has been widely rejected. For Helmut Thielicke those who "die in Christ" live on due to the operation of the Holy Spirit and not due to a naturally immortal soul, and they enjoy a life of personal fellowship with Christ. But he fails to offer any explanation *how the same person* continues to exist after death and in 'what form' this person enjoys the fellowship of Christ. J. M. Shaw maintains that those who "die in Christ" immediately are "clothed" with a spiritual and immortal body that is the gift and work of the Holy Spirit, and that they enjoy a developmental life with varied reward and glory. But he too fails to explain how the *same person* lives on in this new afterlife. Nor does he indicate what happens in his view to the solidly established dogma of a general resurrection at the end of the world. Russell Aldwinckle holds that those who "die in Christ" have an afterlife of personal immortality in an *embodied* form, in which they have the joy that comes from "being in Christ" and in His presence. But this initial resurrection does not eliminate the purpose and importance of the general resurrection. However, in strongly stressing the interim state as one in which moral growth and change of status are possible, he must reject the Catholic doctrine of purgatory and of a particular but final judgment of the individual at death. These four Protestant theologians all base their after-life doctrine mainly on Paul's teaching that those who "die in Christ" here will be "with Christ" there. This is their strength. But much more is needed. They should at least try to explain what it means "to be with Christ," and how the *same person* who died "in Christ" is now "with Christ" somewhere. They should try to explain what happens to those who do not die in Christ, for possibly these constitute a large portion of mankind. They should try to explain why they draw such different conclusions from the same biblical data. If their basic principle of *"sola Scriptura"* leads to such divergent interpretations, perhaps they should think of supplementing it by recourse also to the interpretations of the Fathers and of the Church's Councils and Creeds. Perhaps they should think about reinstating a naturally immortal soul as the only conceivable vehicle of personal identity and continuity in the afterlife.

When we turned to some modern Catholic theologians we found that they too agreed there was an interim state of life after death but they took divergent views of this interim life. For A. Winklhofer in the interim state a naturally immortal soul goes on living in a disembodied condition with a continuing awareness of itself, of its personal identity, and of its links with the cosmos, but with a very limited spiritual activity. This traditional view has many good features but in positing a disembodied soul it fails to explain how the *same person* goes on existing and acting in the afterlife. Pierre Benoit presents a tantalizing view of an interim life with Christ, in which my "spirit" has its embodiment in and from the body of the risen Christ. But he leaves unanswered many vital questions about the nature of this "spirit" and its relationship to me as a person. Ladislas Boros opts for an interim state of immediate but interim resurrection at death, followed at the end of time by a final and complete resurrection in a transfigured universe. This is a very attractive view but it too needs amplification and clarification about the relationship between me and my soul and this embodiment. Gregory Baum offers a view that is generally unsatisfactory as it stands.

What then shall we say about an interim state? There are several things we can say that definitely seem to be beyond doubt. There is such an interim state of life and for *all* men, not just for those who "die in Christ," not just for the good. It is not a state of sleep, but of consciousness and of personal awareness and activity. It is a mode of life which, while human, is very different from earthly life. In this interim state the *same person* who lived before in an earthly mode of life now lives on in a very different interim mode of life. And this *person* is capacitated for this interim life basically by his naturally immortal soul that is endowed with immaterial powers. These are facts, in our estimate. But facts are not meant to stand in isolation. They call for integration, for unification, for a coherent explanation, something that we found lacking in the theologians we studied. Obviously the interim state is a mystery and will remain a mystery a long, long time. But we still can and should make a speculative attempt at some kind of consistent explanation. Mysteries tantalize men and certainly God would want men to explore them as much as they can, using all the powers of mind that He gave them.

So we start from the conviction that the same human person who before lived an earthly mode of life now lives an interim mode of life, and we ponder this human person. Since he had an immaterial soul in his earthly life, to be the same person in the afterlife he must have the same immaterial soul as carrier of personal identity and continuity and as ultimate principle of his interim human activity. (Unless the same immaterial and immortal soul continues in the afterlife it seems impossible to account for this person's continued personal identity and activity). Since a human soul is essentially the form of a body, to continue to exist it seems probable that this human soul must continue to inform a human body, and hence it must be re-embodied at death, with a new but human embodiment that will adapt this person for his interim life and activity. And since this human person in his earthly existence (most probably) was constituted a full human person not just by his immaterial soul but by this human soul embodied in this human body, it seems possible (probable?) that for this same human person to continue to exist in the afterlife it must there consist not only of the same immaterial soul and its new interim embodiment but also of an essential 'core' or 'seed' of the old body which developed into this new interim embodiment. And since *all* human persons, not just the good but the wicked as well, are destined by God to everlasting life (as we have indicated and will indicate again later on), they must all be capacitated by God for everlasting life by a naturally immaterial and immortal soul that is capable of functioning in various embodiments, first an earthly embodiment, then an interim embodiment after death, and finally an everlasting embodiment at the general resurrection.

But the mystery of interim life still remains. What will be the nature of this interim embodiment and how it will function, is mysterious. What is the nature and extent of the soul's 'immortalizing power' is mysterious. Whether the soul has in itself the power of re-embodying itself after the death of its body, or whether only God can and will produce this interim embodiment, is mysterious. What is the complete nature and functional power of the immortal soul is mysterious. Just how precisely I am constituted after death the same person that I was before death, is mysterious. Wherever we turn we encounter mystery, and so it will be all through our pilgrim life, until we encounter face-to-face the ineffable mystery that is God.

There are many other aspects of life in the interim state that still need to be pondered. We shall ponder them in the following chapters.

Notes for Chapter 4

1. O. Cullman, **Immortality of the Soul or Resurrection of the Dead,** (New York, The Macmillan Co., 1958), 48ff.

2. H. Thielicke, **Death and Life,** tr. E. H. Schroeder, p. 213ff.

3. J. M. Shaw, **Life after Death,** (Toronto, The Ryerson Press, 1945), pp. 243ff., 338ff.

4. **The Coming of His Kingdom,** (New York, Herder and Herder, 1963), pp. 61-160.

5. "Resurrection at the End of Time or Immediately after Death," **Immortality & Resurrection, New Concilium,** (New York, Herder and Herder).

6. **Living in Hope,** (Garden City, N. Y., Doubleday Image, 1973), pp. 38-39.

7. **Living in Hope,** (New York, Herder and Herder, 1970), pp. 33ff.

8. "Eschatology," **Chicago Studies,** Fall, 1973, pp. 304-311.

Chapter 5
Is There a Particular Judgment at Death?

Does God judge each individual at death? By a judgment that is definitive and final as far as each individual's eternal destiny is concerned? A judgment that has traditionally been called the "particular judgment" in contrast to the general judgment of all men that takes place at the end of the world? And if there is such a judgment, what form does it take? These are the questions that concern us now.

It has been traditional Catholic and Orthodox doctrine that there is such a judgment, although Catholic and Orthodox theologians have not been in complete agreement about the "how" and the "where" and the "matter of the judgment."

Today this particular judgment is being called into question not only by Protestant theologians, but also by some Catholic writers. Dr. J. A. T. Robinson declares that it appears unjust to make the moment of death the time of final judgment. And he adds that "to be content with the individual eschatology of later Western Catholicism is to betray a sub-Christian view of the Fatherhood of God" (op. cit., p. 44). Prof. Aldwinckle believes that Dr. Robinson's point is well taken, and so he maintains that the final and definitive judgment only takes place at the end of the world, at the parousia (op. cit., pp. 138ff). Some Catholic authors seem a bit hesitant about such a particular judgment, whether out of a deep concern to preserve the unique importance of the general judgment, or because they think that man's final fundamental option for self or for God, which is his own final self-judgment, renders a particular divine judgment unnecessary. Human reason alone cannot answer this question with any certainty. Nor can theological wishful thinking. Only God can tell us with certainty that there is or is not such a judgment at death. So we look for an answer from God in the Sacred Scriptures and in the interpretation of these Scriptures by the Fathers, Councils and great theologians of the Church.

Old Testament

In the Old Testament we find the belief that God is the judge of all men but nowhere do the sacred writers declare that God makes a particular, final and definitive judgment of each individual at death. For the longest time in the Old Testament it was thought that retribution operates within the limits of the present life. God judged man in this life by recognizing his works and the recompense that was proper to them. The signs of God's favorable judgment upon a man were prosperity, posterity, longevity (Ps 1:1-3; 36 (37):18-25; Pr 22:4). To live wretchedly and to be cut off early from life without descendants were regarded as evidence of a bad life and of God's judgment against the man who lived that life (Jb 15:20-21; Ps 139(140):12; Ws chs. 3-5). For the just and the unjust alike God's judgment was lived out in this life. However, it was often extremely difficult for Old Testament men, as in the case of Job (Jb 9:22), to see how God's judgment achieved justice in this life. It is possible to find some passages in the Old Testament that suggest a personal judgment after death (Si 21:9; Jb 17:4; Is 14:11) but today interpreters see in these only the developed doctrine of a later time read back into these texts.

New Testament

The New Testament, like the Old Testament, nowhere teaches *explicitly* that there is a particular judgment of each individual at death, but it does *imply* that there is such a judgment. In the Gospels such a judgment is implied in the teaching that the departed souls immediately after death receive their reward or punishment. In the story of Lazarus and the rich man the definitive separation of the two supposes that a definitive sentence has been passed upon them and committed to execution right after their deaths (Lk 16:19-31). We can detect implications of this judgment at death in the admonitions to penance and good works in this life. Only repentance in this life can save a man from the wrath to come (Mt 3:7-10; Lk 3:7-9), and hence at death his judgment is completed and his fate settled. In the light of the coming judgment men are urged to enter by the narrow gate . . . "When the master of the house has entered and shut the door, you will begin to stand outside . . . saying, 'Lord, open for us.'. . . And he shall say to you . . .'I do not know where you are from. Depart from me, all you workers of iniquity.' There will be weeping and gnashing of teeth when you shall see Abraham and Isaac and Jacob . . . in the kingdom of God, but yourselves cast forth outside" (Lk 13:24-28). If we strip away the cultural envelope of those times, the underlying implication of such passages is quite clear: at death men are definitively judged and separated according to their works, good or bad.

In St. Paul there is no explicit declaration of a particular and definitive judgment of each individual at death. But in several passages that indicate that at death a man's fate is settled and the good and the wicked are separated, there is a fairly strong implication of a particular judgment at death by which each man's eternal fate is settled and the good are separated from the wicked and sent to their reward then and there.

John, some say, contradicts this, for he teaches that judgment has already occurred in this life (Jn 5:25; 12:31). And thus there are only two judgments, one in this life whereby the unbeliever judges himself and is judged by his very unbelief in Christ, the other by God or Christ at the end of the world when those who refuse to believe in Jesus will rise to the resurrection of judgment. It is true that John does teach these two judgments of condemnation, judgments that involve a manifestation of a man's disbelief in Christ, first in this life and then at the end of the world. But the judgment in this life *implies* another judgment, a particular judgment at death. For just as a man is judging himself in life by his rejection of Christ, so God is and must be provisionally judging him by this rejection of Christ. And when a man finally judges himself at death by a final decisive rejection of Christ, God too finally and definitively judges him and separates him from those who accepted Christ.

Early Church

When we turn to the early Church we find some affirmation of a particular judgment at death, but not a great deal. Nearly all the earliest Creeds explicitly declare that Christ is to come again to judge the living and the dead (DS 42, 44, 76, 125, 150), but what they have in mind is the general judgment at the end of the world. A few of the early Fathers directly attest a particular judgment at death, such as Chrysostom, Jerome, Caesarius of Arles and Augustine. About 420 Augustine spoke explicitly of a judgment that awaits the soul as soon as it leaves the body, and he distinguished this from the great judgment after the resurrection. He appealed to the parable of the rich man and Lazarus, and regarded the denial of such a judgment as an obstinate refusal to listen to the truth of the gospel (*anim.* 2.4.8, CSEL 60.341). Many of the Fathers, however, gave no explicit affirmation of a particular judgment at death, and some thought the final and definitive blessedness of heaven and condemnation of hell did not come till the general judgment at the Parousia. But there was a fairly general conviction that at death the good and the wicked are definitively separated from one another and receive reward and punishment, and such a definitive separation necessarily seems to imply a definitive judgment by God that determines and implements the eternal destiny of each one.

General Councils

In the earliest general councils of the Church we find nothing about a particular judgment at death. Only in the two great reunion Councils of Lyons II (A.D. 1274) and Florence (A.D. 1439), and in the Benedictine Constitution (A.D. 1336) does a particular judgment begin to surface in the solemn teaching of the Church. And even in these dogmatic documents (DS 854-859, 1304-1306, 1000-1002), the particular judgment is only *im-*

plied, but not explicitly declared. What these documents declare explicitly is that right after death the wicked go to hell while the just either go to heaven directly or first to purgatory if they need cleansing. But this definitive separation of the good and bad at death and their immediate consignment to heaven, hell or purgatory, evidently implies a particular judgment of each one by God at death by which the just are separated from the impenitent sinners and by which each one is given his due.

It seems quite certain then in the light of this evidence that there is a particular judgment of each individual by God at his death. But this doctrine of a particular judgment is not a Catholic dogma, since it is not solemnly defined by the magisterium but is only inferred from solemn magisterial declarations and based on a solid scriptural and patristic foundation. Theologians, however, rather generally consider it a theologically certain Catholic doctrine.

Recently some of our theologians seem to be manifesting a tendency to down-grade God's role as judge and to up-grade man's. They seem to think that man's final assessment of himself, his final decision for or against God, is all that is needed. Man becomes man's judge, not God. One wrote: "Judgment and purgatory must now appear, despite their interest for Christian tradition, only as marginal. Death brings an end to the time-place conditions of our present life, and in finding our true selves we shall know what is of eternal value and meaning in ourselves. But we shall also, unfortunately, have to admit what is false and selfish, what in ourselves is alienated from God. This disclosure constitutes what is meant by 'judgment': man's assessment of himself in the presence of God, and the awareness of personal non-fulfillment comes acutely as a 'judgment' and as a definitive one" (Patrick Fannon, *The Catholic Mind,* April 1974, p. 22).

This tendency to downgrade God and upgrade man is an interesting phenomenon. It seems to be a reaction against what they consider an excessive stress on God in past theology. And to oppose this excess they go to the other extreme. From an "excessive" stress on God they move to an excessive stress on man. They do not seem to realize that the golden mean should apply in theology also. If the older view of the particular judgment was excessive, this newer view is just as excessive. It is right enough to take away the trappings of the old view, the court-room trappings, but it is utterly wrong to take away the judgment itself from God and hand it over to man. Possibly a man can make an adequate assessment of himself in death, an adequate assessment of what in him is of eternal value and what is false and selfish. Does this mean that he can also make an adequate assessment of what he deserves, of where he belongs, where and how he should spend his interim and final state? All this is part of the traditional particular judgment. Should we picture each man drifting around looking for his proper "place" or a "place" that suits him? This procedure might fit a Spiritualist's concept of the afterlife, but hardly anyone else's. Only the God who made every man and watched him live out his earthly life, is competent to judge every man, to assess what he has been and done and what he is in death. Only God is competent to assign to every man the reward or punishment that he deserves. Only the God who determined that there should be an afterlife for every man is competent to assign to every man his proper place or state in that afterlife. The biblical injunction is still true: render to Caesar what is Caesar's and to God what is God's.

To say that God cannot judge anyone is to play a word-game that is hardly worthy of a theologian. For that God not only can but does and will judge is basic biblical doctrine, a doctrine that has been canonized in our dogmatic creeds and councils. If some-one wishes to limit the concept of judgment to "condemnation," he should say so clearly, but then he should also indicate that biblically and traditionally judgment has meant more than merely a "judgment of condemnation." If someone wants judgment to mean merely "condemnation," then in a sense it is true that God cannot judge, i.e. condemn a man eternally and arbitrarily (though Calvin seems to have thought otherwise). But it is also true that if a man provisionally judges, i.e. condemns himself in life, so must God. However, while God's judgment was provisional during a man's lifetime, just as was man's judgment of himself, now God's judgment at death is no longer provisional but completely definitive and irrevocable. This is the particular divine judgment. And it is needed that it may be made utterly clear to this and every individual that it is God, not man, who has the final word. After all God has made man—made him in his own image and likeness. Man should not try to remake God in the image and likeness of this man or that.

WHAT IS THE NATURE OF THE PARTICULAR JUDGMENT?

Often in our devotional literature in the past the particular judgment was painted in vivid courtroom colors. As a judicial process in which accusations were made and a defense was offered. In which the guardian angel and patron saints of the individual being judged pleaded his cause, while devils piled up charge on charge so that they might carry him off to hell. Meanwhile Christ the judge listened to both sides and at length pronounced a just and final sentence from which there was no appeal. Today theologians view the particular judgment very differently (cf. J. H. Wright, "Judgment," *The New Catholic Encyclopedia*, pp. 30ff). They strip away all the courtroom apparatus and proceedings, and retain only the most essential features. Thus they envision the particular judgment as taking place wholly within the individual's soul and mind by the power of God's mind and will which effectively join the final dispositions of the individual with their appropriate realization. The judgment does not so much occur in a place as it effectively puts the soul in a place or state that is heaven, hell or purgatory. By the free choices a man has made in life and in death he has fitted himself to occupy a certain "place" or "state" in the plan of God. God's judgment makes clear to each man what he has made of himself and gives him that place in the total design of His wisdom and love that the man has fitted himself to fill. If, in the theory of death as final decision, we say that a man judges himself by his final decision for or against God, then God's particular judgment unmistakably manifests to the man the implications and the consequences of this final decision and implements them. The particular judgment at death is final and irrevocable not so much from God's arbitrary decision to make it final but rather because a man's final decision for or against God is definitive and irrevocable, when a man is in fullest lucidity and freedom and in fullest possession and control of himself. Intrinsically, then, the finality and irrevocability of man's status comes from man's own decision and self-judgment, extrinsically it comes from God's judgmental will ratifying and implementing man's decision. When the man makes his final, complete, irreversible response to God's loving initiative, his state of pilgrimage is over, and God's judgment assigns him his fitting reward or punishment in the interim state that perdures from death until the general resurrection.

Chapter 6
Is There a Purgatory?

Is there really a purgatory in the afterlife? A temporary state of purification? Or only an eternal hell and heaven? For a long time purgatory has been a bone of contention between Catholic and Orthodox Christians, between Catholic and Protestant Christians, and to some extent it still is today.

The doctrine of purgatory has had an interesting history. That there is a purgatorial place or state of purification in the afterlife is not taught explicitly in the Old Testament or in the New Testament. However, in the early Church there was a widespread practice of praying for the dead, a practice that seems to imply a belief that some of the dead were neither in heaven nor in hell but in a temporary state of purification in which they could be helped by prayers of the living. Then Origen in the East and Augustine in the West began to explicate an idea of purgatory, which Gregory the Great developed and presented as a doctrine that "ought to be believed." Western Catholic and Eastern Orthodox Christians developed somewhat differing views of purgatory over the years but in two reunion councils, Lyons II and Florence (A.D. 1274 and 1438-1445), they agreed on a solemn definition that "souls are cleansed after death in purgatorial cleansing punishments" and that "the suffrages of the faithful can be of great help in relieving these punishments." The great Reformers, Zwingli and Calvin, Luther and Melanchthon, rejected purgatory, and so do Protestants rather generally today. Ever since Lyons II and Florence Catholics have proposed the doctrine of purgatory as a dogma of the faith, and they have painted purgatory in very lurid colors and laid a heavy stress on its punishing "fire." Today, however, some Catholic theologians seem to be down-grading purgatory and saying that "this piece of medieval theology" is "particularly in need of revision."

Is there any solid evidence for the existence of purgatory? Obviously human reason by itself cannot detect or demonstrate purgatory. If it exists, it is beyond the reach of science, astronomy and cosmology. Spiritualism and Theosophy have not offered any solid empirical evidence in this matter. The only one who can give us solid certainty in this matter is God. Has He?

Old Testament

In the past theologians regularly turned to the Second Book of Maccabees where it speaks of prayer for those fallen in battle (2 M 12:38-46). They argued that this practice of prayer implied that those fallen were neither in heaven nor in hell, but in an intermediate state of purification in which they could be helped by the prayers of the living (cf. Herve, op. cit., 546-7). More recently theologians and biblicists have increasingly rejected this interpretation as unfounded. But rather surprisingly J. McEleney has recently written that "this doctrine, thus vaguely formulated, contains the essence of what would become (with further precisions) the Christian theologian's teaching on purgatory" (JBC 27:82).

New Testament

In the past many theologians found some evidence of purgatory in two passages of Matthew's Gospel, Mt 5:26 and 12:32. But it was especially to 1 Cor 3:11-15 that they turned for inferential evidence of purgatory. From the fact that Paul there declared that "each man's work will become manifest: for the Day will disclose it, because it will be revealed with fire, and the fire will test what sort of work each one has done" (3:13), they argued to a state of purgation by "fire" after the particular judgment. Later exegetes generally tended to reject this purgatorial interpretation of the passage. But two recent Catholic Commentators see once again purgatorial implications in this passage. Thus R.

Kugelman, C.P., writes: "although the doctrine of purgatory is not taught in this passage, it does find support in it. The metaphor suggests an expiatory punishment—which is not damnation—for faults, that although not excluding salvation, merit punishment. When Paul wrote this epistle he was still hoping for the coming of the Lord's Day in his lifetime. Consequently, he locates this expiatory punishment at the final judgment" (JBC 51:23). And W. Rees says that "the last words clearly imply some penal suffering, and as Paul connects it so closely with God's judgment, it can hardly be confined to suffering in this world, but it seems to include the idea of purificatory suffering after this life, i.e. in purgatory."[1] Thus, while there is no explicit doctrine of purgatory in either the Old Testament or the New Testament, there is some support for this doctrine in both the Old Testament and the New Testament. Will the early Church Fathers and writers develop this germinal doctrine of purgatory?

Early Church

In the early Church this germinal doctrine of purgatory developed gradually. And it developed primarily, it seems, from reflection on a widespread practice of praying for the dead, on an 'immemorial' custom of offering prayers and the Holy Sacrifice for the dead. That this was a very widespread practice is evident from the testimony of Tertullian, Origen, Cyprian, Ephraem, Ambrose, Chrysostom, Augustine, Caesarius of Arles, Gregory the Great. Tertullian mentions anniversary masses for the dead (De corona mil. 3) and advises a widow "to pray for the soul of her husband, begging repose for him, and . . . to have sacrifice offered up for him every year on the day of his death" (Monogamia 10). This same custom is confirmed by many sepulchral inscriptions found in the catacombs, in which the departed ask for the prayers of their surviving friends or beg God for "peace and refreshment." In the Acts of St. Perpetua we read that she beheld her brother Dinocrates, who had died a heathen and was "suffering terrible torments, released from the place of punishment through her prayers" (Acta Mart. S. Perp. et Soc.).

St. Augustine appealed to his friends to pray for his mother, St. Monica, and instructed them as to the most effective way of helping her soul (*Confess.* IX, 13).

Some of the early writers gave more direct testimony. Thus St. Basil affirmed the existence of a "place for the purification of souls" and of a "cleansing fire" (In *Is* IX, 19). St. Gregory of Nyssa said that "after egress from the body (a soul that is not fully pure) . . . will not be able to participate in divinity, unless the purgatorial fire will have purged away all stains on the soul" (Or. *de mortuis*, RJ 1061). St. Augustine said that "some of the faithful, according as they have more or less loved passing goods, will be more slowly or quickly saved through a certain purgatorial fire" (*Enchir.* 6). And elsewhere he added: "that the dead are aided by the prayers of holy Church, by the salutary sacrifice, and by the alms which are poured out for their souls" (*Sermones* 172; cf. *Enchir.* 60). F. Cayre, an eminent Patrologist, wrote that "Saint Augustine gave a very exact outline of the doctrine of purgatory, at least as regards its existence, which he establishes on 1 Cor 3:11-15. He recognized that there is temporal punishment in the next life, by which souls are purified and which will come to an end with the judgment. He speaks of purifying fire. He hesitated perhaps to give any exact definition of the nature of this fire, but there is no doubt that he admitted the existence of purgatory."[2]

That this practice of praying for the dead implied a belief in a state of purification for the just after death became fairly obvious in the early Church. The early Church did not believe that in each and every instance the eternal beatitude of the just began immediately after death. Rather the just fell into two groups, the first made up of apostles, martyrs, prophets, who were with Christ in paradise, and the second made up of ordinary Christians, for whom the Church prayed. For it remembered that our Lord and the apostles had stated clearly that no one enters heaven unless he is sinless. The early Church did not seem to be very clear about *where* these souls were or *how* prayer would help them, but she definitely knew that prayer and Sacrifice could be of benefit for these faithful Christians. She built her purgatorial doctrine on "three truths firmly grounded on Scripture and religious experience. The first is an unshakable faith in God's holiness which cannot stand contact with what is not pure and holy (Rv 21:27) ... Then a true understanding of the stark realities of life led to a perception that not all the dead have attained absolute purity. Lastly a keen realization of the mystical body of Christ, that is, the mysterious oneness of all the faithful with Christ, at once suggested the idea of intercession for the departed."[3]

In summing up the patristic development of purgatorial doctrine, B. Bartmann wrote: "The Fathers hardly try to prove the existence of purgatory—they take it for granted—and the texts of Scripture to which they refer are used less as proofs than as means by which to explain and clarify the notion of purgation after death ... If we study the development of the belief in purgatory in the Catholic Church in the writings of the Fathers, we find that it originated with the practice of prayer, intercession and the offering of the Eucharistic sacrifice for the dead. ... To this practice was allied the secret belief, which in the course of time became vocal, that the souls of the departed are benefited by our devout remembrance of them at the Eucharistic sacrifice. This conviction is reflected in the definitions of the Councils" (op. cit., pp. 160ff).

Church Councils

With their views about purgatory differing so much, it might have seemed impossible that the Eastern Orthodox and the Western Catholics could find any purgatorial formulation on which they could agree. But they did—at the two reunion councils of Lyons II and Florence (probably for partly political reasons). In the first place both Greeks and Latins found that they agreed on the utility of prayer for the dead. But they were not able to agree on the existence of a purgatorial fire, for the Greeks regarded this as an Origenist doctrine of a fire in which all were saved. However, they were able to agree on a rather remarkable purgatorial doctrine. This is the way they formulated and defined their common doctrine in the reunion council of Florence in 1439, in the decree for the Greeks: "If those who are truly penitent, die in the charity of God, before they have done sufficient penance for their sins of omission and commission, their souls are cleansed after death in purgatorial punishments: and they are helped to be relieved from these punishments by the suffrages of the living faithful, the sacrifices of Masses, the prayers and alms and other pious deeds which the faithful are accustomed to offer for other faithful according to the institutes of the Church" (DS 1304). Almost 200 years earlier in 1274 at Lyons II, also a general and reunion council, practically the same doctrine was enunciated in the dogmatic Profession of Faith of the Emperor Michael Paleologus (DS 856). Thus the Latins and Greeks were agreed on two essential aspects of purgatorial doctrine: (1) the souls of truly penitent just who have not done sufficient penance for their sins before death, are cleansed after death in purgatorial punishment; (2) the suffrages of the faithful on earth can be of great help in relieving these punishments. But in their declarations they said nothing about purgatory as a place, about a fire of purgatory, about the duration of purgatorial punishments, about how the suffrages of the faithful on earth can help these souls. They singled out what they considered the essential elements of purgatorial doctrine, and these they defined as common doctrine to be believed by West and East.

The Council of Trent (1563) redefined these two very basic points of purgatorial doctrine, (1) that there is a purgatory and (2) souls detained there are helped by the suffrages of the faithful on earth. In a recent study of "Trent's Temporal Punishment," P. J. Beer, S.J. noted that "the Council itself firmly upheld the usefulness of and need for suffrages on behalf of those in purgatory" (*Theological Studies*, Sept. 1974, pp. 471ff). He added that "it seems that according to this conciliar view God provides for the remission of the debt of temporal punishment of those in purgatory ordinarily through the charity of the faithful on this side of the grave. No longer able to merit or to sin, as those at

Trent saw it, those in purgatory long with fierce intensity for the happiness they know to be theirs and which the faith, love and intercession of the Church obtains for them" (ibid.).

In recent years there has been much critical discussion of ecumenical councils and their "definitions," and especially of those of the Council of Trent. And the result has been a strong tendency on the part of some theologians to maintain that some (many?) of their "definitions" were not definitions at all, for in proposing them the Council Fathers were merely repeating what they *supposed* to be the traditional doctrine, and not defining it themselves. The Council Fathers, it was urged, could not give a definitive answer to something that was not in question at the time they made their pronouncements. Though this argument itself is of dubious validity, it should be noted that it does not apply in the case of the Tridentine "definition" of purgatory. For when the Fathers of Trent defined purgatorial doctrine they were well aware that this doctrine had been called into question and denied by the Reformers, and hence they were *not just supposing* a traditional doctrine: they were *defining* a doctrine that was being questioned and denied at that time. And because the Reformers claimed that the doctrine of purgatory had no foundation in Scripture and Tradition the Council declared: "The Catholic Church, by the teaching of the Holy Spirit, in accordance with Sacred Scripture and the ancient tradition of the Fathers, has taught in the holy councils, and most recently in this ecumenical council, that there is a purgatory and that the souls detained there are helped by the prayers of the faithful and especially by the acceptable Sacrifice of the Altar." And the Council added, "therefore this holy council commands the bishops to be diligently on guard that the true doctrine about purgatory, the doctrine handed down from the holy Fathers and the sacred councils, be preached everywhere, and that Christians be instructed in it, believe it, and adhere to it. But let the more difficult and subtle controversies, which neither edify nor generally cause any increase of piety (1 Tm 1:4), be omitted from the ordinary sermons to the poorly instructed" (DS 1820).

Purgatory, then, has been and still is a dogma of the faith. It is a doctrine that has been solemnly defined by two general and reunion councils, by Pope Benedict XII in the famous Benedictine Constitution (DS 1000) and by the general council of Trent. These councils did not just suppose this doctrine: they defined it. In the time of the reunion councils the doctrine was questioned by the Greeks, in the time of Trent by the Reformers. In both cases the purgatorial pronouncement was a solemn definition promulgated by a general council. It was meant to be an irreversible declaration and it is. This dogma involves two basic points: (1) some just souls are cleansed after death in purgatorial or cleansing punishments, (2) the suffrages of the faithful on earth can be of great help in relieving these punishments. Fire, place, duration, are not part of the dogma. Today the tendency among theologians is to eliminate anything like a material fire, to shorten the duration of purgatorial punishments, and to do away altogether with the idea of purgatory as a "temporary hell."

Theological Questions Today

Today theologians are asking various questions about purgatory and taking a different view of it. One of the basic questions is: *why* is there a purgatory? And here there is rough agreement among the theologians, though they may express this a bit differently. They seem agreed that there is a purgatory because some of the just at death are not ready for immediate entry into heaven. But to the questions, *how* does purgatory make them ready, and *how quickly*, they respond in ways that are quite different.

R. Guardini thinks purgatorial purification comes largely by way of *realization*. When a man enters into God's light, he comes to see himself as God sees him. The pain of this realization is inconceivable, but it is very effective. In this pain man's disposition is purified and expanded until the man attains the needed readiness for communion with God. In surrendering to the re-creating will of God he endures death on death, death to pride and vanity and evasion and indifference and imperfect love till he becomes newly made and perfect, ready for eternal communion with God.[4]

K. Rahner views purgatory as a process of maturing and change, but of change that in no way conflicts with the dogma of the Church. This dogma, he feels, does not require us to think of purgatory as a purely passive endurance of vindictive punishments which, when "paid for", release man in exactly the same condition in which he commenced the state of purification. Not every "change" or "process of maturing" necessarily implies growth in grace, increase of merit, advance in the degree of glory. Such a change in the degree of maturity can just as well be conceived of as an integration of the whole stratified human reality into that free decision and grace which, having been made and won in this life, is in itself definitive. The many dimensions of man do not all attain their perfection simultaneously and hence there is a full ripening of the whole man "after death," as his basic decision penetrates the whole extent of his reality. In this concept . . . the remission of punishment (is not) a mere abstention from punishing but rather . . . the process of painful integration of the whole of man's stratified being into the definitive decision about his life, taken under the grace of God . . . We cannot indeed picture to ourselves how in particular such a process of maturing can develop in different ways in the life after death; but *that* such a thing is conceivable will be very difficult to dispute a priori. How do indulgences fit into this picture? They do not help the departed souls to "pay" the temporal punishment, but they do help them "prepare" for heaven, not by an increase of merit but by making them more perfect for heaven.[5]

P. Fransen views the pain and joy of purgatory in terms of God's love. "Purgatory," he says, "constitutes for us the beginning of the most intense, total, and final living of our spiritual selfhood . . . For in it we are appearing before the absolute glory of God's majesty, not yet in the beatific vision of the saints, but still knowing ourselves to be in his immediate presence shining through us and bearing us up. If we are a punishment for ourselves, it is because we see, in the light of God's own love for us, which we have answered so hesitantly but which is now triumphantly taking possession of our hearts, how deeply we have offended his holiness, and we feel the unspeakable weight of his pure and all-holy anger. But it is not only God's anger that weighs upon us. It is his love that causes our greatest pain, pain far greater than any we can bear on earth. It scorches up in us all the remnants of our self-love, ingratitude and refusal. But at the same time it penetrates us totally—which is why purgatory is also a joy more intense than anything we can experience on earth."[6]

Probably the most advanced view of purgatory is that of L. Boros. He finds only one thing about purgatory absolutely certain theologically: that every sin a man commits entails a debt of punishment (*reatus poenae*) which cannot simply be paid each time by turning away from the crime committed and doing nothing else. Hence the essential thing in the process of purification consists in paying this debt of punishment through the pains of satisfaction (*satispassio*). What of the *reatus culpae*, the guilt of unforgiven venial sins that must be forgiven before the man may enter heaven? The two most common answers, that they are forgiven in purgatory itself or by an act of perfect charity made in the first moment *after death*, he rejects as unacceptable. Instead he opts for the theory of the final decision in death and so in the very act of death he sees a flaring up of charity that would effectively offset all a man's sins and open his heart to God's forgiveness. The only thing remaining then would be the debt of temporal punishment in the paying of which defined doctrine sees the essential nature of purgatory. What of purgatory itself? Here he makes a twofold reduction in the idea of purgatory, reducing (1) the place of purgatory to a process and (2) the process to a personal encounter, so that God himself, our meeting with him, is our purgatorial fire. The place of purification, he maintains, cannot be some kind of torture chamber or cosmic concentration camp. Purgatory is the meeting with Christ, having to sustain the fire of his loving gaze which is our ultimate purification. That gaze burns into the innermost, most secret essence of human reality. To meet God in the flame of Christ's gaze is indeed the highest fulfillment of our capacity for love, but at the same time it means the most terrible suffering in our very essence. The harder and more stubborn our layers of egotism, the more painful the eruption of the love of God, and the more purifying the meeting with Christ. Human beings would thus personally undergo at the moment of death a process of purification which would differ in intensity for each. Instead of a difference in the time spent in purgatory, there would be a difference in the degree of intensity of the purification.[7]

Of these differing views obviously the most attractive is that of L. Boros. For in it purgatory is over in an instant. And then comes immediate entry into glory. Christ's intense flaming gaze of love penetrates to our deepest depths and burns out our egotism and all that impedes our entry into glory. And then our purgatorial cleansing is over and we are ready for the beatific vision. This view fits nicely into our contemporary stress on the God of love. Would a God of love punish vindictively and for a 'long time' those whom He loves, those who love Him greatly and who died in His love? Would a God of love torture those who died in His love and make them go on and on in painful suffering until they had paid their debt of temporal punishment to the last farthing? Did not St. Augustine, too, hold this view in the long ago when he 'made' purgatory very brief but very severe?

Attractive this view is, but is it acceptable? If we accept it what must we say about an old tradition in the Church that purgatory is often of very long duration? Will we simply say that that tradition was erroneous? Can a "new theory" so simply eliminate an old tradition? Were the faithful and the Church so wrong in their interpretation of Scripture and tradition? If we accept this view, what must we say about the second essential point of the purgatorial dogma, that the suffrages of the faithful on earth can be of great help in relieving these purgatorial punishments? This point of belief goes back to the early Church and it was accepted and defined by both Latins and Greeks in their reunion councils. And it was often expressed by anniversary Masses that were offered year after year for the repose of the soul of the faithful departed. Was that point of belief and definition a mistake, an error? Can an attractive new theory eliminate such a point of dogma? Or can it be reconciled with this dogmatic point? It is hard, if not impossible, to see how it can be so harmonized. How can the suffrages of the faithful be of any help in relieving such instantaneous punishment? How can they affect the burning gaze of Christ? Traditionally these suffrages were considered to somehow shorten the 'duration' of purgatorial punishments. But if each one's purgatory is over in an instant, how can our suffrages, our prayers, our Masses, help in any way to shorten or relieve these instantaneous punishments? It seems utterly futile to answer as L. Boros does: "For God all is present: for him our prayer and the death of the person for whom we are praying coincide; for him, the human being whom we love and whose decision we want to make easier by the support of our prayer is dying at the moment when we are praying for him. The situation is of course similar to that which holds in the widespread devotional exercise in honor of the Sacred Heart, the 'Holy Hour.' "[8] The situation is in no way similar to that of the "Holy Hour"! And the suffrages that the purgatorial dogma mentions are not prayers to help make someone's *decision* before death or *in death easier* than it would otherwise be. They are prayers meant to help someone *after death, after* he has made *his final decision*, to help relieve his purgatorial punishments. If these purgatorial punishments, whatever form they take, are over in an instant, how can our suffrages in any way *relieve these punishments?* The only conclusion seems to be that this theory, however attractive it may be, is unacceptable as it stands. Whether it can be harmonized with the second point of the purgatorial dogma and with the traditional belief of the faithful, is not clear. Only time and better theological reflection will tell.

At present the only acceptable view seems to be that which holds that purgatory is not over in an instant but is a state of longer or shorter "*duration*" according to each one's condition at death. It is thus a gradual process, not an instantaneous effect. Where there is in a man more to be purified, more to be perfected, there a man's purgatory will be of longer duration, understanding duration, of course, in some other sense than that of our time-space world. When a man's sins have left evil consequences deeply implanted in his soul and its faculties, when "persistent habits of sin or uncontrolled desires have left deep spiritual scars on the

faculties of the soul, that penetrated below the level of consciousness into the very fibre of the personality,"[9] then this man's purgatorial cleansing will be of longer duration. "There are many
dimensions of man," K. Rahner wrote, that "do not all attain
their perfection simultaneously," and so there will be "a full ripening of the whole man 'after death,' as his basic decision penetrates
the whole extent of his reality." Thus there will be a longer or
shorter "process of painful integration of the whole of man's
stratified being into the definitive decision about his life" (loc.
cit.). By this painful integration each one will reach the full
maturity and the full ripening that will ready him for entry into
the eternal vision and love and companionship of God and angels
and saints.

Obviously this view fits easily enough into the traditional
belief in a purgatory of longer or shorter duration. But can the
suffrages of the faithful and of the Church on earth help those
in purgatory, if their purgatory is a maturing process? It would
be easy enough to see how suffrages could help departed souls
to "pay" the temporal punishment that is due, for God could
accept them as "part payment." But how can suffrages, prayers,
Masses, alms, help departed souls to "mature" in purgatory, to
become "perfect" for heaven? It is not easy to give an answer to
this question, especially since "we cannot . . . picture to ourselves
how in particular such a process of maturing can develop in
different ways in the life after death" (K. Rahner, loc. cit.). But
we can give a tentative answer if we build on something that
K. Rahner says in his article on Indulgences.[10] Thus charity, justi-
fying charity, would be present in those who go to purgatory
(otherwise they would go to hell). But this charity would not
be perfect in all respects, it would not have integrated into itself
the manifold dimensions of man's being (else this man would go
immediately to heaven). In purgatory, then, as a maturing process,
this charity will become perfect in all aspects and will integrate
into itself the manifold dimensions of man's being. And suffrages
could be a very important aid, an intercessory aid for the grace
needed for maturing into perfect charity. Just what form this
grace would take would be hard to say. But probably it would

take the form of illumination and inspiration. An illumination to see the deep-down defects and imperfections and inordinations and an inspirational impulse to elicit a more intensely purifying love that would burn out these defects and imperfections.

In L. Boros' theory the flaming loving gaze of Christ would burn out all defects in an instant. But this would seem to do psychological violence to man's nature and personality, and man would passively undergo this 'burning.' But if purgatory is a process of maturing, then the burning out of defects and imperfections would be more gradual and would be effected by a gradual intensification of the man's purifying love, until it would have burned out all, even the deepest, defects and imperfections. More suffrages would mean more intercessory aid for the grant of more grace to intensify a man's purifying love so that it would more quickly and painfully burn out the last traces of defect and imperfection left over from the sins of his pilgrim life. Thus the faithful on earth by their suffrages, God by His grant of grace to intensify love and the person in purgatory by his intensified purifying and integrating love would all cooperate, each in his own way, to bring the person in purgatory more quickly to the full perfection of charity in all its aspects which would ready him for immediate entry into glory. Those for whom no suffrages were offered by pilgrim faithful and pilgrim Church would take longer, it would seem, to reach the integrating charity needed for entry into glory. Unless God in His mercy and for reasons of His own would arrange otherwise.

Is Purgatory Avoidable? Infants, of course, who die in the grace of God, can and do avoid it, for they have no sins, no evil consequences of sin, no debt of temporal punishment. But can adults? Or can adults have their 'purgatory' in this life? In the past theologians taught that adults could avoid purgatorial punishments after death, if they died without venial sins on their souls (unforgiven) and without a debt of temporal punishment. And to die thus, they added, did not depend on achieving the highest degree of sanctity. For one with very great sanctity might have a long purgatory but a very "high place" in heaven. While one with a much lower sanctity might avoid purgatory altogether, if he frequently used the Church's power of indulgences, performed many acts of charity and self-abnegation, grew in the love of God and neighbor, lovingly accepted the sorrows of life and the pain and separation of death.[11]

Can we still say someone can avoid purgatory altogether, if purgatory is viewed more as a maturing than as a debt-paying process? Why not? If someone can "pay off" the debt of temporal punishment in this life, why can he not achieve in this life the maturity and perfection of charity required for immediate entry into glory? As martyrs do. Why not others? Pains, sorrows, sufferings of all kinds come to people as they grow older, and these can have tremendous purifying and maturing power, if they are lovingly accepted. Better prayer, greater love, more fervent reception of the sacraments can bring them grace on grace to realize their defects and imperfections and gradually eliminate them. Sometimes we meet people who have learned to accept more and more lovingly and contentedly great physical and mental suffering. Like Our Lord in His passion they have experienced agony and loneliness, contempt and abandonment. They have come to accept their lot and their sufferings more and more peacefully, out of a deeper and deeper love of God that has blossomed into a warm love of all those around them, even those who hurt them deeply. If a saintly maturity is needed, they seem to have achieved it. If a perfection of charity in all its aspects is needed, they seem to have achieved it. And so they could have their purgatory here on earth and at death go immediately into the glory of heaven. *Pie creditur.*

And thus one of the finest ways of charity to older people, one of the finest spiritual works of mercy, could be to help them have their purgatorial punishments here on earth by lovingly accepting the pain and sorrow and sufferings, the loneliness and contempt and abandonment, that come their way. To help them reach that full maturity, that full perfection of charity in all its aspects which would ready them for immediate entry into glory. To help them die like Christ, with Christ, in Christ, loving God and neighbor with all their mind and will and soul.

Notes for Chapter 6

1. **A Catholic Commentary on Holy Scripture,** (Edinburgh, Thomas Nelson and Sons, 1953), p. 1087.

2. **Manual of Patrology,** (Tournai, Desclee and Co., 1936), v. 1, p. 712.

3. B. Bartmann, **Purgatory,** (London, Burns, Oates and Washbourne, Ltd., 1936), ch. xvi.

4. R. Guardini, **The Last Things,** (New York, Pantheon, 1954), pp. 46-48.

5. **Theological Investigations** IV, (Baltimore, Helicon Press), pp. 347-354.

6. "The Doctrine of Purgatory," **Eastern Churches Quarterly,** no. 13, 1959, p. 106.

7. **The Mystery of Death,** (New York, Herder & Herder, 1965), pp. 129ff.

8. "Death, A Theological Reflection," **The Mystery of Suffering and Death,** M. J. Taylor, S.J., ed., (New York, Alba House, 1973), pp. 147-148.

9. R. J. Bastian, S.J., "Purgatory," **New Catholic Encyclopedia,** v. 11, p. 1037.

10. "Remarks on the Theology of Indulgences," **Theological Investigations IV,** pp. 347-354; cf. **Sacramentum Mundi 3,** p. 127.

11. Cf. J. P. Arendzen, **Purgatory and Heaven,** (New York, Sheed & Ward, 1960), pp. 31-36.

Chapter 7
Is There a Limbo for Infants?

One of the most difficult problems in theology has been the afterlife of unbaptized children. If we include all such children from the beginning of mankind, the number must be astronomically great. What happens to them after death? This question has disturbed theologians down the centuries. For they believed that a God of love had destined all of them to an endless life after death. From the New Testament they knew that God sincerely willed all men to be saved and to reach the eternal joy of heaven. And for that purpose He had sent His Son into the world of men to live and suffer and die and rise for them so that they might be saved. But they also knew from the New Testament that God apparently had said that without faith in Christ, without the baptism of water and the Holy Spirit, without justification, no one could enter the kingdom of heaven. What, then, would happen to children who die unbaptized? Would they go to hell for all eternity? Or to some other mysterious "place of punishment"? Was there any possibility that all or some of them might go to heaven?

St. Augustine said all unbaptized infants would go to hell. Catholic theologians after the Middle Ages rather generally said they would not go to heaven or to hell or to purgatory but to limbo, a place where they would lack the beatific vision of God but would enjoy a high degree of natural happiness. Many Protestant theologians held that all these children would go to heaven. Perhaps a historical survey of this question of the destiny of infants who die unbaptized can give us a better grasp of the implications of the problem, and why it has recently been so widely discussed by theologians (G. J. Dyer's works have been most useful and we have drawn from them most heavily: *Limbo: Unsettled Question*, Sheed and Ward, N. Y., 1964; "Limbo, A Theological Evaluation," *Theological Studies*, 19 (1958); "The Unbaptized Infant in Eternity," *Chicago Studies* 2, (1963).

East

If we look to the East for early foreshadowings of the later limbo, we can find them in the two Gregorys, Gregory of Nazianzus and Gregory of Nyssa. If children died unbaptized, they taught, they would receive neither reward nor punishment, neither the happiness of heaven nor the pain of hell. They would not go to hell because they had done nothing to deserve this. They would not go to heaven because their personal innocence would not qualify them for it. Ultimately, Gregory of Nyssa thought, these children would become capable of the life of heaven and be admitted to it. Here we can see a limbo of sorts, but not the later limbo that was based on the guilt and punishment of original sin, for neither Gregory seems to have realized the implications of original sin and of the effect of baptism.

West

In the West one of the earliest foreshadowings of the later limbo doctrine is found in Vincentius Victor's view that children who die unbaptized will be admitted to heaven at the resurrection of the dead, a view very like that of Vincent Wilkin, S.J., in recent times. But it was the Pelagians and Augustine who made the most important contributions to the problem of unbaptized children. The Pelagians denied original sin and its consequences. They insisted that all sin was the product of (human) freedom. And if it was, they argued, then there could be no original sin in children for they lacked freedom and so could not incur the guilt of original sin. And if there is no original sin in them, then they do not need baptism to remit this sin. But here the Pelagians faced a serious difficulty, for in their time infant baptism had come to be a rather universal practice. To answer this difficulty they came up with an interesting distinction between the kingdom of heaven and eternal life. Baptism, they said, was necessary for the one, not for the other. For Christ had said that baptism was necessary for entry into the kingdom of heaven, not for eternal life. Hence if a child died before baptism he would be excluded from the kingdom of heaven but he would not be condemned to hell for he had done nothing to deserve hell. But neither could he enter the kingdom of heaven, for this was beyond the powers of his nature. Instead he would spend his eternity in a *place* (or state) somewhere between heaven and hell. There he would enjoy eternal life, a measure of happiness in keeping with his natural powers.

Was this Pelagian intermediate "place" our later limbo? No, though some later theologians would think so. For in some respects it resembled our later limbo in that it was neither heaven nor hell but a place of natural happiness. But there was a basic difference between the Pelagian intermediate place and the later limbo of infants. For in the Pelagian intermediate place the children were in a state of *innocence,* and "eternal life" was the natural reward for this state of innocence. But in the later limbo the children were in the state of original sin, and as such were "children of wrath," in a state of damnation, and punished by the deprivation of the beatific vision of God.

It was Augustine who vigorously attacked this Pelagian doctrine and largely brought about its condemnation, but in doing this he ended up by consigning to hell all children who died unbaptized. In the Matthean description of the "last judgment" (Mt 25:31-46), he noted, all the nations would be gathered and men would be placed either at the right hand of the King and welcomed into the kingdom of God, or on his left hand and condemned to eternal fire. Christ thus had indicated there would be only two ultimate destinies for men, heaven and hell, not three. Without faith, without baptism, without reception of Christ's body and blood, a child who died unbaptized could not be placed at the right hand of the judge, could not go into eternal life. Such a child could only go into "the eternal fire," into "eternal punishment." Though Augustine painted a dismal picture of the future life of an unbaptized child, he did try to mitigate it as much as possible by adding that such a child's punishment would be the slightest, the mildest.[1]

A Council of Carthage (XV or XVI) held in A.D. 418, formulated 8 (or 9) canons against the Pelagians and submitted these to Pope Zosimus for approval. One of the canons ascribed to this council rejected the Pelagian notion of eternal life for unbaptized infants, in these words: "If anyone says that the words of Our Lord, 'There are many mansions in my Father's House,' must be understood in this sense that there exists in the kingdom of heaven or elsewhere an intermediate place where the children who die without baptism live happily, while without baptism they cannot enter the kingdom of heaven . . . let him be anathema. Consequently what Catholic would hesitate to call him a co-heir of the devil who has not merited to be called a co-heir with Christ? He who is not at the right of Christ will surely be at his left" (DS 224). Even though there is no conclusive evidence that Pope Zosimus ever endorsed this canon (DS 222-230, Introduction), it gives us an indication of the mind of the African Church at that time.

Middle Ages

As we move into the Middle Ages we find the limbo of infants beginning to take shape. Back in the East toward the close of the fifth century, Pseudo-Dionysius had suggested that original sin was not the presence of something, but rather the privative absence of something, the privation of the "original excellence conferred on our first parents." This idea that original sin is privative rather than positive was picked up and developed by Anselm of Canterbury, but he did not draw from it the logical conclusion that if original sin is only a privation it should only be punished by a privation; instead he followed Augustine and said that original sin is punished by damnation in the hereafter. It was left for Peter Abelard to draw the logical conclusion: "In my opinion," he said, "(their) punishment consists in this alone, that they are in darkness, i.e. that they are deprived of the vision

of the divine majesty without any hope of attaining it." Thomas
Aquinas carried this thought a step further and assigned to the
limbo of children a double darkness, to denote their lack both
of divine grace and of the beatific vision. But in that limbo the
children do not suffer the torments or anguish of the damned,
though they are eternally deprived of the beatific vision. These
children, he later concluded, would not be disturbed over their
loss of the vision of God because they would not know what
they had lost. They would be happy because they would be
united to God by their native ability to know and love Him.
Where would this limbo be? Aquinas envisioned a fourfold
inferno, which at its deepest level was the hell of the damned,
at its next higher level was the limbo of the children, at the next
higher level was purgatory, and at the topmost level was the
limbo of the Fathers, where the Old Testament just had awaited
the coming of Christ. Suarez is sometimes said to have brought
the doctrine of limbo to its ultimate refinement. Limbo, he declared, will not hold these children forever. These infants die
as infants but at the general resurrection they will rise as adults,
possessing not only the use of their reason but full physical maturity as well. As young adults they will stand before the tribunal
of Christ to see there the divine pattern into which their lives have
been woven and the whole plan of God's providence unfold.
After the resurrection of the dead and the judgment, the world
will be swept away and the very air will burst into flames, consuming the earth, purging it of every impurity, leaving behind
a new world gleaming in brilliant splendor. On a renovated earth
in this new universe that will be a congenial climate for the vigor-
ous natural resources they possess, they will live out their eternal
exile from the kingdom of God. Their bodies will be those of
adults, completely adapted to the full and perfect use of reason.
They will be free of any need for food or drink, free from the
strife of concupiscence and the rebellion of passions. Their minds
will bring to perfection in themselves every natural virtue: justice, wisdom, courage, prudence. They will be happy in the possession of God by their natural powers of intellection and volition. Their minds will be able to contemplate God, their wills

to love Him above all things. Their destiny will not be an eternal horror but an eternal paradise—and all this due to the merit of Christ (G. J. Dyer, op. cit.).

The Great Reformers

The Great Reformers did not accept the theory of limbo. Luther saw no middle ground between heaven and hell for unbaptized infants. Zwingli taught that baptism was not necessary for infant salvation and that all who die in infancy are elect and hence saved. Calvin seems to imply that some but not all infants are saved, when he writes: "As to infants, they seem to perish, not by their own fault, but by the fault of another. But there is a double solution. Though sin does not yet appear in them, yet it is latent; for they bear corruption shut up in the soul, so that before God they are damnable". . ."That infants who are to be saved (as certainly some of that age are saved), must be previously regenerated by the Lord is clear" (*Institutes*, iv, xvi, 17). The Synod of Dort in 1619 offered assurance to godly parents but not to ungodly parents when it declared: "Since . . . the children of believers are holy, not by nature, but in virtue of the covenant of grace in which they together with their parents are comprehended, godly parents have no reason to doubt of the election and salvation of their children whom it pleaseth God to call out of this life in their infancy" (First Head of Doctrine, art. xvii). The Westminster Confession of 1648 said: "elect infants dying in infancy are regenerated and saved by Christ through the Spirit, who worketh when and where and how he pleaseth" (x, 3). Recent Protestant theologians are no more attracted by the theory of limbo than were the great Reformers. In 1903 American Presbyterians said of the Westminster Confession: "It is not to be regarded as teaching that any who die in infancy are lost. We believe that all dying in infancy are included in the election of grace, and are regenerated and saved by Christ through the Spirit." While some theologians of the Church of England say we have no assurance of the salvation of unbaptized infants, Daniel Poling has declared: "Of course they will be saved. If they are not saved, I don't want to be" (cf. Buis, loc. cit.).

The Magisterium of the Church

The Magisterium of the Church has never given the doctrine of limbo any clear and definitive endorsement, though some theologians have at times inclined to think that it had. For Pope Innocent III in 1201 wrote to the Archbishop of Arles that actual sin is punished by the endless torment of hell but original sin is punished by the loss of the vision of God (DS 780). And the general councils of Lyons II and Florence defined that "the souls of those who die in mortal sin, or with original sin alone, shortly go down to hell, to be punished with different punishments" (DS 858, 1306). Did they thus implicitly define the existence of limbo? It seems not, for they did not define that anyone did die in original sin alone. And what is more, within a few centuries after these definitions, we find at least four differing interpretations of these definitions, namely that Lyons and Florence (1) teach that there are those who actually do die guilty of nothing but original sin; (2) only teach what will happen should someone die in original sin; (3) are canonizing the limbo of the medieval theologians; (4) are endorsing the opinion of St. Augustine. And if we turn to the Council of Trent we find that it defined that all are born in original sin and that this sin is removed by baptism in "re aut voto" (DS 1512, 1513, 1524), but it did not define that anyone died in original sin alone. And hence these councils did not define that there is a limbo of infants and a limbo that has occupants. However, it is sometimes affirmed that Pope Pius VI in 1794 affirmed or approved the doctrine of limbo, when he condemned the Jansenist teaching that the limbo of the theologians was nothing but the old Pelagian fable of an intermediate state of innocence and eternal life between heaven and hell (DS 1526). But it should be obvious that by this condemnation the Pope did not affirm the existence of limbo or approve the current doctrine of limbo. He merely denied that the limbo of the theologians was nothing but the old Pelagian fable of an intermediate state of innocence and eternal life between heaven and hell. Thus far, then, the Church has neither affirmed nor denied the existence of a limbo of infants; she has neither approved nor rejected the theologians' doctrine about this limbo. She has refrained from taking sides in the theological debate over this limbo, and permitted theologians to defend or to reject the doctrine. She conceded the orthodoxy both of Augustinians who rejected limbo and of Jesuits who defended it. She has left the matter open to theological discussion.

Catholic Theologians

And so Catholic theologians have poured out one theory after another to explain the salvation of infants. Angel Santos[2] urged that the law of the Gospel and hence the law of baptism had not been sufficiently promulgated everywhere, and so where it had not been proclaimed children of pagan parents could be saved by the "sacrament of nature," a sign of an implicit faith in Christ the Redeemer.[3] Cardinal Cajetan suggested that a baptism of desire on the part of Christian parents might sanctify and save a child dying in the womb. One of the most influential theories is that of P. Glorieux.[4] In this theory death is the final moment of choice for every man. In death, not before and not after death, every human being has a final choice between good and evil, between choosing or rejecting God. Because a choice is the work of an instant, that choice may be compressed within the first instant of death which is the last instant of life, and so still pertains to the period of probation and of merit. Thus in the instant of death the unbaptized child (and every man) would begin immediately to exercise the rich intellectual and volitional life of a disembodied soul and choose his eternity (cf. G. Dyer, loc. cit.).

Regularly these salvation theories stopped at death, since death was generally regarded as the end of merit and demerit and conversion. But two theologians offered theories of *salvation after death*. M. Laurenge (*"Esquisse d'une etude sur le sort des enfants morts sans bapteme,"* "L'Annee Theologique Augustinienne,"

XIII, 1952) argued that if salvation by way of baptism was impossible for a child during its life, God's sincere salvific will would provide the child with a means of salvation after death. If Scripture said that adults must save their souls before death, its words should not be applied to infants. Hence when a child's intelligence awakens after death, God gives it the grace to orientate itself toward its final goal. If the grace is efficacious, the child is saved; if it is merely sufficient, the child freely turns from his final end and damns himself to hell.

Vincent Wilkins, a Jesuit,[5] likewise envisioned the salvation of unbaptized children *after* their death. Not that such children could choose or merit salvation after death. But at the general resurrection at the end of the world these children would be recapitulated in Christ and thereby saved. At the parousia and the general resurrection the whole economy of original sin comes to an end. So the unbaptized child then will go to heaven unless the will of God or the will of Adam or the will of Satan or the will of the child keeps it out. But none of these wills does. And so at the general resurrection the unbaptized child comes forth from limbo and is reborn not only to physical life but also to supernatural life in Christ and so goes to heaven for all eternity. Till the end of the world, then, these unbaptized children remain infants in the sense that they remain incapable of assuming responsibility for their eternal future. But after the general resurrection they will be adults and in the final state of mankind, it seems, there will be only adults, no children.

How shall we *evaluate* these and other theories about the salvation of unbaptized infants? Do all children who die without baptism have a chance to be saved and to reach the happiness of heaven? Theologians have given many different answers, and we have considered a few of them. But of the many theories that have been proposed, the most important would seem to be those that apply to *all* children who die without baptism whether before or after Christ. Among these six stand out, i.e. the theory of (1) Universalists who say all men, and so also these children, are ultimately saved somehow, (2) Augustinians who say they all go to hell, (3) limbo theologians who send them all to limbo,

(4) Laurenge who gives all such children *after* their death a free choice of their final destiny, (5) Wilkin who consigns all these children to limbo till the general resurrection and then sends them to heaven, (6) Klee and Glorieux who have all these children make a final and irrevocable decision for or against God, not before death nor after death but *in death*. How shall we evaluate these six theories?

The Universalist theory, as far as it maintains that all *adults* are ultimately saved somehow, seems to be theologically unacceptable as we shall indicate in more detail when we discuss hell in our next chapter. But as far as it says all children who die unbaptized are somehow saved, it seems in our opinion to be acceptable, as we shall indicate when we evaluate the theory of a final option for or against God in death.

The Augustinian theory that all such children are consigned to hell is largely, if not entirely, abandoned today. For its basic arguments, that actual baptism is the only means of salvation for such children, and that unbaptized children all die in original sin and in consequence must go to hell, are widely questioned today. It has become increasingly clear that neither the Scripture passages nor the conciliar texts nor the papal statements that seemed to affirm or imply the absolute necessity of baptism for the salvation of infants, really "prove" such an absolute necessity. What is more, even if all such children were in original sin at death, this would not prove that they must automatically go to hell, since limbo is a tenable theory never condemned by the Church.

What of the doctrine of limbo? In the past many theologians considered it theologically certain that children who died without baptism went to a limbo of infants, where they 'suffered' the pain of loss of the beatific vision but not a pain of sense, and enjoyed substantially a natural beatitude. This doctrine has never been condemned by the Church but neither has it been officially approved, only tolerated. For a long time it was held in high repute by many outstanding Catholic theologians as the best answer to the harsh theory of Augustine. For though it "saved" none of these children, brought none of them to heaven, neither did it damn any of them to hell. Today it is not in such high repute, and is rather widely rejected as merely a scholastic invention. But the strongest objection to it is drawn from the *real universality* of God's salvific will and of Christ's *universal* redemptive activity. If God really wills *all* men to be saved and if Christ really died for *all* men, it is argued, then this immense number of children must have a *real chance of salvation*, which it does not have in the limbo theory. There must be a real means of salvation available for each and every human being. Actual baptism is not and cannot be this means for all men. So there must be and there is, it is contended, another means of salvation for those who cannot achieve actual baptism, and this must be a *baptism of desire* that involves a free and final personal option for or against God. So that all men go into eternity either with God in heaven or without God in hell.

The Laurenge theory, in which such children are enabled *after* their death to make a free choice of their final destiny, has found few followers for it goes against a solid and traditional doctrine of the Church that death is the end of man's probation and that after death he can do nothing by way of merit or demerit to change or determine his final condition.

The Wilkin theory of a temporary limbo followed by heaven after the general resurrection, is in some ways most attractive for it ultimately saves all children who die without baptism. But it is not widely favored. For it too runs counter to the solidly traditional doctrine that a man's eternal destiny is settled at his death. To interpret this to mean that an unbaptized child cannot after death by an act of his own free will merit eternal salvation but can achieve this salvation automatically through a "vivifying" rebirth at the general resurrection of the dead, seems to be a highly dubious interpretation of this traditional doctrine. If God really wants every man to be saved, it is urged, then he really wants every man to be able freely to achieve salvation in a way that befits man, i.e. by freely and finally choosing or rejecting God. In the Wilkin theory, however, these children are practically robots, automatically sent to limbo till the general resurrection, then automatically sent to heaven. However, it can be urged against this objection that it is of the very nature of children to be unable to determine and work out their own destiny, and so this can properly be done for them by Christ who made them and redeemed them and died for all of them that they might have eternal life with Him in heaven. The value of this last contention is hard to assess precisely in the matter of salvation, but it should at least move us not to reject this theory too quickly. It is a fascinating theory that deserves further study.

But the theory that seems to be in the ascendency today among Catholic theologians is that of a "final fundamental option" for or against God made by every man "in death," a theory that seems to trace back to *H. Klee* and *P. Glorieux,* if it applies both to infants and adults. More and more theologians are adopting it in one form or another. For it makes God's salvific will really and effectively universal and it makes Christ's death for all men really operative for every man. So that every man in death has a grace-given, fully free and highly lucid moment in which to make his final and irrevocable decision for or against God, for or against Christ. This does not mean that all unbaptized children will opt for God in death and so be saved and immediately receive the beatific vision of God. At least this seems to be the view of some theologians. But to me it seems most probable, if not certain, that all such infants will opt for God. What reason could they have for rejecting God? The God of love who made them and who redeemed them on the Cross? In them there is no personal sin, no evil habit, no passion, no concupiscence, at least no sinful concupiscence. They were made to rest in God for all eternity and into their very nature God has put a supernatural orientation toward the beatific vision. It seems incredible that they would not opt for God, would not opt for Christ.

A frequently urged objection to this theory of a final option for God on the part of unbaptized children is a statement made by Pope Pius XII in 1951 to a group of Italian Catholic midwives: that in the present dispensation there is no other means of communicating supernatural life to the child who has not yet the use of reason—than baptism. In this statement the Pope added that while in an adult an act of love may suffice to obtain for him sanctifying grace and so supply for the lack of baptism, this way is not open to the child still unborn or newly born. Does this papal statement really prevent the application of this theory to unbaptized infants? Not today, it would seem. In years gone by it was regarded by quite a few theologians as closing the door of this theory against children who died unbaptized. But today a papal statement of this caliber is much less impressive, when some theologians are even questioning the obligatory force or relevance of some conciliar definitions. What is more, this papal statement was in no way intended to be a definitive, infallible statement of doctrine. The aim of the statement was disciplinary rather than doctrinal. For the Pope was urging those midwives not to delay baptism, since the only sure means of salvation for children is baptism, and it would be foolhardy to put off a sure means of salvation for these children and rely on a speculative theory of a baptism of desire that was in no way certain. Further, even if the theory is taken literally and interpreted rigorously, it does not prevent the application of this theory. For the Pope merely says that a child still unborn or newly born cannot make an act of love that may suffice to obtain for him sanctifying grace and so supply for the lack of baptism. The theory in no way denies this. For it maintains that in the moment of death the child is "adulted," i.e. is intellectually and volitionally capacitated to make a fully free final decision or to elicit a fully free act of perfect love of God.

It is hard to say what will be the future of this theory. But it has many advantages over any other theory that has been proposed. It applies to all unbaptized infants of all times and it explains realistically how God can truly be said to will effectively the salvation of children who through no fault of their own die unbaptized. If this theory is correct, there never was and never will be a "limbo of natural happiness" for children who die unbaptized. Most probably all such infants opt for God in death and go with Him into His heaven of eternal happiness.

Notes for Chapter 7

1. J. G. Dyer, **op. cit.**; H. Buis, **The Doctrine of Eternal Punishment,** (Philadelphia, Presbyterian and Reformed Pub. Co., 1957), pp. 137-140.

2. "Infancia y Bautismo," **Estudios Ecclesiasticos, XXXI,** 1957.

3. Cf. J. M. Herve, **Manuale Theologiae Dogmaticae,** III, pp. 525-526.

4. "Endurcissement final et graces dernieres," **Nouvelle Revue Theologique,** LIX, 1932.

5. **From Limbo to Heaven,** (New York, Sheed & Ward, 1961).

Chapter 8
Is There a Hell of Everlasting Punishment?

Is there a hell of everlasting punishment? Blaise Pascal (1623-1662) was perhaps the most fascinating genius in a century that counted many. It is said of him that at 12 he created mathematics, at 16 wrote his treatise on conic sections, at 18 invented a calculating machine, at 20 demonstrated the phenomena of air-pressure. He is famous, too, for his 'immortal wager': even if there is only one chance that God exists and 10,000 chances that there is no God . . . choose for God and thus insure yourself against the hazard of damnation.

The "hazard of damnation" has haunted men for a long, long time. Is there really a hell of everlasting punishment for the wicked? In the past when most Christians lived in a sin-centered world with a sin-centered God, they firmly believed in such a hell and feared greatly that they might end up there. For theologians generally taught that in the plan of the 'predestinating God' most men were destined for hell. Today we live in a love-centered world, with a love-centered God. But the existence of a hell of everlasting punishment is still a most disturbing matter for Christians. They find it so hard to understand, so hard to explain to others. How can it be reconciled with the God of love and mercy that Christ taught and manifested? And yet the same Christ who died that men might not go to hell, this very Christ stressed hell again and again.

But it is not only Christians who are haunted by the fear of hell. Hindus, Buddhists, Taoists, Persians, Babylonians, Orphic Greeks—all believed in some sort of hell. Even Sheol in the Old

Testament, though at first it was viewed simply as the land of the dead, later on was 'compartmented' into a Gehenna for the wicked and a Paradise for the good. The Pharisees taught eternal punishment for the wicked. Rabbi Shamai held that the perfectly wicked were immediately consigned to Gehenna, while the other wicked went down to Gehenna for a time and then came up again. Rabbi Hillel declared that sinners went to Gehenna for 12 months and then their bodies and souls were burned up. In the first century A.D. the rabbis taught eternal punishment, in the second century temporary punishment, in the third century eternal punishment. And Moslems believe in an inferno that is a place of fire for all infidels but a temporary place of purgation for Moslems.

There are many who reject hell. Mormons say the wicked will be punished but not forever. Congregationalists and Episcopalians seem to have an implicit belief in universal salvation. Jehovah's Witnesses say that the wicked instead of going to hell will be annihilated. Protestant Liberals tend to substitute for hell a sort of purgatory, whose pain is not endless and is disciplinary and remedial, rather than vindictive. Spiritualists, Theosophists, Christian Scientists reject hell.

Many Protestants today still believe in a hell of everlasting punishment. But there seems to be a growing drift toward Universalism or Annihilationism.

Universalism traces back to Origen and his famous doctrine of apocatastasis, i.e. the ultimate restoration of all men (and devils?). Friedrich Schleiermacher gave a great impetus to this view by his argument that "through the power of Redemption there will result in the future a general restoration of all human souls" (*Der Christ. Glaube*, ii, p. 506). Tennyson's *In Memoriam*, some have said, "probably did more than the writings of any theologian of his time to break down the belief in the historic doctrine of eternal punishment and to popularize Universalism."[1] More recently Paul Tillich, Emil Brunner and Karl Barth have been interpreted by some as having come very close to Universalism, if they have not actually espoused it.

Annihilationism perhaps traces back to Tatian who seemed to

think that the souls of the wicked are annihilated at death until the last day, or to Rabbi Hillel who declared that the bodies and souls of sinners went to Gehenna for 12 months and then were burned up. Modern Annihilationists hold that after death the wicked undergo a period of punishment: then those that remain in rebellion against God cease to exist. A man's sin and obstinacy however great can in no way, they argue, demand or deserve an eternity of vindictive punishment. A God of infinite love and mercy could not permit this. Recently Prof. Aldwinckle wrote that "there is nothing to prevent the deduction that at the final judgment the stubbornly impenitent will be allowed by God to pass out of existence, not because He desires this but because such people have declared their unwillingness to exist in the kind of world God has created. . . . Whether any or many will be finally impenitent in this sense is a question not to be dogmatically answered" (op. cit. 116). The way he came to this position is interesting. His study of the Gospels told him that Jesus did at times use the word "Gehenna." But since he could not precisely determine what Jesus meant by this word, he turned to Jesus' view of God—as a God of holy love. This God of holy love, he feels, will give the wicked an opportunity to be converted after death, but if they stay wicked and rebellious, they will cease to exist at the parousiac end of the world (ibid. 107ff.).

What of Catholics? Are they too reconsidering the traditional doctrine of Hell? Robert Nowell writes that "Hell in particular raises difficulties for the Catholic who is trying to think out his or her faith in the aftermath of Vatican II . . . Thanks to the ferment engendered by Vatican II and especially the clearer ideas about sin that are now in circulation . . . we no longer have a catalog of mortal sins which will lead us (or others) straight to hell. And about hell, itself, we feel we can no longer be quite so certain as we once were. Are there any human beings simply that bad . . . but genuinely responsible for their own badness to an extent that merits eternal damnation?"[2] Gregory Baum tells us that "these teachings (about heaven, hell and purgatory) are not information about a future world but a message about the present-as-well-as-the-future . . . The doctrine of hell reminds us of the chaos from which God's grace saves us. It makes us aware of the possibility of total loss . . . reveals to us the seriousness which lies in moral decisions."[3] Ladislas Boros writes that "hell is not something that simply happens from outside; it is not something that God imposes on us afterwards for our misdeeds . . . It is the mode of existence of a human being who is satisfied in himself, for all eternity; he has nothing more and desires nothing more than himself. . . . There is no tragic grandeur about hell, because fundamentally there can not be any 'place' which is hell. There is only a state of heart."[4] Patrick Fannon thinks that "death, judgment, hell and heaven continue to be dressed in such primitive thought forms as to offend both reason and moral sensitivity. . . . Hell must be understood as a symbol, for the eternal possibility of man's present and future existence. Even now hell is experienced as present in the torment and suffering of a man's experience of failure or inability to love God, man, or even himself. Hell is not a place. Nor is it an eternal destiny running parallel to heaven . . . hell is simply destruction and death, the failure to enter into eternity, into the eternal life of God."[5]

These new views are interesting in many ways, but most of all perhaps for their wonderful subjectivity. Traditional interpretations of Sacred Scripture, handed down by a long line of Church Fathers, Councils and theologians, are blithely brushed aside as incompatible with the findings of 'modern science and exegesis,' and irrelevant for 'contemporary man.' The way that modern men and writers *feel* about hell, seems much more important than what Christ and His Church have said about hell. Of course, we must adjust to changing times and to new discoveries of "truth" in science and biblical exegesis, if they really give us truth. Perhaps we must be open to a new, "secularized" theology. But it must be a real theology, not just wishful thinking or emotional reaction. An excessively reactionary theology, intent mainly on scrapping the past, is hardly likely to be 'real' theology. Theologians must try to keep past, present and future in proper balance, something that is extremely difficult—always has been and always will be. So these new views are interesting, but they must be very carefully evaluated so as to find the grains of truth they may contain. And evaluated in the light of 'traditional doctrine,' not just in the light of 'modern' man's mind-set, science, exegesis, for who knows how long these will continue to be relevant or valuable.

What is the 'traditional Catholic doctrine' about hell? Is hell a 'dogma' of the Catholic faith? Theological manuals of the past declared that the existence of an eternal hell is a dogma, a truth to be believed by divine and Catholic faith (cf. J. M. Herve, op. cit. IV, 565). And recently B. Lonergan has written: "the dogmas are permanent in their meaning. . . . What permanently is true, is the meaning of the dogma in the context in which it was defined" (*Method in Theology*, Herder and Herder, 1972, 320-325). Karl Rahner in his article on "Hell" in *Sacramentum Mundi* (3, p. 7) wrote: "In its official teaching the Church has defined the existence of hell (DS 72, 76, 801, 858, 1306) and its eternity against the doctrine of the apocatastasis as put forward by Origen and other ancient writers (DS 411). The Church affirmed that entry into hell takes place immediately after their death (DS 858, 1002), and made a certain distinction between the loss of the vision of God (*poena damni*) and the pain of sense (*poena sensus*) (DS 780), but apart from this there is no official declaration on the nature of the pains of hell, though the difference of punishments in hell is mentioned" (DS 858, 1306).

Thus that the Church has defined the existence of hell is beyond doubt from the documents cited above. But only one document is cited for the *eternity* of hell, and that reads as follows: "If anyone says or holds that the punishment of devils and wicked men is temporary and will eventually cease, that is to say, that devils or the ungodly will be completely restored to their original state: let him be anathema." And from this document it is not at all clear that hell's *eternity* is a dogma of the faith. For first of all the wording of this canon is ambiguous. Secondly, this canon was not a part of the Second Council of Constantinople (cf. *Conciliorum Oecumenicorum Decreta*, 82), and hence it draws no dogmatic value from this general council. Thirdly, it is not at all certain that Pope Vigilius approved this canon of the Edict of Justinian[6] and hence it cannot derive dogmatic value from this pope.

Is it, then, really a dogma of the faith that there is an *eternal* hell, a hell of everlasting punishment? It is. For at Lyons II, a general and reunion council, the Eastern Emperor, Michael Palaeologus, subscribed through his ambassadors to a dogmatic creed (DS 858) which professed that soon after death the souls of those who die in mortal sin go down into a hell of punishment. Another general and reunion council, that of Florence, repeated this profession of faith in its Decree for the Greeks (DS 1306). Still another general council, that of IV Lateran (Ds 801) and a dogmatic creed, *the Quicunque* (DS 76), declare that "at his coming all men are to rise with their own bodies . . . those who have done evil will go into everlasting fire, to receive perpetual punishment." Further the general council of Trent often speaks of "eternal punishment" (DS 1539, 1543, 1575), and of "eternal damnation" (DS 1705) for mortal sin. These pronouncements are too many and too clear to be brushed aside. They leave no room for Universalism or Annihilationism. Even granting that they come out of an apocalyptic historical culture, they still offer a solemn core-affirmation of a hell of everlasting punishment for those who die in mortal sin.

But are these definitions based on a correspondingly solid biblical foundation? Do they define divinely revealed truth? It has in fact been maintained that this doctrine of an eternal hell is really a Jewish apocalyptic doctrine, and that the punishment it involves is not everlasting but of limited duration. Do the Sacred Scriptures of the Old Testament and the New Testament really teach that there is an everlasting hell?

Old Testament

The Old Testament, it must be admitted, gives no clear witness to a widespread belief in the everlasting punishment of the wicked after death. Certain passages can seem to point in that direction, such as Judith 16:20-21; Is 66:24; Ws 3:10, 17-19; 6:44ff. and Dn 12:2. But only Daniel gives us a relatively clear reference to the punishment of sinners after death: "Many of those who sleep in the dust of the earth shall awake; some shall

live forever, others shall be an everlasting horror and disgrace."
But even this passage is open to many questions and is in no way
probative.

Intertestamental Literature

If we turn to the Jewish apocalyptic literature of the intertestamental period for a possible development of this Old Testament thought about the punishment of the wicked, we find in
the Book of Enoch a vivid picture of punishment—by fire, worms,
ice, cold, chains, darkness. But two things must be noted. First,
the concern is not with the wicked in general or even with ordinary sinners of Israel, but mainly with the persecutors of Israel or
with traitors within Israel. Secondly, although terms like 'eternal,'
'everlasting,' 'forever' are freely used, these terms are used loosely
and rarely, if ever, connote everlastingness. Sometimes the word
"eternal" means for 70 generations or 500 years (ibid. 10:5; 10:10).
Hence at best we have here a belief in the punishment of some
wicked people for a long time after death.

New Testament

In the New Testament the main testimony to an everlasting
punishment of the wicked is found in the Synoptics, especially in
Matthew, where the term for our "hell" is "gehenna." Gehenna
is mentioned seven times in Mt; three times in Mk; one time in Lk;
one time in Jm. It is a place of "fire" (Mt 5:22; Jm 3:6), of
"unquenchable fire" (Mk 9:43), a "pit" (Lk 12:5), a place where
the wicked are destroyed body and soul (Mt 10:28). Gehenna
is also supposed in other passages which describe the place of
punishment as a prison and a torture chamber (Mt 5:25-26), a
place of misery, of "weeping and gnashing of teeth" (Mt 8:12)
or as the grave "where the worm does not die" (Mk 9:48) or as
a place of "everlasting punishment" (Mt 25:46) (Thus J. L. Mc-
Kenzie, op. cit. 300). In Lk 16:23 the rich man was in torment, in
flame in "Hades," a place of torment, "scarcely to be distinguished
from Gehenna" (ibid. 801).

Most of this testimony we find issuing from the lips of Jesus

Himself. Again and again He is presented in the Synoptics as threatening sinners with the punishment of hell. If it is true that "we shall never know for certain whether we find in these sayings of Jesus an accurate report of the words of our Lord,"[7] yet it seems very hard to believe that such repeated threats of hell were not made by Jesus Himself but only attributed to Him by the Synoptic writers without a real foundation in fact.

But it is not only the Synoptics that testify to the punishment of the wicked after death. *John* says the punishment of sin is accomplished through judgment (3:8; 5:24ff; 12:31, 48); through death (5:29; 8:24; 10:28; 11:25f), i.e. through exclusion from the eternal life communicated by the Son (J. L. McKenzie, op. cit., 300); and through darkness (8:12; 12:44-46). And the "final destination of all the wicked is the pool of fire" (Rv 19:20; 20:9-15; 21:8; cf. 2 P 2:4; Jude 6f.), which is the second death. *Paul* declares that the wicked store up wrath for the day of wrath when the justice of God will burst forth (Rm 2:5). Sinners have no share in the kingdom of God (1 Cor 6:10; Gal 5:19-21). The impious will be punished with "eternal destruction from the face of the Lord and from the glory of His might" (2 Th 1:9). For obdurate sinners there lies ahead only judgment and the blazing consuming anger of God; it is fearful to fall into the hands of the living God (Heb 10:26-31).

What can be said of this testimony today? Scholars are interpreting it differently. Many have pointed out that in the New Testament hell is conceived according to the views prevalent in later Judaism.[8] J. L. McKenzie has noted that "comparison of these New Testament passages with the passages of the apocryphal books cited above shows that the Synoptic Gospels, Jude, Jm, 2 P and Rv employ the language and the imagery of contemporary Judaism. It is remarkable that this language and imagery does not appear in other New Testament writings. These passages suggest that the apocalyptic imagery . . . is to be taken for what it is, imagery, and not as strictly literal theological affirmations" (op. cit. 300). K. Rahner writes that "the metaphors in which Jesus describes the eternal perdition of man as a possibility which threatens him at this moment are images (fire, worm, darkness), taken from the mental furniture of contemporary apocalyptic. . . . Even such a term as 'eternal loss' is in the nature of an image" (*Sacramentum Mundi*, 3, 7-8).

Obviously if imagery is imagery and metaphor is metaphor, they are not taken as strictly literal theological affirmation. Just as obviously, if there is imagery, must there not be an underlying belief or affirmation or meaning that is being imaged forth? This "belief" very definitely seems to be a belief in an everlasting hell of punishment for the wicked. Cut off (or demythologize) the apocalyptic imagery of *fire, pit, prison, torture chamber, worm that does not die, weeping and gnashing of teeth* and you are left with a definite belief underlying this imagery that *after death* and *after the parousia* the wicked are punished by a painful and everlasting separation from God. All these images "mean the same thing, the possibility of man being finally lost and estranged from God in all the dimensions of his existence . . . eternal loss . . . indicates the cosmic, objective aspect of loss which is outside the consciousness. . . . Loss means a definitive contradiction of the abiding and perfected world, and this will be a torment" (K. Rahner, loc. cit.) "In other passages of the New Testament," J. Michl has written, "this ultimate punishment of sinners is not characterized in figurative language or in imagery but simply as God's wrath and anger (Rm 2:8), as evil (2 Cor 5:10), as death (Jn 8:51ff), as the second death (Rv 2:11; 20:6), as destruction (Mt 7:13; Gal 6:8), as eternal destruction (2 Th 1:9). Exactly what this punishment is remains a mystery which is not revealed anywhere in the bible" (loc. cit.). Primarily hell means eternal separation from God and His glory, not eternal torture.

The Last Judgment parable has often been cited as the mainstay of the doctrine of hell in the past. Is it still a valid witness to the hell of everlasting punishment? Its words are blunt enough: "Then (the King) will say to those at his left hand, 'Depart from me, you cursed into the eternal fire prepared for the devil and his angels.'. . . And they will go away into eternal punishment, but the righteous into eternal life" (Mt 25:41, 46). Some scholars say this title of the "Last Judgment" is misleading, because there is not a word about judgment in the passage. And yet the reality of judgment is so obviously and necessarily implied: If the separation of the sheep and goats is not a "judgment," what is it? If the distinction of *blessed* and *cursed* is not a judgment, what is it?

Another writer declares that "even if we have here Jesus' own thoughts and words faithfully reflected, we have no right to read into the language used the idea of everlasting torment. Apart from the fact that the symbolism of 'fire,' even if characterized as 'eternal fire,' suggests ultimate destruction or annihilation rather than everlasting continuance of that which is corrupt, the phrase 'eternal punishment' need not necessarily mean punishment of unending duration or everlasting torment, but simply 'age-long' or 'lasting for an aeon'."[9] It is quite true that the phrase "eternal punishment" need not necessarily mean punishment of everlasting duration. But that is not the point. The point is: does that phrase mean "punishment of everlasting duration" *in this passage?* And the obvious parallelism between 'hell' and 'heaven' indicates clearly that it does. If heaven is everlasting, then so is hell. If interpreters see here a witness to an "everlasting heaven," then they should also see here a witness to an "everlasting hell." Even if in the Book of Enoch the term "eternal" often means "a long time," and rarely if ever connotes everlastingness, and even if this Matthean parable reflects or is borrowed from Jewish apocalyptic teaching . . . in the book of Enoch, that in no way 'proves' that the term "eternal" does not mean "everlasting" here—in *this* passage. The parallelism between an "everlasting heaven" and an "everlasting hell" is too blunt. We must either reject an "everlasting heaven" or accept an "everlasting hell." C. R. Smith maintains that "in the texts where the adjective *aionios* (eternal) is used (Mt 18:8; 25:41; Mk 3:29; Jude 7; 2 Th 1:9; Heb 6:2) there is nothing to suggest that it has any other meaning than in the LXX and other New Testament passages, i.e. 'belonging to the (future) age,' and 'age' that in the minds of all Jews was everlasting. 'Depart from me' is a negative phrase, but 'into everlasting punishment' is positive. Jesus' hearers would take it so, and he knew that they would.". . . It seems impossible "if the evidence is considered objectively, to deny that there is a doctrine of 'everlasting punishment' in the New Testament."[10] X. Leon-

Dufour declares that "Jesus must be taken seriously when He uses SS images of hell that are most violent, most merciless, because these affirmations are uttered by the very man who has power to cast into hell. He does not speak of hell only as a threatening reality. . . . He Himself will pronounce the curse, 'Begone from me, ye cursed, into everlasting fire' " (op. cit. 206).

In the light of this biblical evidence for hell, can the position of the Universalists claim solid biblical support? Many of the Universalists think it can. They appeal especially to two passages from Paul and John: "As in Adam all die, so also in Christ shall all be made alive" (1 Cor 15:22-28); "When I am lifted up from the earth, I will draw all men to myself" (Jn 12:32). But they also cite in their favor (Lk 15:4; 1 P 4:6; 2 Cor 1:19f; Ep 1:10; Ph 2:9ff.). And from the Johannine affirmation that "God is love" (1 Jn 4:8) they draw one of their most moving arguments: "since God is love, He saves man; since He is omnipotent love, He will save all men." Hell cannot be eternal, they argue, for it will last only as long as men are disobedient: but God's love is stronger than man's disobedience, and will eventually bring all men to salvation.[11]

Do these Scripture passages really say or imply that God will actually save all men, and hence there is no hell of everlasting punishment? Not one of them says explicitly or implies necessarily that all men will ultimately be saved. Not one, as far as I know, has been given such an interpretation by the great Fathers or theologians or Scripture scholars of the Church. The Pauline passage about Adam and Christ merely means that "all who are in Christ at death, shall rise with Him to eternal life" (JBC 51:84). In the Johannine text that says that Christ, when He is lifted up, will draw *all men* to Himself, "all" is not to be understood numerically, but rather so as to exclude every distinction of race or people. Thus the text means that Christ's death *makes possible* the salvation of all men: it does not say or mean that His death brings about the actual salvation of all men. The other texts similarly indicate that Christ's death makes it possible for all men to find unity and salvation in and through Him, to give Him adoration. They do not say or mean that all men will actually do this.

Much less do they imply that after death the wicked will be given a further opportunity for salvation. If we take these texts in their context, most of them clearly indicate that Christ's death makes possible the salvation of all men in this life on earth, not in an after-life. If we add in the texts that were used above (Part III) to show that death is the end of merit, demerit, conversion, and the points that were made in showing that right after death there is a definitive and irrevocable judgment of every man, there can be no doubt that Universalism has no solid foundation either in Scripture or in tradition.

The argument from God's omnipotent love admittedly has an appeal and a fascination for most all of us. Our 'hearts' call to us to hope that God's love will capture the love of every man. But the argument is more wishful than cogent, if measured against the full teaching of Scripture and tradition. At most it indicates that the God of love will offer all men an opportunity for salvation, perhaps even a very abundant opportunity for salvation, before death or in death. But not after death. And C. H. Thompson, who seems to envision the possibility of conversion of the wicked after death, yet feels compelled to write: "if we take freedom seriously, we must at least theoretically admit the possibility to make a final choice against the right . . . a possibility of the final rejection of the love even of the Sovereign God. All we know about human personality points in the direction of a growing fixedness, toward a more certain permanence. The longer we persist in a direction, the less likelihood there is of radical change. The longer we live the more we become what we have chosen to be. Is there any likelihood that this tendency will be reversed in the next life? We may certainly believe that the God of universal love wills the salvation of all men, and that the finally lost are lost entirely through their own action in defiance of His will. The final rejection, persistence in rebellion against divine love, is not a divine failure. It may even be regarded as a divine victory: to sustain the free soul in its full range of possibilities—until divine love has literally exhausted itself both in personal suffering on Calvary and subsequently in its persuasive resources—and still the recalcitrant soul says 'No.' I have come to be sympathetic with a view which asserts that all may not eventually submit to love's entreaty . . . For those who refuse—there will be the existence involved in their eternal necessity, created by their own sins. . . . They exist under necessity, the necessity of their own creation. Every soul must choose what his service of God will be—either in freedom of love or bondage of lostness."[12]

We might note, further, that God is not only the God of love, but also the God of justice and holiness, and the God who has given men the tremendous gift of freedom from coercion and determination in making his basic and important decisions and the tremendous power to make a final irrevocable fundamental option for or against God Himself.

Turning to Annihilationism, is there any biblical evidence for it? Some scholars have thought that the idea of annihilation is perhaps to be found in Mt. 10:28: "do not fear those who kill the body but cannot kill the soul: rather fear him who can destroy both soul and body in hell." Generally, however, Annihilationists draw most of their support from St. Paul, who wrote that (1) immortality is conditioned on fellowship with Christ (Ph 3:1-4; Rm 8:11) and that (2) the ultimate fate of the wicked is *death, destruction, ruin* (Rm 9:22; Ph 3:19; 1 Tm 6:9; 2 Th 1:9). They argue that these words indicate Paul's belief in the ultimate annihilation of the wicked. In their judgment the New Testament teaches that only those will live forever who have what it calls "eternal life." Hence the wicked, since they lack this "eternal life," will be ultimately annihilated.

However, this alleged biblical support is far from convincing. If the New Testament does say that those who have "eternal life" will live forever a life of blessed fellowship with Christ, it does not say that those who lack this "eternal life" will be annihilated. The parable of Dives and Lazarus indicates that they are not annihilated at death but live on in torment after death. The parable of the Last Judgment indicates just as clearly that they are not annihilated at the end of the world but "go away into everlasting punishment." Paul does say the ultimate fate of the wicked is "death" or "destruction," but he does not say that death or destruction mean annihilation. Rather they mean for him "spiritual death," the privation of the eternal life of fellowship with God and eternal banishment from His presence.[13] Their "punishment is eternal (unending) destruction, a deprivation of the presence and glory of Christ, which is the lot of the faithful; their continued existence is presupposed" (JBC 48:30). "Death is not the physical, bodily death of man, the separation of body and soul, but denotes the spiritual death as the definitive separation of man from God, the unique source of life" (JBC 53:54). It is not hard, then, to see why C. R. Smith wrote that "extinction is not a biblical concept" (op. cit. 220) and why A. Jones declared that "the idea of annihilation of the soul would be strange to Jewish theology" (*A Catholic Commentary on Holy Scripture*, p. 870).

Since, then, the wicked are not ultimately saved nor ultimately annihilated, but undergo an unending punishment in hell, we are faced with a number of very disturbing questions. Why is there such a hell? What kind of hell is it? How many sinners go there? Obviously we can give little but conjectural answers, since hell is a baffling mystery. But to one basic question that is often asked we can give a quick, factual answer. "Is it possible to reconcile a hell of everlasting punishment with the God of love and mercy?" is the way this basic question is often put. The simplest response seems to be: Yes! For Christ did and so did His Saints, and so does His Church. And Christ is the one who knew God best and most clearly revealed to us that God is a God of love and mercy, a God who sincerely "desires all men to be saved" (1 Tm 2:4).

Why is there a hell, is a much harder question to answer. Many philosophers argued that God made hell to be the efficacious deterrent and sanction that would bring men to observe His law and to practice virtue. St. Augustine viewed hell in the perspective of original sin. For him as a result of original sin mankind becomes a *massa damnata*, and from this *massa damnata* God marks out some men for salvation and these are infallibly saved. The rest are not positively rejected by God but are permitted to consign themselves to perdition by reason of their sins. For Calvin, unlike Augustine, there is a double predestination, a predestination to life for some, to death for most. He calls predestination "the eternal decree of God by which he has determined in himself what he would have become of every individual of mankind. For they are not all created on equal terms, but eternal life is fore-ordained for some and eternal damnation for others. Every man, therefore, being created for one or the other of these ends, we say he is predestined either to life or to death" (III xxi.5; OS IV.374.11-17). In his theology God is absolutely sovereign and free, free to damn His creatures for His own glory. He can have no other motive for His action than His own proper glory. So before the beginning of time He decreed immutably that men should be predestined to manifest this glory, some by their gra-tuitous election, many more others by their damnation (cf. *Instit. chret.*, III, 21, Opera t.IV, p. 454).

However, most Catholic theologians today stress hell much more as man's creation than as God's. R. Gleason wrote: "We should not think of it as God's vengeance upon the unrepentant souls who desert Him, for hell is much more their creation than His . . . The man who dies in unrepented mortal sin damns him-self. For hell does not issue from an arbitrary decision of God. It is the direct and logical prolongation of man's own will to sin. If a man fixes himself in opposition to God, then hell is only the logical working out of this everlasting opposition."[14] Patrick Fannon declares: "it is not a question of God condemning a per-son to hell but rather of this person freely choosing, totally and definitively, to reject Christ. . . . Hell should not be seen as a punishment for past sins perhaps now bitterly rejected, but as an enduring attitude of rejection of Christ's love: an affirmation of sin as such. The will of the damned is not to love God; that is their hell."[15] Or as L. Boros sees it, "no one is damned by chance merely, because he was suddenly called to eternity by an accident or because he had never properly come to know God in his life-time, or because he was born into a family where he never knew what love is and so could never understand what God Himself is, or because he turned against a God of the law, a dreadful tyrant, or because he was hated, rejected, wounded to the heart by men and so rebelled against everything, including God. No one is damned unless he has decided against God with his whole being, in full clarity and reflection."[16] And J. Ratzinger writes that "the depths we call hell man can only give to himself. Indeed, we must put it more pointedly: hell consists in man's being unwilling to receive anything, in his desire to be self-sufficient. . . . Hell is wanting-only-to-be-oneself; what happens when man barricades himself up in himself."[17]

What kind of hell do theologians envision today? The traditional picture of hell was horrible, as painted by Catholics and Protestants alike. It has been called "terror in technicolor." Lucy, one of the children involved in the Fatima apparitions and revelations, said on one occasion: "And we saw as it were a great sea of fire. Plunged in this sea were demons, and souls in human shapes, blackened and burnt; they were glowing like embers. The flames were tossing them into the air, like sparks from a great conflagration, and they were falling everywhere, weightless and purposeless, and from them came screams and howls of agony and despair. . . . The devils were different from the humans; they had the horrible and revolting forms of strange and frightful animals; they too glowed like embers. The vision lasted only an instant. . . Then the Blessed Virgin said to us gently and sadly: 'You have seen hell, the place where poor sinners go. It is the wish of our Lord that, in order to save them, there be set up in the world, devotion to my Immaculate Heart'."[18] A Lutheran, C. J. Södergren, quotes the lurid description of a Protestant pastor: "When thou diest, thy soul will be tormented alone—that will be a hell for it—but at the judgment day thy body will join thy soul, and then thou wilt have twin hells. Body and soul shall be together, each brimful of pain, thy soul sweating in its inmost pore drops of blood, and thy body from head to foot suffused with agony; conscience, judgment, memory, all tortured; but more, thy head tormented with racking pains, thine eyes starting from their sockets with sights of blood and woe; thine ears tormented with sullen moans and hollow groans, and shrieks of tortured ghosts; thine heart beating high with fever . . . thy limbs cracking like the martyrs in fire, and yet unburnt; thyself put in a vessel of hot oil, pained, yet coming out undestroyed . . . every nerve a string on which the devil shall ever play his diabolical tune of Hell's unutterable Lament."[19]

Today theologians take much different and much less horrible views of hell, if they consider it at all, for they realize that the Church has made no official declaration on the nature of the pains of hell, and that the apocalyptic imagery of the New Testament is not to be taken literally. Exactly what the punishment of hell is, they say, "remains a mystery which is not revealed anywhere in the bible" (J. Michl, loc. cit.). But the traditional punishments of hell, the pain of loss and the pain of sense are retained, although differently presented by various authors.

Regularly they view the pain of loss as the sinner's eternal separation from God, his eternal deprivation of the beatific vision that constitutes the essential happiness of the blessed. For A. Winklhofer "the loss of God, which is the essence of hell and damnation, is but the prolongation in eternity . . . of mortal sin in which a person died. . . . For now the earthly sin, persisting to the end of life, has become as it were deliberate rebellion, and has brought about the loss of all that could possibly give meaning to life . . . If he has betrayed it for the sake of a lesser good, he must necessarily hate it . . . his worst plight . . . is that he knows that through communion with it . . . he would have been raised up to his own real self" (op. cit. 83-84). P. Fannon writes that "this deliberate separation from God produces a twofold discord: an inner conflict which comes from this—that the inescapable relationship each of us has to God is now joined to an inescapable and eternal godlessness" (op. cit. 89).

Just as regularly the pain of sense is no longer viewed as a pain of "fire," but as a pain of conflict with a hostile universe. "Fire is a symbol of a hostile effect of the whole material creation . . . on the reprobate whose whole relationship with creation is upset and distorted. . . . Everything is turned into fire. . . . The whole cosmos is for him a furnace from which he can never emerge purified, since he is no longer susceptible of transformation" (Winklhofer, op. cit. 93-94). "The universe bears the stamp of the God who created it . . . and the damned find themselves in conflict with all that surrounds them and which afflicts them

in the depths of their being" (P. Fannon, op. cit. 89). For K.
Rahner "fire is a metaphorical expression for something radically
not of this world—but this does not mean that fire is to be given
a merely psychological explanation. It does mean the cosmic,
objective aspect of loss, which is outside the consciousness, a
definitive contradiction of the abiding and perfected world, which
will be a torment" ("Hell," *Sacramentum Mundi* 3, p. 8). In a
Teilhardian perspective "the damned are not excluded from the
pleroma but only from its luminous aspect, and from its beatifica-
tion. They lose it but are not lost to it. The existence of hell, then,
does not destroy anything and does not spoil anything in the
divine milieu whose progress all around me I have followed with
delight."[20]

Is hell *a place?* Karl Rahner answers bluntly: "speculation
about the 'place' of hell is pointless; we can't insert hell into the
empirical world around us" (loc. cit.). Maybe we can't insert hell
into our empirical world. But does that mean that speculation
about the 'place' of hell is pointless? Other theologians do not
think so. One declares that although it is not a matter of faith
that hell is a place, yet "the Catholic can scarcely deny the existence of a 'place,' impossible though it is to localize damnation."[21]
Another admits that "we shall search in vain to locate hell: the
geography of the next world belongs to a Christian mythology
rather than to the Christian message." But he adds: "heaven and
hell are more than states. We can speak of a 'place' in an analogous
sense to mean the social dimension of the next life. Heaven includes a fellowship among the blessed and hell the company of
the damned" (P. Fannon, loc. cit.). Simple reasoning points in
the same direction. If there are damned, then they are somewhere,
not nowhere, and "somewhere" for them is not heaven and not
our empirical world. They are "someplace else" where they are
alive, conscious, think, will, remember, suffer and are punished
by separation from God and from the blessed and from us. If
they have an "interim embodiment," then it would seem that they
are in a trans-empirical world of their own, or in a trans-empirical
dimension of our world. If the whole material creation exercises
a hostile effect on them, then somehow material creation is in

contact with them and they with it. In this connection A. Winkl-hofer has an interesting thought. "If it is reasonable," he writes, "to understand by heaven the entire transfigured creation, and hell-fire as the creation as inimical and alien to the damned, we may well assume that hell is, by God's mercy, a place set apart, 'a prison' (Rv 20:7), bounded not by walls but by incapability of the damned soul to apprehend other parts of the cosmos. . . . The whole vast creation may well be, for the damned it torments, far smaller and more restricted than it is for the blessed, whose unimpaired faculties perceive and experience it in its totality. Hell would then be, not a place within the cosmos, 'above' or 'below,' but a particular constricted relation to the cosmos . . . 'places' in the next world are a metaphysical, not a spatial char-acter. No 'way' leads to them, and neither is there 'distance' from them. We must be content to say: Hell is the damned person himself; where he is, there is hell" (op. cit., 96-97).

Far from being pointless, then, speculation about the place of hell is very much in order, *if* one really believes that there are men in hell. But if one shies away from the thought of an "occupied hell," then clearly enough speculation about the "place" of hell is pointless.

And Karl Rahner definitely seems to shy away from thought about *"occupants of hell."* All he seems to see in the biblical state-ments about hell are *threats* of the *possibility* of a man being finally lost and estranged from God in all his dimensions. He sees no evidence that anyone actually is in hell. This is an excessively narrow view of the matter.

It may be true enough that the New Testament gives no clear-cut witness to any particular person being in hell. But the clear *implication* of the biblical statements is that there is a hell and it is not just an abstract threat, an "abstract possibility of perdi-tion," but a concrete reality with actual occupants. That our Lord and the Apostles, the early Christian writers and Fathers, believed that hell had actual occupants, seems to be beyond doubt. That they were all mistaken in this belief, is a contention that needs solid proof, proof that so far has not been adduced by anyone.

Preachers often urge the point that "the Church has never

officially said that anyone was in hell." This is true enough. But it seems to be equally true that the Church has never officially said that anyone was in Purgatory. And yet the Church has permitted prayers to and for the "souls in purgatory," and officially declared that such souls can be helped by the suffrages of the faithful. So the fact that the Church has not officially said that any particular person is in hell, does not at all imply that she thinks hell is unoccupied. Rather, if she has declared that there is a hell of everlasting punishment for men, does this not imply that someone, that some men, are everlastingly punished there?

If death is the end of merit, demerit, conversion, as we have shown above, then an unoccupied hell seems to mean that nobody dies in mortal sin. Is this a theologically tenable position? The answer definitely seems to be NO. For the Old Testament, the New Testament, the early Christian writers and Fathers, affirm or imply this. And so do the Church's definitions. That is why another theologian wrote recently: "it would be useless to claim . . . that no human being is to be found there. . . . It is . . . certain that the definitions of the Church's Magisterium presuppose the presence of human beings in hell. The pains of hell never end: that is all that is of faith . . . but in fact will any men be obliged to suffer them? It would be temerarious to deny it. It is at least a certitude" (Becque, op. cit.). What deterrent-value, what threat-value could hell have if no one would ever be in it?

If there are and will be men in hell, is it proper to ask: *how many?* John Shea would probably say No. For he writes: "that all men will be saved is the Christian hope . . . The conception of hell as 'eternal torment' is the cultural picture of another time and another place. Today the possibility of hell seems to equal the possibility of annihilation" (op. cit. pp. 77-78). But is it responsible theology to brush off so glibly a question that has moved and tormented Fathers and theologians and Saints down the centuries, on the grounds that this belongs to "the cultural picture of another time"?

For long, long years the Fathers of the Church, Saints, theologians, all felt they had to ask this question and try to answer it. And they answered it rather terrifyingly: "*Major pars hominum damnatur*," the majority of mankind is damned. This grim view represented the common opinion of Basil the Great, John Chrysostom, Gregory of Nazianzus, Hilary, Ambrose, Jerome, Augustine, Leo the Great and Bernard, of Aquinas, Molina, Bellarmine, Suarez, Vasquez, Lessius, Alphonsus. As they read the New Testament this was its clear teaching. Did it not say: "many are called, few are chosen" (Mt 22:14); "strive to enter by the narrow gate, for many seek to enter but cannot" (Lk 13:23); "the gate is wide and the way is easy, that leads to destruction, and those who enter by it are many. For the gate is narrow and the way is hard, that leads to life, and those who find it are few" (Mt 7:13-14)? Did it not add that without faith it was impossible to be saved? (Heb 11:6; Rm 1:16-17; 3:26-28). And was it not a patent fact that most men from the beginning of time did not have this faith in Christ? Did it not say that without baptism no one could enter the kingdom, and was it not obvious that most men would never achieve baptism? Did not salvation require charity, the love of God above all things, and did not most men lack this charity? And was it not a solidly traditional doctrine that "outside the Church" there was no salvation? And was it not obvious that the majority of mankind had been, was and would be "outside the Church"? To the Fathers, to the theologians, to the Saints, then, the evidence for the eternal damnation of most men was overwhelming.

Today this traditional view is being widely—and properly—abandoned by theologians. For it was based, they argue, on an interpretation of the New Testament that is no longer acceptable, on a failure to distinguish between explicit and implicit faith, between baptism of water and baptism of desire, between explicit and implicit charity, between actual and votal membership in the Church, between a narrow and a broad view of the Church. God's salvific will, they urge, is broad enough, and the grace of Christ is so abundantly and universally distributed to men, that it is quite possible for men to achieve salvation with only "implicit" faith and charity, with votal membership in the Church.

This traditional view was based also on a much too rigoristic interpretation of the New Testament (e.g. of Mt 7:13; 22:11ff.; Lk 13:22ff.), an interpretation that today is either rejected or strongly questioned by many Scripture scholars (cf. JBC 43:50; *A Catholic Commentary on Holy Scripture*, pp. 865, 890, 957; *New Testament Reading Guide on Matthew* by D. M. Stanley, p. 71; *Word of Salvation* by A. Durand, p. 126ff). Yves Congar has pointed out that "there is to be found in the New Testament a whole series of texts which open up wider possibilities of salvation or at least of 'non-damnation,' those namely in which it is said that God will render unto each 'according to his works'" (e.g. Ps 62:13; Job 34:11; Mt 16:27; Lk 14:14; 2 Cor 2:6; Ep 6:8). "Moreover," he adds, "St. Paul also says that the man who does not have the Law of Moses, does have his own conscience for law, and that it is on this basis that he will be assessed before God's judgment seat. And for all those who obey God's law as heard by them in the voice of conscience and consequently perform good works (not without the help of grace), Paul does envisage a reward at the end of time to which we can give no other name but that of salvation (cf. Ep 1:9-23; Col 1:15f.; 2:9). . . . And a man can miss encountering the positive fact of Christ without himself being at fault; perhaps it is even possible never to encounter the fact of God as such . . . but to attain him only under what amounts to a travesty of himself. . . . In such men of good will the 'intention of faith' would really be present, but it would reach its goal only on the eschatological level, perhaps at the moment of death."[22]

Thus the strongly "rigoristic" patristic and theological tradition is heavily down-graded in these days, as based on an inaccurate exegesis of the New Testament, on a very inaccurate view of the world and its population.

Today the drift is in the other direction: to maintain that the majority of mankind is saved, not lost. A. Winklhofer argues that if God sent His Son to redeem the world, this redemption could hardly be said to be accomplished if the majority of mankind is lost. And would Satan be really "cast out" (Jn 12:31) if he is still to be victorious over the greater part of mankind? Could Christ really be the victorious Redeemer if most men are lost? If the grace of Christ is so abundant and so powerful, and if it was already active before the time of Christ, would the majority of mankind finally and definitively reject it? If God's mercy is no less than His justice, would it not be more probable that most men would reach salvation? If God so loved the world as to send His Son to die for it, and to die that men might have eternal life, is it not most probable that most men will respond to the love of God and to the grace and love of Christ? If we add to this argument, Yves Congar's teaching about the possibility of salvation through faith in and love of a "substitute for God," and Karl Rahner's teaching about "Anonymous Christians" and about "Christianity and Non-Christian Religions," it should be quite clear that theologians today have moved strongly away from the rigorist view and toward the view that the majority of mankind is saved. Vatican II leans strongly in this same direction when it states: "those also can attain to everlasting salvation who through no fault of their own do not know the Gospel of Christ or His Church, yet sincerely seek God and, moved by grace, strive by their deeds to do His will as it is known to them through the dictates of conscience. Nor does divine providence deny the help necessary for salvation to those who, without blame on their part, have not yet arrived at an explicit knowledge of God, but who strive to live a good life, thanks to His grace" (Abbot, op. cit. 35). And it adds that "some, even very many, of the most significant elements or endowments which together go to build up and give life to the Church herself can exist outside the visible boundaries of the Catholic Church: the written Word of God; the life of grace; faith, hope and charity, along with other interior gifts of the Holy Spirit and visible elements" (ibid, 345).

If, then, we must believe that there is a hell of unending punishment for grave sinners, we need not believe that most men will end up in this hell. We can hope that most men will be saved and we can know that this is not just wishful thinking. We can know that this is a solid theological position backed up by many responsible theologians, by sound theological reasoning, and by the drift of the teaching of Vatican II. Can we express the Christian hope, as some do, that all men will actually be saved? At present this seems biblically and traditionally unrealistic.

CONCLUSION

What conclusions can we draw from our study of hell? First of all, hell exists, a hell of everlasting punishment. Of this there is solid and convincing biblical evidence, while there is no such solid and convincing biblical evidence for either Universalism (all men are ultimately saved) or for Annihilationism (the wicked are ultimately annihilated). For the evidence adduced for these two positions does not stand up when taken in the total context of New Testament teaching. Further, the biblical evidence for the existence of hell is backed up by solid patristic evidence and by dogmatic definitions on the part of the Church's solemn magisterium. As long as these dogmatic definitions are "in possession" (and they still are), there can be no proper doubt about the existence of hell. If some Catholic theologians are not as certain about this today as they once were, perhaps they should examine their present attitudes towards the Church's role and competence in the matter of biblical interpretation and definition. If they are Universalists or Annihilationists, they should say so. If they think that the existence of an everlasting hell has not been solemnly defined by the Church, they should say so. If they think this has been solemnly—but mistakenly—defined by the Church, they should say so. If they think that the traditional interpretation of Scripture that issued into these solemn definitions, was a mistaken interpretation, they should say so and back up their contention. If they think that a modern Catholic is free to believe or disbelieve whatever he wants, is free to accept or reject whatever he wishes from the Church's dogmatic definitions, they should say so. And then declare just what they think a modern Catholic can believe and disbelieve and still be a Catholic. Otherwise they are not doing justice to their duties as responsible Catholic theologians.

Secondly, we conclude that hell not only exists but is a "place," not in the sense that we can localize it or insert it in our empirical world, but in the sense that the damned are not nowhere, are not with the blessed in the heaven of God, are not with us empirically in our empirical world, but are "someplace else," in a "place" or "dimension" set apart.

Thirdly, hell is not just an abstract threat or possibility. It is an actuality and it has and will continue to have actual occupants. Unless one wishes to be a Universalist or an Annihilationist, it seems rash to deny this. But it seems quite probable that of all mankind only a minority will "occupy" hell, and we can hope that this minority will be very small, indeed.

Fourthly, we conclude that hell is not a great sea of physical fire and darkness, in which souls howl and scream in endless agony because a vindictive God arbitrarily chose to punish them in this way forever for their grave sins. Hell is the eternal separation from the beatific presence and vision of the God of Love who had called them to eternal and beatific union with Himself. And since the damned are thus eternally in disharmony with the God of Love, they are also eternally in disharmony with His world, and "suffer" thereby. They were meant for beatific communion with God but they definitively rejected Him and His love and so they are eternally closed in on themselves and wrapped up in their lonely pride, like the Dark Prince of Loneliness. They prided themselves on their freedom, their freedom to choose to be and do just what they wanted. Now they are what they wanted to be, and they will be that forever.

Why is there such a hell? Not because of an arbitrary decision of a vindictive God. Hell is much more the creation of the damned than of God. In their final and irrevocable and utterly free decision in death they opted for themselves and not for God, for themselves and not for Christ. They wanted "self," not God nor Christ. That is what they will have for all eternity. That is hell.

Notes for Chapter 8

1. H. Buis, **The Doctrine of Eternal Punishment,** (Philadelphia, Presbyterian and Reformed Pub. Co., 1957), pp. 93ff.

2. **What A Modern Catholic Believes about Death,** (Chicago, Thomas More Press, 1972), pp. 8, 9.

3. "Eschatology," **Chicago Studies,** Fall, 1973, p. 309.

4. **We Are Future,** (Garden City, N. Y., Doubleday, 1973), p. 155.

5. "And After Death," **Catholic Mind,** April, 1975, pp. 12-25.

6. Cf. **Enchiridion Symbolorum,** p. 140; **The Church Teaches,** by J. F. Clarkson et al., (B. Herder Book Co., 1955), p. 345.

7. J. T. Addison, **Life Beyond Death,** (New York, Houghton Mifflin Co., 1932), pp. 215ff.

8. J. Michl, **Sacramentum Verbi,** (New York, Herder & Herder), v. 1, pp. 369-371.

9. J. M. Shaw, **Christian Doctrine,** (New York, Philosophical Library, 1954), p. 69.

10. C. R. Smith, **The Bible Doctrine of the Hereafter,** (London, Epworth Press, 1958), p. 200.

11. Cf. J. Shea, **What A Modern Catholic Believes about Heaven and Hell,** (Chicago, Thomas More Press, 1972), pp. 74-76.

12. **Theology of the Kerygma,** (Englewood Cliffs, N. J., Prentice-Hall, 1962).

13. B. Vawter, **New Testament Reading Guide, I and II Thessalonians,** (Collegeville, The Liturgical Press, 1960), p. 56.

14. **The World to Come,** (New York, Sheed & Ward, 1958), pp. 115ff.

15. **The Changing Face of Theology,** (Milwaukee, Bruce, 1968), p. 89.

16. **Living in Hope,** (Garden City, N. Y., Doubleday, Image Books, 1973), pp. 30-31.

17. **Introduction to Christianity,** (New York, Herder & Herder, 1970), p. 239.

18. Georges Panneton, **Heaven and Hell,** (Westminster, Md., The Newman Press, 1965), p. 169.

19. **The Future Life,** (Minneapolis, 1935), pp. 31-32.

20. D. L. Fleming, "Pilgrim of the Future," **America,** April 12, 1975, p. 281.

21. M. and L. Becque, **Life after Death,** (New York, Hawthorne Books, 1960), pp. 104ff.

22. Cf. **The Theology of Salvation,** (Boston, St. Paul Editions, 1960), pp. 68ff.

Chapter 9
Is There a Heaven of Everlasting Happiness?

Is it too much to think that in every man at one time or other during his life there is a thought, a dream, a wish, a hope for a heaven of bliss where the pain and sorrow and agony and frustration of this life will be followed by everlasting joy and happiness? If we look back to earlier and earlier times, most everywhere we find men picturing some kind of heaven and looking forward to it hopefully.

For earliest India there was the Vedic heaven, where Yama the King of the dead rules over all the departed who have lived worthily. His realm is the radiant light of the outer sky, where men may share the unbounded love of celestial life, food and drink and the pleasures of love. Clothed in glorified bodies that magnify every delight of the senses, the spirits sit at table with the gods, enlivened with the sound of flute and song, where pleasure and bliss dwell together and all desire is satisfied (Addison, op. cit. 248ff; much of what follows also comes from Addison). Later Hinduism had five heavens in ascending order. (1) The heaven of Indra, where souls will find dancing girls and musicians. (2) The heaven of Shiva, where the great god dwells with his wife and sons. (3) The heaven of Vishnu, built wholly of gold and adorned with pools covered with blue and red and white lotuses. (4) The heaven of Krishna where its ruler amuses himself with the cowherds and the lovely cowgirls. (5) The heaven of Brahma, the highest heaven of all, where man can enjoy the society of the celestial nymphs. Mahayana Buddhism had three realms. (1) The realm of Desire—with material worlds and pleasures of eating, drinking and sex. (2) The realm of Form which is to be attained only by meditation and where the lusts of the flesh are left behind and bodily existence is ethereal. (3) The realm of Formlessness where all trace of mere matter is dispelled and spirit abides in a state of ecstasy. Beyond this realm no further achievement is possible save the perfection of Nirvana itself.

In Persia we find the domain of the supreme God of goodness, Ahura Mazda. There he dwells with all who have chosen to serve him by living a righteous life. This Zoroastrian heaven was devoid of sensual pleasures but it brought happiness through the gradual approach to Ahura Mazda and the joy of abiding in his presence. There were three stages of progress toward the ultimate vision, the paradise of Good Thoughts in the Stars, the Paradise of Good Words in the Moon and the Paradise of Good Deeds in the Sun. In all these regions the righteous are immortal, unalarmed and undisturbed, full of glory, delight and happiness. Beyond the sun is the Highest Heaven, the Heaven of Endless Light, where Ahura Mazda reigns with angels and archangels.

In Greece the Orphic paradise to which all believers might look forward, was a blissful region in the underworld, known as the Elysian Fields. It was a land of flowery meadows, fruitful trees, feasting and drinking, sacred song and dance.

IS THERE A HEAVEN?

A heaven of eternal happiness with God? Human reason can perhaps tell us that there should be a heaven as a reward for the good deeds that man does in his earthly life. But it cannot demonstrate that there really is such a heaven. Only God can tell us that there is a heaven and what sort of heaven it is. So we turn again to Sacred Scripture for a witness to God's revelation and to the Church as interpreter of this biblical witness.

Old Testament

The Old Testament gives us no clear-cut testimony that there is a heaven of eternal happiness for all who die justified by God's grace. It tells us that 'heaven' is God's abode (Dt 26:15; Ps 2:4) and that Israel looked to heaven as the source of salvation and of all blessings (Gn 49:25; Dt 33:13; 1K 8:35), and longed for the day when God would rend the heavens to bring salvation to earth (Is 63:19; 45:8). Perhaps it hints that salvation would somehow consist not only in a descent of God to earth, but also in a return of man to God in heaven (Is 55:10-11). For Daniel attests a bodily resurrection to eternal life: "Many of these who sleep in the dust of the earth shall awake; some shall live forever. . . . But the wise shall shine brightly like the splendor of the firmament, and those who lead the many to justice shall be like the stars forever" (Dn 12:2-3). And where 2 Maccabees tells of the glorious martyrdom of the seven brethren and their mother we read: "For my brethren, having now undergone a short pain, are under the covenant of eternal life" (2 M 7:36). The book of Wisdom tells of the bliss and peace of the souls of the just, who rest in the hand of God and live with Him forever: "But the souls of the just are in the hand of God, and no torment shall touch them . . . they are in peace . . . their hope full of immortality; chastised a little, they shall be greatly blessed, because God tried them and found them worthy of himself and . . . took them to himself . . . they shall judge nations and rule over peoples, and the Lord shall be their King forever. . . . But the just live forever and in the Lord is their recompense. . . . Therefore shall they receive the splendid crown, the beauteous diadem from the hand of the Lord" (Ws 3:1-9; 5:15-16).

Intertestamental Literature

If we turn to the *Book of Enoch* we find a heaven with a wall built of crystals, a ceiling like the path of stars, a greater house built of flames of fire, a lofty throne on which sat the Great Glory and his raiment shone more brightly than the sun. In the *Secrets of Enoch* we find the *Seven Heavens* so familiar in later Jewish and Christian tradition. The first heaven is a great sea, the dwelling place of 'the elders'; the third is the celestial paradise with its tree of life from whose roots four streams flowed with milk, honey, wine and oil: this is the eternal abode of the righteous;

in the sixth are the seven orders of angels and archangels who rejoice as they sing before the Lord; in the seventh the Lord is seated on his lofty throne surrounded by worshipping hosts of angels.

New Testament

The New Testament tells us a great deal about 'heaven' in a setting of ancient cosmology and in the language of imagery that was characteristic of those times. If we look beneath the imagery for the reality that is imaged forth, we find the fact of a blissful heaven and intimations of some of the elements that enter into this mysterious heaven. One of the finest presentations of heaven in the New Testament is found in an article by J. Plastaras ("Heaven in the Bible," *New Catholic Encyclopedia*, 6, 968-971), in which he offers a sweeping survey of the place of heaven in salvation history and then indicates some of the more specific aspects of heaven that are stressed by Jesus, by Paul, by John.

His survey shows an Old Testament desire and a New Testament realization knitted together. In the Old Testament there was a hint that salvation would somehow consist not only in a descent of God to earth but also in a return of man to God in heaven, coupled with a strong desire for the day when God would "rend the heavens and come down" (Is 63:19ff; 55:10-11). In the New Testament this desire is fulfilled in the coming of Jesus Christ. At the beginning of His ministry "the heavens were opened" (Mt 3:16) that salvation might descend to earth (Ac 2:2). Of himself man could not ascend to heaven to behold the revelation of 'the mystery hidden in God' (Ep 3:9; Jn 1:18; 3:13; Rm 10:6). So God sent His Son to bring this revelation to earth (Mt 11:27; Jn 1:18; 3:11-19; 14:9). Then Christ returned to the Father in heaven (Jn 6:62; 13:1; Heb 9:11-12) as the first among many brethren (Rm 8:29). As forerunner He entered heaven to prepare a place for His followers (Jn 14:3). His ascension into heaven inaugurated a period of eager expectation of His parousia from heaven (Mk 14:62; Mt 25:31; 1 Th 1:10; 4:16; 2 Th 1:7), when He will seek out His own (1 Th 4:17; Ph 1:23; 2 Cor 5:6-8) and introduce them into the kingdom of the Father (Mt 25:34; 1 Cor 15:24), the New Jerusalem (Rv 3:12; 21:3, 10-14). Heaven is thus the consummation of salvation history when the world will be transformed into a new heaven and a new earth (Is 65:17; Rm 8:19-23; 2 P 3:13; Rv 21:1) and God will be all in all (1 Cor 15:28). This survey, it should be noted, embraces heaven as it is now in the interim state of mankind and as it will be in the final state of mankind after the end of this world.

Jesus in the New Testament depicts the happiness of heaven under the picture of a wedding feast (Mt 25:10; 22:1ff; Lk 14:15ff.), and calls it life, or eternal life (Mt 18:8ff.; 19:29; 25:46; Jn 3:15ff.; 4:14; 5:24; 6:35-39; 10:28; 12:25; 17:2). He compares the reward for good works with treasures in heaven which cannot be lost (Mt 6:20; Lk 12:33), and speaks of "eternal dwellings" (Lk 16:9).

Paul speaks of eternal bliss as "an incorruptible crown" (1 Cor 9:25) and says that "every man shall receive his own reward according to his own labour" (1 Cor 3:8; 15:41ff.). He declares that the just receive as reward eternal life (Rm 2:7; 6:22ff.) and a glory which bears no relation to the sufferings of this world (Rm 8:18). He stresses the mysterious character of future happiness: there are things "which no eye ever saw and ear ever heard and which never occurred to the human mind, which God has provided for those who love Him" (1 Cor 2:9). One of his very attractive views of heaven is as being at "home with the Lord": "I know well that as long as I am at home in the body I am away from the Lord . . . yet I am confident, and I prefer to leave my home in the body and make my home with the Lord" (2 Cor 5:7).

But the aspect of heaven for which he is perhaps most noted is that of the vision of God, the immediate vision of God that takes the place of the imperfect knowledge of God we have in this world: "We see now through a mirror in an obscure manner, but then face to face. Now I know in part, but then I shall know even as I have been known" (1 Cor 13:12). This expression "face to face," understood in terms of an eschatological knowledge of God, is unique in Paul's writings, although it is a common Jewish theme (Rv 22:3-4: Mt 5:8). In comparing the knowledge we now have in this world of God with that hoped for in the world to come Paul is comparing the "mirror-knowledge" of God we have here through charismatic gifts with the "face-to-face" vision of God hereafter. The image of God manifested to the Christian in this life is through a medium, through faith (Col 1:12; Jn 1:17f.; 14:9; Heb 1:3). The vision of God for which the Christian is destined, however, is much more intimate and is immediate (cf. I Cor 13:12; 2 Cor 3:18). When he has this vision the Christian will indeed be like Christ, whose relation to God is unique (Jn 6:46; Mt 11:27; cf. JBC 51:78).

John. Just as Jesus and Paul, so John too stresses eternal life, and he indicates that this life begins *here* for believers and goes on after death, for he says: "whoever believes in the Son 'hath life everlasting, and cometh not into judgment, but is passed from death to life'" (Jn 5:24). He indicates that one attains to eternal life through a *belief in Jesus,* the Messiah and Son of God (Jn 3:16, 36; 20:31; 1 Jn 5:13), through *baptism,* through *love,* through the *Eucharist.* He does not explicitly say eternal life consists in the immediate vision of God but his thought and his words definitely point in that direction, for he says, "This is eternal life that they may know thee, the one true God and Jesus Christ, whom thou hast sent" (Jn 17:3). And he adds, "We know that when he shall appear we shall be like to him, because we shall see him as he is" (1 Jn 3:2). What is more, he seems to connect entry into the kingdom with entry into this eternal life, for he writes: "unless a man be born again of water and the Spirit, he cannot enter into the kingdom of God . . . For God so loved the world that He gave His only-begotten Son that those who believe in Him may not perish, but may have life everlasting" (Jn 3:5, 16).

If we try to gather together what we find in Sacred Scripture we realize that the concept of heaven is not simple but rather a very complex one, with many elements that are not easy to integrate perfectly. Heaven means bliss and peace, a wedding feast, an incorruptible crown, a mystery. It means being at home with the Lord, being like Christ. It means seeing and entering the kingdom of God. It means an immediate vision of God. It means the resurrection of the flesh (1 Cor 15). It means in summary the total fulfillment of man, perfect fulfillment of his spiritual and his bodily nature in eternal life.

The Fathers

The Fathers of the early Church conceived heaven as somehow constituted by the vision of God. For some of them this meant that God would be seen with bodily eyes, but for most of them it was the eyes of the mind that would see God. But what would they see of God? Would they see His very essence? Would they see Him as He is in Himself, one and triune? Some of the Greek Fathers thought the blessed would not see the very essence of God but only His light or radiance or splendor or glory, and this view was strongly defended later on by the Palamites and other Orthodox Christians. Many of the Western Fathers, however, believed that the blessed saw God Himself according to His essence and in this vision of the divine essence they found the very essence of heavenly happiness. Augustine placed the consummation of heaven in the beatific vision of God and he described this beautifully in his *City of God*. But to the question whether the blessed are in heaven enjoying the beatific vision *now*, the Fathers gave contrasting answers. Some said they will only be in heaven and have this vision after the last judgment at the end of the world. Others said they are in heaven now and have the beatific vision now.

The Church

What did the Church say about heaven in its solemn declarations? At Lyons II, a general and reunion council, the Eastern Emperor, Michael Palaeologus, subscribed through his ambassadors to a dogmatic creed (DS 857) which professed that "the souls of those who have not committed any sin at all after they received holy baptism, and the souls of those who have committed sin but have been cleansed . . . are promptly taken up into heaven." The council of Florence, also a general and reunion council, declared that "the souls of those who have not committed any sin at all after they received baptism, and the souls of those who have committed sin, but have been cleansed either while in the body or afterwards . . . are promptly taken up into heaven and see clearly the Triune God Himself, just as He is, some more perfectly than others according to their respective merits" (DS 1305). And Benedict XII in the Benedictine Constitution solemnly defined: "by this constitution which is to remain in force forever, we, with Our apostolic authority, make the following definition: all those souls, not needing purification, soon after their death, and after purification if they needed it, are in heaven, in the kingdom of heaven and the celestial paradise with Christ, joined to the company of the holy angels . . . even before these souls take up their bodies again and before the general judgment, and *do see the divine essence with an intuitive and even face-to-face vision,* without the interposition of any creature in the function of object seen; rather, the divine essence immediately manifests itself to them plainly, clearly, openly. The same thing is true of the souls of children who have been reborn with the baptism of Christ. . . . We also define that those who see the divine essence in this way take great joy from it, and because of this vision and enjoyment . . . are truly blessed and possess life and eternal rest. . . . And we define that after this intuitive and face-to-face vision has or will have begun for those souls, the same vision and enjoyment remains continuously without any interruption or abolition of the vision or enjoyment and will remain up till the final judgment and from then on forever" (DS 1000-1001).

WHO ARE IN HEAVEN NOW? AND WHAT ARE THEY DOING THERE?

These are questions that cannot but come to mind. And in the Benedictine Constitution Benedict XII gave us an answer: Christ, the angels and just souls are in heaven. First of all we ponder Christ. For both the Niceno-Constantinople Creed and the New Testament tell us of His ascension to heaven and His exaltation there. The Creed says very simply "he ascended into heaven, sits at the right hand of the Father" (DS 150).

The New Testament tells us something about this ascension of our Lord in language that fitted its times and culture. "But now

I am going to Him who sent Me; I go to the Father; I came from the Father and have come into the world; again, I am leaving the world and going to the Father" (Jn 16:5, 10, 28). "Then He led them out as far as Bethany, and lifting up His hands He blessed them. While He blessed them, He parted from them and was carried up into heaven" (Lk 24:51). "And when He had said this, as they were looking on, He was lifted up, and a cloud took Him out of their sight. And while they were gazing into heaven as He went, two men stood by them in white robes, and said . . . This Jesus who was taken up into heaven from you, will come in the same way as you saw Him go into heaven" (Ac 1:9-11). These passages can seem to present a mythical heaven, but actually they tell us of a heaven that is independent of the so-called 'three-storeyed mythical' world. "The ascension of Jesus is the transfer of His risen, glorious body to 'heaven,' i.e. to the world of the divine; it implies His corporeal survival, His final glorification, His departure from the material universe" (J. L. McKenzie, op. cit. 59). Pere Benoit points out "that the essence of the mystery of the ascension is the invisible transcendent accession of Jesus in His physical presence to the world of the divine" (ibid, 60). We can "recognize in this mystery two connected but distinct aspects: on the one hand, the celestial glorification of Christ which coincided with His resurrection; on the other hand, His final departure after a period of apparitions—a departure and return to God which the apostles witnessed on the Mount of Olives" (X. Leon-Dufour, op. cit. 26).

The New Testament also tells us of Jesus' exaltation: "the God of our Lord Jesus Christ, the Father of glory . . . raised Him from the dead and made Him sit at His right hand in the heavenly places, far above all rule and authority and power and dominion, and above every name . . . and He has put all things under His feet and has made Him the head over all things for the church, which is His body, the fulness of Him who fills all in all" (Ep 1:20; cf. Col 3:1; Rm 8:34; Ac 2:33; 5:31; 7:55). "In order to sit there at the right hand of God (Heb 1:3; 8:1; 10:12f; 12:2) above the angels (Heb 1:4-13; 2:7ff.), the high priest has gone up first, passing through the heavens (Heb 4:14) and penetrating behind the veil (Heb 6:19f.) into the sanctuary where He intercedes in the presence of God" (X. Leon-Dufour, 25). This celestial enthronement indicates that the human Jesus participates in the kingly power of God, is installed in regal authority as the Lord to whom all power is given in heaven and on earth (Mt 28:18). It is the sign and seal of His ultimate accomplishment of His mission.

WHAT IS JESUS DOING IN HEAVEN?

Most of the things He is doing are wrapped in mystery. A few we can touch on. He is sending the Holy Spirit to us and will continue to do so until the end of time: "when the Counsellor comes, whom I shall send you from the Father, even the Spirit of truth . . . He will bear witness to Me" (Jn 15:26); "when the Spirit of truth comes, He will guide you into all the truth; for He will not speak on His own authority, but whatever He hears He will speak, and He will declare to you the things that are to come. He will glorify me, for He will take what is mine and declare it to you. All that the Father has is mine; therefore I said that He will take what is mine and declare it to you" (Jn 16:13-15).

He is engaged in His high-priestly ministry. "When Christ appeared as a high priest of the good things that have come . . . He entered once for all into the Holy place (i.e. heaven; JBC 61:51) taking . . . His own blood, thus securing an eternal redemption" (Heb 9:11-12); "for Christ has entered, not into a sanctuary made with hands . . . but into heaven itself, now to appear in the presence of God on our behalf" (Heb 9:24); "He holds His priesthood permanently, because He continues forever. Consequently He is able for all time to save those who draw near to God through Him, since He always lives to make intercession for them" (Heb 7:25). And what is His prayer for us but the great high-priestly prayer recorded in Jn 17: "that they may all be one, even as thou, Father, art in me and I in thee, that they also may be in us . . . may be one even as we are one . . . that they also may be with me where I am, to behold my glory which thou hast given me in thy love for me before the foundation of the world" (Jn 17:17-24).

He is the Head of His body, the Church: "the God of our Lord Jesus Christ, the Father of glory . . . when He raised Him from the dead and made Him sit at his right hand in the heavenly places . . . made him the head over all things for the church, which is His body, the fullness of Him who fills all in all" (Ep 1:17, 20, 22). In Christ we are redeemed and saved (Rm 3:24; 2 Tim 2:10), we are sanctified (1 Cor 1:2), we are blessed (Ep 1:3f.), we receive "newness of life" (Rm 6:4). And "Christ is not only the agent-instrument by which new life is conferred; He is also the sustaining cause, the principle by which the new life endures" (J. L. McKenzie, op. cit. 436). He is for Christians (and others) a principle of grace and virtue, of the love of God and spiritual enrichment and freedom and strength and faith (Rm 8:39; 1 Cor 1:4, 5; 2 Cor 5:21; Gal 2:4, 17; 1 Tm 1:14). He is the principle of their resurrection (1 Cor 15:22).

Vatican II gives an excellent description of the function of Christ as Head of the (Mystical) Body in *Lumen Gentium*. "The Head of this body is Christ, the image of the invisible God . . . in Him all things hold together. By the greatness of His power He rules the things of heaven and the things of earth, and with His all-surpassing perfection and activity He fills the whole body with the riches of His glory (Ep 1:18-23)." "He continually distributes in His body, that is, in the Church, gifts of ministries through which, by His own power, we serve each other unto salvation so that, carrying out the truth in love, we may through all things grow up into Him who is our head (Ep 4:11-16)." "Christ loves the Church as His bride (Ep 5:25-28) and fills the Church with His divine gifts (Ep 1:22-23) so that she may grow and reach all the fullness of God (Ep 3:19)." He "ceaselessly sustains here on earth His holy Church, the community of faith, hope and charity as a visible structure." "In that body the life of Christ is poured into believers who are united through the sacraments in a hidden and real way to Christ who suffered and was glorified." "Through baptism we are formed in the likeness of

Christ (1 Cor 12:13) and united with His death and resurrection (Rm 6:4-5)." "Truly partaking of the body of the Lord in the breaking of the Eucharistic bread, we are taken up into communion with Him and with one another (1 Cor 10:17)." "In this way all of us are made members of His body (1 Cor 12:27) but severally members one of another (Rm 12:5)." "All the members ought to be moulded into Christ's image until He is formed in them (Gal 4:19). Made one with His sufferings . . . we endure with Him, that with Him we may be glorified (Rm 8:17)."

ANGELS

The Benedictine Constitution (A.D. 1336) declared that just men in heaven will be "joined to the company of the holy angels" (DS 1000). At that time the existence of angels was hardly questioned. But today it is questioned, and not only questioned but often denied outright. By many scholars who maintain that angels are merely "mythical" entities conjured up out of primitive man's ignorance and misinterpretation of the world and its natural agencies and phenomena. Some historians of religion say the concept of "angels" came from Babylonian and late Iranian ideas, then moved into the Old Testament and from the Old Testament into the New Testament and Christian doctrine and piety.

There may be elements of truth in this view. Karl Rahner has written: "Revelation does not really introduce into the realm of human existence a reality in relation to God and His saving action in man, because that reality is already there . . . Where revelation proper, especially in the New Testament, does occur in regard to the angels through reference to the word of the prophets and other primary bearers of revelation, or to inspired Scripture, it nevertheless has an *essential function of selection and guarantee*. 'Archaic' angelology of alien origin prior to revelation was purified or kept free of elements incompatible with the real content of revelation (the unicity and truly absolute character of the God of the Covenant and of Christ as a person and mediator of salvation). The residue was confirmed as human experience legitimately handed down, preserving such knowledge for men as an important factor in their religious life which otherwise might be lost" (*Sacramentum Mundi*, 1, "Angel," 29, 30). J. L. McKenzie has written that "the belief in heavenly beings runs through the entire Bible and exhibits consistency. In some instances (e.g. Rv) the influence of apocalyptic literature can be traced and mythological allusions appear in their description; but the biblical conception of these heavenly beings is in general remarkably restrained compared to Jewish literature. In the New Testament as in the Old Testament the angel is sometimes no more than another word for a divine communication or a divine operation personified" (op. cit. 32).

If, then, we regard the *selective development* and basic continuity of angelic doctrine in the Old Testament and the New Testament and its strong link with the salvation of man and with the nature and work of Christ, it is not hard to see why K. Rahner declares that "the existence of angels and demons is *affirmed* in Scripture and not merely assumed as a hypothesis which we could drop today" (loc. cit. 32). However, a demythologization of "mythological, historically conditioned representational material" is quite in order today.

Besides this biblical evidence, there is strong ecclesial evidence for the existence of angels (incorporeal spirits). The Nicene Creed declares God to be the "maker of all things visible and *invisible*" (DS 125). Lateran IV defined against the Albigenses and Cathars that God is "creator of all things visible and invisible, spiritual and corporeal; who by His almighty power . . . created both orders of creatures in the same way out of nothing, the spiritual or angelic world and the corporeal or visible universe. And afterwards He formed the creature man" (DS 800). And even if we agree with P. Schoonenberg that this Lateran statement "presupposes but does *not directly affirm their existence*," we must also admit with A. Darlap "that these definitions *imply* the existence of personal non-human beings and that this is guaranteed by the ordinary magisterium and tradition" (*Sacramentum Mundi* 2, "Devil," 71). Karl Rahner declares that "the existence of angels cannot be disputed in view of the conciliar declarations (DS 800, 3002) on the creation of spiritual beings, angels, in addition to men (cf. DS 3891), and statements of the creed about

invisibilia created by the one God. It cannot be said that the conciliar statements only mean *that if* there are such personal spiritual
principalities and powers, they like everything else are creatures . . . though this, the ultimate import of the affirmation, is
what is finally decisive" (*Sacramentum Mundi*, 1 "Angel," 34).
And if we ask him what these angels are he says that "as regards
their essence, the angels are to be thought of as spiritual, personal, 'principalities and powers.' This is what is always implied
in the official doctrinal pronouncements of the Church (e.g.
DS 800, 3003, 3891). And they are 'principalities and powers'
of the cosmos in virtue of their very nature . . . and like man
they have a supernatural goal of grace in the direct beatific
vision of God" (ibid. 33, 34). (Cf. also K. Barth, *Church Dogmatics* III, 238, 374).

WHAT ARE THESE ANGELS DOING?

Old Testament

In the Old Testament we read that they watch over men
(Tb 3:17; Ps 91:11) and present their prayers to God (Tb 12:
12); they preside over the destinies of nations (Dn 10:13-21).
They receive names corresponding to their functions: Raphael,
"God heals" (Tb 3:17; 12:15); Gabriel, "Hero of God" (Dn
8:16; 9:21); Michael, "Who is like God,"? the leader of all,
to whom the Jewish community is entrusted (Dn 10:13, 21;
12:1).

New Testament

The New Testament tells us of archangels (1 Th 4:16),
cherubim (Hb 9:5), thrones, dominations, principalities, powers
(Col 1:16), virtues (Ep 1:21) but it is not easy to differentiate
them and their functions. Jesus mentions the angels as real and
active beings who, while watching over men, see the face of
the Father (Mt 18:10). Although they do not know the date
of the last judgment, which is known to the Father alone (Mt
24:36), they will be its executors (Mt 13:39, 49). They will

accompany the Son of Man at the day of His parousia (Mt 25:31). From the time of the passion they are at His service, and He can demand their intervention (Mt 26:53). The Pauline corpus tells us the angels are inferior to Jesus (Heb 2:7; 1:6), subject to Him (Ep 1:20f), created by and in and for Him (Col 1:16) and will form His escort on the last day (2 Th 1:7). Angels continue to accomplish for men the tasks attributed to them by the Old Testament. They are messengers from heaven to earth (Lk 1:19, 26: Gabriel). A heavenly group intervenes the night of the Nativity (Lk 2:9-14). Angels help Christ in the work of salvation (Heb 1:14). They guarantee the protection of men (Mt 18:10; Ac 12:15). They present to God the prayers of the saints (Rv 5:8; 8:3). They continue the fight against Satan (Rv 12:1-9).

In addition to these God-ward and man-ward functions, Karl Rahner gives the angels a cosmic function. "We cannot and do not need to think of them," he says, "as a collection of immaterial spirits . . . active in the material, human world at will, or else solely as a consequence of special divine commissions, but without any really intrinsic permanent and essential relation to the world. But the angels can be regarded as incorporeal . . . principalities and powers, essentially belonging to the world, i.e. the totality of the evolutionary spiritual and material creation; in other words as conscious (and therefore free and personal), created, finite principles of the structure of various parts of the cosmic order. . . . Wherever in nature and history instances of order, structure and meaningful patterns emerge which—at least conjecturally and when envisaged without preconceptions— do not appear to be purely mechanical, material compositions 'from below' nor to be planned and produced freely by men, and when such meaningful patterns in nature and history exhibit even for us at least traces of non-human intelligence and dyna- mism, it is meaningful to regard these as grounded on and guided by such 'principles.'. . . This does not exclude a function of the angels as guardian angels. For every spiritual being (and consequently the angels too) has a supernatural vocation and therefore each in its own way has or had a history of salvation or perdition, and so even through its natural function itself, each spiritual being is of importance for every other. . . . And if the angels' natural relation to and operation in the world has its ground in principle in their essence and not in any personal decision of theirs, it is also clear that through them as principles of partial structures of cosmic order the certainty and exactitude of the natural sciences is not called in question". . . "At the present time when people are only too ready to think it reasonable to suppose that because of the tremendous size of the cosmos there must be intelligent living beings outside the earth, men should not reject angels outright as unthinkable, provided they are not regarded as mythological furnishings of a religious heaven, but primarily as 'principalities and powers' of the cosmos" (loc. cit. 28, 29).

JUSTIFIED SOULS

Justified souls are in the heaven of God, according to the Benedictine Constitution, along with Christ and the angels, and there they enjoy the beatific vision of the divine essence. Is this the root of their happiness? Some theologians seem to root their happiness in "being with Christ," some in the "beatific vision of God," some in unending growth and progress, some in the fellowship of the blessed. Basically all seem to agree that heaven's root happiness lies in supreme union with God and with Christ and with all those who are "in Christ." But their stresses often are very different.

"To be with Christ"

This is heaven in the view of many. For this is what St. Paul stressed, what he wanted: "to leave my home in the body and make my home with the Lord" (2 Cor 5:7). And the Benedictine Constitution declared that they "are in heaven with Christ." But theologians are not sure just what it means "to be with Christ" and how this can be said to constitute a heaven of everlasting joy for men both in the interim and in the final state of mankind. Many theologians simply say it means to be "in union with Christ," in "special proximity with Christ." H. Thielicke says "being with Christ" indicates "indissoluble communion with Christ," "personal fellowship with Christ." R. Aldwinckle sees it as a conscious awareness of Christ's presence through the indwelling Spirit and a joy that comes from being in Christ and in His presence. P. Benoit views this life "with Christ" as "a new, supernatural, mysterious yet real life" drawn from a "spirit" placed in man at baptism by the new creation and the indwelling of the Spirit of Christ. In it the just retain, he thinks, "a mysterious but vital link with the risen body of Christ and find in Him the source and means of supernatural and blissful activity."

All this is good and true as far as it goes. But it does not go very far. "To be with Christ" is definitely a real aspect of heaven. But as these theologians present it, it hardly seems to constitute "heaven" as we have envisioned it. For we are already "with Christ" here on earth through faith and baptism and the Eucharist, but we are not "in heaven." The Apostles saw Him "face-to-face," walked and talked with Him, loved Him and were in intimate fellowship with Him, and were seen and loved by Him in turn while He and they were on earth, both before His resurrection and to some extent even after it, but they were not thereby "in heaven." And as R. Aldwinckle has perceptively noted, "the very idea of continued existence 'in Christ' after death can present a picture of eternal boredom which is intolerable" (op. cit. 169). "To be with Christ" must mean much more than these theologians have expressed, if it is to be a major part of our being "in heaven." Sir William Robertson Nicoll was convinced that Christ would be our great Instructor in heaven, teaching "the redeemed to love God as they have never loved Him before" (*Reunion in Eternity*, New York, 1919, p. 85). Ulrich Simon sees life in heaven as "a procession behind and the adoration of the Lamb. Where he goes, the blessed people go; whatever he does they emulate; what he wills they give" (*Heaven in the Christian Tradition*, Harper & Brothers, 1958, p. 230). "To be with Christ" in these ways is not enough to constitute heaven. And heaven must be much more than just "being with Christ." That is why the Benedictine Constitution and Catholic theologians have stressed heaven as the 'beatific vision of God.'

The beatific vision of God

The beatific vision of God Triune is the highest form of divine knowledge possible for men (and angels). It is a supreme participation in the very knowledge that God has of Himself, in the very life of God. It "deifies" men in the highest degree possible to men outside the hypostatic union. It supremely transcends the highest form of divine knowledge that a man can achieve in his pilgrim state. In his pilgrim state man can and does have various "knowledges" of God, differing in degree and intensity and extension. He can know God by "faith" quickened by "charity" and thus share in an initial degree in God's life of knowing and loving Himself. But this does not put him in heaven. He remains a pilgrim. His faith and love of God can grow more and more intense and all-pervading, but neither does this put him in heaven. Martyrs, confessors, virgins, loved God with a most intense and consuming love, but this did not put them in heaven.

The highest form of divine knowledge in man's pilgrim state is the "infused contemplation" of the true mystic. It is such a high form of divine knowledge and union that mystics find it impossible to describe it conceptually and call it ineffable. It can be transient or permanent. It can bring rapture and ecstasy. One of the best attempts at describing it, is that of J. de Guibert, S.J. in *The Theology of the Spiritual Life*. It is a sheer gift of God, he says, whereby "man feels that he is entering into immediate contact with Infinite Goodness, not as the result of his own efforts but rather as the result of a call; and this contact is without imagery, without reasoning, but not without light" (305). By his own efforts, strive as he will, a man cannot acquire it. "It consists in a deep and intense intuition that is at once simple and most rich. The will is snatched up and, as it were, held in one simple act by which it cleaves wholly to God. The experience is ineffable and either enlightenment of the mind (cherubic contemplation) or stirring of the will (seraphic contemplation) may prevail in it. It may be so intense that the soul may be more or less completely deprived of the use of the senses. It may give the keenest pleasure" (306).

The object of this infused contemplation is God Himself, and at times the Triune God. But "there is no *direct* intuition of God but only an intuition "as in a glass," as in a "mirror," through an objective medium. And this objective medium, this "mirror" in which the mystic intuits God is "the supernatural gifts already present in the soul" (i.e. sanctifying grace, the infused virtues, the gifts of the Holy Spirit). By an "infused light of contemplation" the soul is "made directly and immediately conscious of these gifts as present in it." "One must not conclude, however, that the object of infused contemplation, is not God Himself but only His gifts. . . . These gifts are only a *mirror* or medium through which the soul reaches God. It does not attain to Him by a dialectical or reasoning process but by intuition, just as, for example, when a person sees some object in a mirror, he does not fix his attention on the mirror but rather on the object seen therein. In like manner during contemplation both the mind and the will are carried to God and do not come to rest in attending to or taking pleasure in the supernatural gifts which are the medium of this contemplation" (319-320).

"There are three principal degrees of infused contemplation. 1. *Recollection and quiet*—in which the infused light shows only the supernatural character of the acts of faith and especially of charity. In this the soul feels that its *will* is passively fixed on God . . . but the intellect can still be distracted. 2. *Full union* (or simple union)—in which God lays hold of *all* the powers of the soul and renders them fully passive, so that the soul no longer has any distractions and need make no effort to preserve the union. There are two forms of this: the non-ecstatic in which the use of the external senses and the ability to move may be rendered more difficult but not wholly taken away; the ecstatic in which one may be totally deprived of them. 3. *Transforming union* (spiritual marriage, permanent union) consists in this that the soul *habitually*

experiences that God is present and acting in it: under the influence of this grace the soul cannot doubt that the Divine persons
are present in it, and it is almost never deprived of Their
company" (332-334).

But high and sublime as this mystical knowledge, love and
union with God may be, however permanent it may be, however
rapturous and ecstatic it may be, it does not put a man "in heaven."
He is still a pilgrim, a wayfarer, on his way to the heaven of the
beatific vision. For he still does not see God face-to-face: he sees
Him not as He is in Himself but as He is reflected in the mirror
of His supernatural gifts. He intuits Him at most indirectly, in
this created mirror. And while that mystical intuition can give
a man rapture through ecstatic knowledge and love of God, can
unite him most intimately with God, in it there is still between
man and God, between man's soul and mind and will and God,
an objective medium, a created mirror. Beyond this mystical
knowledge and intimacy and union with God there lies a far, far
greater knowledge and intimacy and union with God that comes
only 'in heaven,' through a man's beatific vision of God's essence
and persons.

But can man, tiny finite creature that he is compared with the
Infinite God, ever really see God face-to-face, can he ever intuit
the very essence of God directly and immediately? Gregory of
Palamas and most of the Orthodox theologians say this is impossible: in His divine essence God is absolutely unknowable and
incommunicable. Only in His divine operations and energies is He
knowable and communicable, never in His divine essence. And so
in their view the blessed only see God's light and glory and splendor, and heaven is the beatific vision of God's light and glory, not
of God as He is in Himself.

Yet the Benedictine Constitution solemnly defined that the
blessed souls in heaven "do see the divine essence" (DS 1000-
1001), and the Council of Florence, a reunion council of East and
West, solemnly defined that the blessed "see clearly the Triune
God Himself, just as He is" (DS 1305). And what is still more
staggering, the blessed do not see the divine essence and persons
in a created mirror, through an objective medium, as the pilgrim

mystics do, but they see God clearly just as He is, directly and *immediately*. For the Benedictine Constitution declared that they see "the divine essence with an intuitive and even face-to-face vision, without the interposition of any creature in the function of object seen; rather, the divine essence immediately manifests itself to them plainly, clearly, openly.... And because of this vision and enjoyment of the divine essence they are truly blessed and possess life and eternal rest . . . forever" (DS 1000-1001). If, then, mystics through their "mirror-intuition" of God can achieve an ecstatic and rapturous union with God, what must be the intimacy and intensity and rapture and ecstasy of this face-to-face vision of God in His very divine essence and persons, not just in His gifts? How very much greater must be their union with God, their love and enjoyment of God? How much greater must be their deification, their god-likeness than that of the highest mystic? What must be the height and depth of God's love for the blessed, to let them share in His divine life to this incredible degree? Nothing in man's nature and power could in any way bring about this beatific vision of God. Only God can give it to a man. Only God's ineffable love leads Him to grant this incredible share in the very life of the Triune God.

What will be the effect of this beatific vision on the blessed? May we not say it will be somewhat like the effect it has on the three divine persons? For these divine persons have this beatific vision of the divine essence and attributes in an infinitely perfect degree, and this vision is of the very essence of God Triune. If they have an infinitely perfect knowledge of the divine essence and of themselves, then they also have an infinitely perfect love of the divine essence and persons. And this infinite knowing, loving, enjoying, is the very life of the Triune God, and it makes the three persons endlessly and infinitely happy. The blessed, then, who share the very life of God, not only see the Father, Son and Holy Spirit face-to-face but share endlessly in their love and joy, their divine happiness.

Heaven, then, means for the blessed a completely new dimension of life and a completely new dimension of love. A life and a love that fulfills all their desires, all the "reaches" of their spiritual nature. And as they now, so we one day will see God as He sees Himself. We will love Him as He loves Himself. We will enjoy Him as He enjoys Himself. And we will be loved by God in turn with a love that is higher, deeper, richer, more intense than His love for the greatest saint or mystic on earth, with a love that will go on throughout eternity, with a love that will never diminish. There will be a reciprocal love between us and God of an intensity that we in our present condition can not imagine, but which will make us utterly impeccable. Long ago St. Augustine said it beautifully: "Thou hast made us for thyself, O God, and our hearts are restless till they rest in Thee." In the beatific vision, love and enjoyment of God, the blessed find their eternal rest, their eternal fulfillment.

What will the blessed see?

The mystics do not seem to "intuit" much of God. But the blessed will see the very essence of God, the infinite divinity that makes God to be God. They will see the attributes of God, God's goodness and holiness, His mercy and His justice, not as abstract concepts but in the fullness of their concrete divine realization and harmony. They will see the Three Divine Persons in themselves and in their relations to one another and to us and to our world. They will see creative love of God pouring itself out on the world of men and things. They will see His salvific will and love at work, gracing and calling men to respond to His grace and love. They will see His fatherly providence at work in hidden and mysterious ways, drawing men in the Spirit, through the Son to the Father, so that ultimately all may be one with one another and with the God of love, Father, Son and Holy Spirit. They will *see* the mysteries they believed as pilgrims, the Incarnation, the Redemption, Grace, the Eucharist, the other sacraments of union with Christ and His Church, the Church, the Mystical Body of Christ, the Communion of Saints. They will see God as the infinite fullness of all being, the ground of creation, growth, consummation of the world; as the fullness of beauty, goodness, holiness, power, majesty, glory. At the first unveiling of God's essence and beauty and glory they will be caught up in ecstatic contemplation of God and in supreme union with God. Eternity will never change this ecstatic union, never dim the light of it, never diminish the love and the joy of it. There will be a never-ending freshness to their vision and love and enjoyment of God, because that is the way it is with God's vision and love and enjoyment of Himself, and the blessed will eternally share that life of God, each in his or her way and degree.

What else are the blessed doing in heaven now—in this interim state of mankind? This is not an easy question to answer, for the matter is wrapped in mystery. The essence of heaven for them now as throughout all eternity is the beatific vision. Is there any other activity for them, whether they are disembodied souls or re-embodied souls? W. M. Smith thinks that "perhaps the first great and continuous activity for the redeemed will be worship of the Triune God" (op. cit. 190). For the book of Revelation tells us that "a voice came forth from the throne saying, Give praise to our God, all ye his servants, ye that fear him, the small and the great. And I heard as it were the voice of a great multitude, and as the voice of many waters, and as the voice of mighty thunders, saying, Alleluia: for the Lord, our God, the Almighty, reigneth. Let us rejoice and be exceeding glad, and let us give the glory unto him" (Rv 19:5-7). "And they sing the song of Moses, the servant of God, and the song of the Lamb, saying, 'Great and wonderful are thy deeds, O Lord God the Almighty! Just and true are thy ways, O King of the Ages'" (Rv 15:3). Archbishop Whately stresses the fellowship of the blessed: "The highest enjoyment doubtless to the blest will be the personal knowledge of their great and beloved Master. Yet I cannot but think that some part of their happiness will consist in an intimate knowledge of the greatest of His followers also" (R. Whately, *A Future State*, 1857, pp. 117-118). Such fellowship, with Our Lord, Our Lady, the Saints and Angels, with relatives and friends, would definitely seem to be a part of the heavenly happiness of the blessed—even now in the interim state. If they have an interim embodiment, communication would be no problem. If they are disembodied souls, communication would still be quite feasible by some form of telepathy and clairvoyance. And fellowship could go on and on—with further and further opportunities to meet more and more persons and to make more and more friendships. Friendship is something every man longs for. To have real friends, true friends, is a heart-hunger in all of us. And so few real friends do we find and keep in this pilgrim life of ours. Even in the interim state there will be an endless opportunity to make friends, keep them, meet them again and again. One of the deepest hungers in the heart of every man can find endless satisfaction even in the interim state. Does this mean there can be *progress* and *growth* in the interim state?

Older theologians loved to define and analyze heaven and to stress its *"static"* dimension of achieved *"immobility"* of mind and will. They defined it as "a state made perfect by the accumulation of all good things" (Boethius) or as "the ultimate perfection of rational or intellectual nature" (Aquinas). They distinguished essential and accidental beatitude and the primary and secondary object of the beatific vision. They admitted the need of a "light of glory" for this vision, but disagreed over the nature and function of this light of glory. They maintained that the blessed see God intuitively but they denied that they could comprehend Him. However they found it very difficult to explain how the blessed could see the utterly simple God intuitively and yet not comprehend Him. They held that perfect beatitude must include our will as well as our intellect, and must involve supreme love and enjoyment as well as vision of God, but they disagreed over assigning the primacy: to intellect or to will? to vision or to love? More recently some theologians were busily engaged in explaining the beatific vision metaphysically, in terms of created actuation by Uncreated Act (de la Taille) or by quasi-formal causality (K. Rahner).

But recently the thought has been growing that a metaphysical analysis of the beatific vision may have interest and value for a metaphysician but very little for anyone else. The thought that a heavy stress on the *immobility* of heavenly beatitude, on the eternal and unchangeable fixation of our mind and will on God and on a perfect happiness that will never increase or decrease, may have value and interest for some Western theologians but very little for anyone else. What attraction can all this have for so-called 'contemporary man,' for whom the major and supremely satisfying part of real life and living is *mobility* and not immobility, *activity* and not rest, *growth* and *progress* and not satiety, striving and achieving and not just retaining, personal growth and fulfillment and not personal fixity and sameness? Modern man wants a heaven that is *dynamic* and not static, a heaven that permits an eternal growth in knowing and loving God and people and things, music and art and science, a heaven where each one can make progress in knowing and loving and doing, where each one can strive and achieve down the endless "years" of eternity.

Is such a heaven possible? If heaven is the satisfaction of every rational desire, then it would seem that it must be not only possible but supremely actual. If an older concept of eternity will not permit this, then modern man seems quite willing to reject or modernize this old concept. Some Protestant theologians have already started to move in this direction. They are stressing heaven as an expanded opportunity, and they think this aspect of heaven can be found in the best theologians of the past. For these modern theologians heaven is not merely a static reward but an expanded opportunity for active service. They view heaven in evolutionary terms and hence it is much more dynamic (and in process?) and gives real opportunity for constant and genuine moral growth and activity. In this heaven change and variety and individuality have free scope, and progress is a reality. Since God is creative love, creative love becomes central in their vision of God and of his saints. Such a view of heaven is very attractive and its basic idea of heaven as an expanded and expanding opportunity for growth in knowing, loving, giving, doing, living, deserves sympathetic consideration. But it needs further study, especially with regard to its concept of "moral growth," for if this means there can be a radical change of status and a basic increase in grace and glory, then the view is unacceptable.

A recent Catholic theologian has been moving in this same direction. Disturbed by a widespread modern indifference to heaven, he feels that this may in part be due to our failure to relate heaven to ordinary life and experience, and to our over-emphasis of certain aspects of heaven that have little appeal today. The concept of *immobility*, he declares, needs to be correctly understood so that heaven will be viewed as essentially an infinite dynamism. In it our initial fulfillment itself will extend our scope and make us more than we are so that we can then be filled even more by the illimitable. Our eternity will be a continual advance further into God. Everything static in heaven will be drawn into a limitless dynamism extending without end. Beatitude will be eternal transformation (L. Boros, *Living in Hope*, 81ff.). There are some good points in this view, but also weaknesses. There is no distinction between heaven in the interim state and in the final state, and many of the statements need considerable qualifi-cation, so that there is a proper balance between the immobile and the mobile elements of heaven and between traditional truth and contemporary appeal.

Another Catholic theologian offers us a heaven for the "mod-ern Catholic." "When time and history are not viewed as terrors," he writes, "but as mediums of human development, heaven will not be viewed as eternal and static perfection. Heaven will be a time for continued growth and moral progress. The project of each man's life which is begun in this world demands more time to develop. In fact, many people cannot conceive of human hap-piness except in terms of growth . . . A heaven where progress is possible seems to appeal to modern man. Heaven conceived as eternal reflects the cultural ideal of static perfection: heaven con-ceived as temporal reflects the cultural ideal of human develop-ment . . . Where interpersonal relationships and family ties are highly valued, heaven is a family and friend reunion . . . Heaven is not only man in union with God but man in communion with other men" (John Shea, *What a Modern Catholic Believes about Heaven and Hell*, pp. 86, 87).

What is to be said of such a heaven? Of this presentation of heaven? This heaven is very attractive, but the presentation seems a bit theologically immature. For it builds too heavily on the principle: give modern man the kind of heaven he wants. In the past theologians gave the men of their times the kind of heaven they wanted, a static heaven. That was bad. So today theologians should give modern man what he wants, a dynamic heaven. That is good. It may seem good, but it is low-grade theology. The theologian is not there to cater to the wishes of modern man. He is there to give him as much theological truth as he can, whether he likes it or not. 'Modern man' has come and gone many times before today. Very likely he will come and go many more times before the end of the world. What appeals to modern man today may not appeal to the modern men of the future. But apart from this unhappy stress on what appeals to modern man, this view of heaven has very much in its favor. Too often the way heaven was presented in the past, it seemed to many to be merely a "place of eternal boredom," with no real "living," with no real growth, with no real developmental activity. An eternity of unchanging contemplation and love and nothing else seemed too little suited to offer men, men of every time, a glorious destiny and fulfillment. It is not surprising that many men chose to build their own heaven on earth. That is why these new trends toward a more 'dynamic heaven' are very good. For a heaven of ever-lasting happiness is man's destiny, and it should not be down-graded. Too much stress in the past on a static and immobile heaven tended to do just that. A more dynamic heaven is worth pondering today. But with a note of caution to today's theologians—not to repeat the error of the past. For if past theologians "built" a heaven that was too static, all-static, there is a danger that today's theologians will build a heaven that is too dynamic, all-dynamic. There is danger that in his hurried effort to stress "mobility" he will eliminate "immobility." Rather regularly in God's plan, it seems, there is a synthesis of opposites, not the elimination of opposites. In man He has put an element of perma-nence and an element of transience, an element of immateriality and an element of materiality. We should not be surprised, then, to find Him building into heaven an element of immobility as well as an element of mobility.

But is such a heaven of growth and progress compatible with what Sacred Scripture and the Church's magisterium have taught us about heaven? A tentative answer seems to be definitely: *Yes.* Nowhere do they seem to have taught that heaven will mean total immobility for man. Nowhere do they seem to have taught that heaven is totally static. They definitely seem to have affirmed or implied that there will be in heaven an element of immobility and an element of mobility, an element of immobility in the union of the blessed with God, an element of mobility in the communion of the blessed with one another. And there seems to be no solid reason so far adduced why immobility and mobility, why eternity and succession, why timelessness and timefulness cannot be harmonized. Immobility can still mean that the blessed are immovably and impeccably attached to God by an unending vision and love of His essence and person. But this need not exclude mobility, growth, progress in an ever-deeper awareness of God's ongoing creative love, an ever greater growth in friendships and fellowship, an ever greater growth in scientific mathematical, philosophical, theological, historical, geographical knowledge through converse with experts in these fields who are gathered together in the heaven of the interim state. Immobility will mean that the blessed will never be able to lose their essential union with God and their essential impeccability. Mobility will mean they can go on growing, learning, doing, loving more and more things and people, striving, achieving, each in his own way and at his own pace and in the direction he wishes. For if the maturing or growth process in purgatory need not mean growth in grace, merit or degree of glory, why should it mean this for the growth process in heaven?

Why should the blessed not be both perfected and yet ever further perfectible? Perfected by the beatific vision and love that unite them to God in an unbreakable beatific union? Perfectible in terms of an ever greater use and development of all their human powers of mind and will? Eternally they will rest in God and nothing will ever disturb or destroy this rest. Successively they will strive and achieve greater and greater knowledge—both theoretical and practical—in a thousand different areas and ways. Successively they will strive for and achieve greater and greater love of thousands and thousands of very different persons. Successively they will develop their personality to a greater and greater degree by greater and greater interpersonal relationships with other persons.

Must we continue to be bound by a static—and unproved—idea of perfection that is achieved in the first instant of heaven and can never grow thereafter? Why not admit a deep down union of mind and soul with God in terms of the beatific vision and love of God that will never change, and at the same time that the human mind of the blessed in its active, productive, ever-perfectible reaches and powers will go on growing and changing throughout eternity? Must we continue to be bound by a rigid concept of an absolutely unchangeable eternal and timeless instant as the distinctive characteristic of heavenly as opposed to earthly life? Why not admit a timeless, unchanging, eternal union of the blessed with God in terms of the beatific vision, and at the same time admit a constant change, growth in the mind's and will's use of its active and productive powers?

Why not let God be an eternal Builder of an ever more glorious world of men and things? If He is creative love why not let Him go on with His work of loving creation throughout eternity? Is there a limit beyond which He cannot build the blessed into ever more perfect sons of God? Ever more perfect in the reach and use of their minds and wills? If the beatific vision gives them their essential perfection of union with the Triune God in the first instant of heaven, must it also be a limit-perfection beyond which God cannot build the blessed into ever more perfect sons and daughters of God? Why cannot He 'father' them more and more down the 'years of eternity' with more and more of His paternal creative love? If by the beatific vision He grants them a share in His divine contemplative and amative life, why should He not go on granting them a share in His creative, building life, so that they go on through eternity being co-creators with God of an ever better world of men and things? Wouldn't God as their Father want this? Wouldn't God as their Brother want this? Wouldn't God as their Friend want this? And what God wants He will do. Would this make God a God in process, as some of the radical process theologians want? No. As far as His divinity is concerned, God is not in process: He is necessary and unchanging. Else He was not and is not the same God yesterday, today, forever. But where His freedom intervenes, He may well be regarded as a God in process. A God in process of endlessly 'creating,' 'building' a better and better world. A God in process of building ever more perfect human sons and daughters of God not all by Himself, but in loving cooperation with these sons and daughters united to Him inseparably by their beatific vision and love of His essence and persons.

There is still another question. A minor question, perhaps, but fascinating. Is heaven a "place?" And "where" is heaven? Some seem to think these are pointless questions. But are they? The New Testament regularly uses spatial terms in talking of heaven: "Behold the heavens were opened and he saw the Spirit of God descending like a dove... and a voice from heaven saying, 'This is my beloved Son, with whom I am well pleased'" (Mt 3:16-17); "No one has ascended into heaven but he who descended from heaven, the Son of Man" (Jn 3:13); "This Jesus, who was taken up from you into heaven, will come in the same way as you saw Him go into heaven" (Ac 1:11). So do the Creeds: "He ascended into heaven, sits at the right hand of God the Father almighty; from there he shall come to judge the living and the dead" (DS 30; cf. DS 125). So does the Benedictine Constitution (DS 1000-1001). So do the Councils of Lyons II (DS 857) and Florence (DS 1305).

Does this use of spatial terms prove that heaven is a "place"? Of course not. For it is to be expected that Scripture, Creeds and Councils would use the spatial and temporal images that were in vogue in their days, so that they might make their message intelligible to their readers. But neither does this use of the spatial terms of an antiquated cosmology prove that heaven is not a place, in some sense of the term "place." For the blessed are not nowhere. They are somewhere, they are some place. They are with God and with Christ and His Blessed Mother, gathered together in a mutual fellowship of knowing and loving and enjoying and doing. They are in some "trans-empirical" place or dimension that does not conform spatially to our "up-there" or "out-there." They are somewhere, not in the manner in which we are "here" but in a manner that corresponds to the way they are· "there." Karl Rahner seems to admit this, though rather grudgingly. For he writes: "If (and so far as) we cannot think of the psychical nature and concreteness of the risen and real person . . . any other way than together with a definite spatial and local determination, then we must think of heaven as a place and not merely as a 'state.' In so far as there are already human beings (the risen Lord, Our Lady and no doubt others: cf. Mt 27:52) who possess a glorified bodily nature, *this place* does already exist as a result, even if not as the presupposition (as the ancients thought) of this transformation of the incarnate spirit.... (But) we do not need to accommodate those in heaven in the physical world system of our experience" (*Theological Investigations* II, Helicon Press, Baltimore, 1963, pp. 214, 215). And we might add that if the blessed are not disembodied souls but re-embodied in an interim embodiment, then there is all the more reason for saying that heaven is a "place."

Can we go a step further and ask *where* heaven is? And *where* it will be at the "end of the world"? Karl Rahner says "it is a priori senseless to ask where heaven is if by this 'where' we are to understand a location in *our* physical spatial world" (ibid. 215). Perhaps it is senseless to ask where heaven is "in our physical world" (though some seem to think it is not as senseless as K. R. thinks). But why should we not ask *where* heaven is? For if heaven is a "place," then it is somewhere, some place either in our world or in another world. And why not in "our world"? Who knows the limits of our world? And all the possible dimensions of our world? And all the possible ways of "being in" our world?

Some theologians used to say heaven is "everywhere," just as God is everywhere. For where God is, they argued, there is heaven, the heaven of God. And in a sense they were correct, for where God is—in a very special way—there is heaven. But they were wrong in thinking that God was everywhere—present everywhere—in that very special way. He is not. He is present in that very special way only to the blessed who are in the company of Christ and His Mother in what we call the "heaven of God." That is *where* the heaven of God is, where the glory of God transfigures them and shines out in all its splendor, where they are "at home with Christ" and His Mother and in the beatific company of the angels and saints, in the radiant glory of the triune God. That is *where* heaven is now.

But *where* will heaven be at the end of the world? If we broaden our concept of heaven a bit, we can say that in the final state of mankind heaven will be wherever the blessed can be. For in the blessed there will always be the beatific vision of God, which is their "essential heaven," their "essential and inamissible happiness." So wherever they may be, they will be in "this heaven of the beatific vision." But where can the blessed be at the end of "this world," in the final eternal state of mankind? It would seem that they could be *in three places,* in the heaven of God where many are now, in the "new heavens and the new earth" (the transfigured cosmos) that the parousiac Christ will initiate at the end of the world, and in the "New Jerusalem" that will come down from heaven at the end of the world, as we shall indicate more fully later on when we consider the final state of mankind that the parousiac Christ will initiate when He comes again at the end of "this world." The "new heavens and the new earth" will not be just a transfigured planet earth and its atmosphere, but the entire universe with all its galactic systems, transfigured to make it a fitting abode for glorified humanity. The "New Jerusalem" that the Book of Revelation proclaims, will not, we think, be just a bit of apocalyptic imagery but a glorious reality underlying this imagery which will constitute the religious center of the entire universe. The "new heavens and the new earth" and the "New Jerusalem" will not be the heaven of God, because the supreme glory and presence of God will not be manifest in them. But they will be heaven or heavenly places or extensions of the heaven of God, because God will be specially and beatifically present to the blessed, basically and interiorly in terms of the beatific vision of the triune God, but also in some sense exteriorly because the countenance of the triune God will shine through a cosmos no longer opaque but now transparent to the glory and radiance of God.

And so those old theologians who said heaven was everywhere were very nearly right. Heaven is not everywhere now, it is true, but at the end of this world, in the final state of mankind, heaven will be everywhere, for God will be very specially present to the blessed everywhere, no matter where they may choose to go, no matter what they may choose to do.

Deep in the hearts and the souls of every man God has put a hope, a desire for "what no eye has seen, nor ear heard, nor the heart of man conceived," the eternal life and happiness that "God has prepared for those who love him" (1 Cor 2:9). In the long days of eternity that desire will be fulfilled in the threefold heaven of the Triune God.

PART V
The Mystery of the Final State

Chapter 10
Is There a General Resurrection of All Men at the End of the World?

Is there a final state of mankind that is distinct and different from the interim state of men that we have just studied? Or is the interim state already man's final state? Some writers seem to think it is, because at death man goes "out of time" and into "eternity," and obviously eternity is man's final state. But we do not understand "final state" in that way. For us final state means the state of man after the end of the world. And the end of this world has not yet come. For at the end of the world come the general resurrection, the parousia, the general judgment, the "new heaven and new earth" and the "New Jerusalem." None of these has yet come. And so the end of the world has not yet come and interim man is not yet in the final state of existence that will be his throughout the ages of eternity.

Precisely when the end of this world will come it is impossible to determine. It may be in the far, far distant future as we reckon time. So some scholars think. It may be not far off. So think some charismatics and healers. But whenever it comes, it will be brought about by God and not by man: that seems to be the biblical view. Then all the dead will rise again. Christ will come again, to judge all men. And establish the eternal kingdom of God with a new heaven and a new earth and a new Jerusalem. This will be the final state of man. Such is the Christian hope, the Christian teaching.

Then man's pilgrim world will come to an end. History will reach its fulfilment and its divinely appointed goal. The Day of Yahweh that Israel looked for will arrive. The Day of the Lord that Paul wrote of will come. Man's history will come to an end, not man himself, but the history of empirical man in his time-space world. Man's pilgrim state and man's interim state will come to an end. Man's final state will begin and continue throughout the endless reaches of eternity. And in this final state of man, Christ, the Lord of history, will be manifest everywhere in the radiance of His glorified humanity.

What will be the first phase of this final state? Will it be the resurrection of the dead, or the parousia, or the general judgment? To talk of a "first phase" may seem to some to be absurd or presumptuous. And yet what else can we do? Three such tremendous "events" can hardly be treated together. It may well be true that the "final judgment must be seen as one with the consummation of the world and history as a whole: as an intrinsic moment of the parousia of Christ and the resurrection of the flesh" (K. Rahner, *Sacramentum Mundi* 4, 345). Yet *we* must assign a priority, we must distinguish a "before" and an "after." And if we do, the resurrection of the dead very likely must come first. Though it might seem that the parousia of Christ should come first, if we take literally what we profess in the Athanasian Creed: "At His coming, all men are to arise with their own bodies" (DS 76). But it seems fairly logical to say that the parousia of Christ presupposes the resurrection of the dead, if Christ will come again to judge the "living and the dead." So we start our consideration of the final state of man with a study of the resurrection of the dead.

History

If we look at History we find that belief in a resurrection of the dead long antedates the Incarnation of Christ. In early Egypt there was a belief that Osiris, son of the earth-god and the heaven-goddess, was killed by his brother Seth but thanks to the help of various gods he was brought back to life. In the pre-dynastic periods the faithful of Osiris hoped to be born again with the god in his Western paradise. Though the nature of this resurrection is not entirely clear, it seems to have implied a "resurrection of a corpse" and a return to much the same kind of life that was enjoyed before death. In ancient Greece in the 6th century B.C. reincarnation was taught by Pythagoras, the Orphics and Plato. This doctrine obviously involved a resurrection, but not a resurrection in the same body, not a resuscitation of a corpse. And it involved an often very long series of successive reincarnations or resurrections in different bodies. But all these reincarnations took place, it seemed, on planet earth, and were subjected to the space-time limitations of this empirical world of ours. Ancient Semitic literature has been thought to show some indications of a belief in a resurrection of the dead. For eminent personages like Ishtar and Gilgamesh were thought to have returned from hell or almost to have achieved immortality. But in the religious literature found through discoveries of Ras-Shamra, a literature whose redaction antedates the Bible and which offers evidence about the religion of a Semitic branch adjacent to the Hebrews, so far nothing decisively favoring belief in the resurrection of the dead has been found. And the impression left by this Semitic literature is that, if one as powerful as the goddess Ishtar or the hero Gilgamesh only escape death by great suffering, then there was no hope that men could ever escape from the grip of the infernal powers. Thus there would be little or no trace of a general resurrection of the dead in this Semitic literature.[1]

Old Testament

If we turn to the Word of God in the Old Testament we find a few instances of resurrection as the resuscitation of a corpse and return from death to pilgrim life, in the stories of Elijah (1 K 17:17-24) and Elisha (2 K 4:18-37; 13:20ff). But only very late in the Old Testament do we find indications of a resurrection to a new and immortal form of life, perhaps due to a general Old Testament silence about an afterlife, or to the Hebrew conception of man that could envisage no afterlife that was not a restoration of life to the body. The first clear affirmation of a resurrection of the body is found in Daniel 12:2-3:

"many of those who sleep in the land of dust shall awake, some to everlasting life, others to everlasting reproach and horror." In 2 M is attested this same belief in a resurrection but only for the righteous, not for the wicked: "we shall be raised up by him, whereas for you there is no resurrection, no new life" (7:9, 14). From this time on a doctrine of resurrection became the common heritage of Judaism and was professed by the Pharisees and the sect that produced the book of Enoch, but denied by the Sadducees (Ac 23:8; Mt 22:23-28).

New Testament

It is in the New Testament, however, that a doctrine of resurrection stands out in full clarity: a doctrine of a twofold resurrection—that of Christ Himself at Easter, and that of all men at the end of the world. The resurrection of Christ is the central event of salvation history. It is the principle of the resurrection of the Christian to the eternal life of glory. It is a basic doctrine of our Christian faith and hope, affirmed by ecumenical creeds and councils of Christendom. So we study it first with two main questions in mind. Did the resurrection of Christ really take place? Can we demonstrate it historically?

THE RESURRECTION OF JESUS

Today the resurrection of Jesus is widely questioned. Was His resurrection really a historical fact, a fact within the reach of modern historical method? And if it was not such a historical event, was it still a real event, something that really happened long ago? Was it a real event that solidly justifies and grounds our traditional faith?

Protestant Theologians

Protestant theologians are divided in their answers. Some are very negative in their response, others are a bit more positive. For Schubert Ogden the bodily resurrection of Jesus would be no more relevant to my salvation than that the carpenter next door just drove a nail in a two-by-four. R. Bultmann denies that the Resurrection is an event which can be proven historically and which occurred the morning of Easter in Jerusalem. He finds an historical fact that involves a resurrection from the dead to be utterly inconceivable. J. Moltmann thinks that leading historians today are in general more open to the historical reliability of the resurrection testimonies, so much so in fact that even the tradition of the empty tomb cannot be quickly dismissed as purely legendary and with no historical core whatever. R. Aldwinckle writes that "the case has not and cannot be closed on the basis of what modern science has said or some positivistic philosophies believe to be the case. . . . Scientific views are themselves subject to constant change and modification. . . . Jesus' resurrection is, to say the least, appropriate to a life and death of such universal significance" (op. cit. 67).

Catholic Theologians

Catholic views today also differ notably from older positions. The older manualists were strongly intent on proving the historicity of Christ's resurrection and on showing that it was a supreme sign of His divine mission. They thought that Christ's resurrection could be demonstrated to be a fact of the historical order (DS 3436). One of the later manualists, J. M. Hervé, maintained that we can get historical certainty of the fact of Jesus' resurrection if we properly prove two points: (1) that Christ truly died and (2) was recalled from death to life in His own proper body. He set about proving this from various "facts": the fact that Christ had predicted His resurrection, the fact of the empty tomb, the fact of the apparitions, the fact of the change in the Apostles and the conversion of the Gentiles, the fact of the testimony of Paul and the Evangelists.[2]

Among more recent Catholic theologians, however, Hervé's conviction that the resurrection of Jesus is historically demonstrable seems largely absent. H. R. Schlette says that the exegetes do not know, nobody knows what occurred at Easter: "I am of the opinion that from methodical grounds it is completely impossible to make historically certain statements concerning what occurred after the death of Jesus and led to the resurrection of faith. I also think that there is little prospect that this uncertainty will be eliminated."[3] J. J. Smith merely says of Jesus' resurrection: "In the language of the historian, it is therefore probably historical."[4] G. Lohfink is cautious in his summation of the resurrection of Jesus: "it is not a 'resurrection' but an 'eschatological event'. . . . As an eschatological event, the actual occurrence of the resurrection does not belong to our empirical space-time world. . . . Our historical considerations have yielded some facts which cannot be explained away—the empty tomb and the appearance phenomena. These facts neither prove nor disprove the resurrection of Jesus. But the data are at least open to the resurrection."[5]

Pere Benoit goes a bit further: "the tradition of the finding of the empty tomb is of great value: it is not a suspect and late invention; it is a primitive datum which can really, with the subsequent apparitions, justify and ground the Christian faith."[6] Werner Bulst and Joseph Schmitt seem to agree that although the Gospels and Acts and Pauline Corpus do not prove that the resurrection of Jesus was a truly historical event, they still offer a very adequate testimony to the fact of the resurrection (*Sacramentum Mundi* 5, 324-329). Hans Küng writes that whether we assert or deny the historicity of the empty tomb, "we all agree that by itself it does not furnish proof of the resurrection. Christian faith appeals to encounters with the living Christ Himself rather than to the empty tomb." To the question whether the Christian belief in the resurrection can "be made psychologically and historically plausible without supposing the appearances," his answer is No. "All the banal psychological explanations contradict what the text itself tenaciously maintains: that the Crucified lives and has shown Himself as Lord to His disciples, that with Him the new time has dawned for the world, that His person and cause belong not to the past but to the present. This is why the disciples believed. From whatever text we start, we invariably come to a radically new encounter of the disciples with the living Jesus after His death. The appearances mean that the resurrection has occurred and the risen Jesus has made Himself known."[7]

What, then, can we conclude from this biblical evidence and commentary? It seems that we cannot make historically certain statements about Jesus' resurrection, if by "historically certain statements" we mean those which can be established by modern historical methods to the satisfaction of modern historians. For if the term "historical" is "limited to what can be established by historical method," E. Pousset, notes, "then the resurrection is not historical because it is the act of passing from death to eternal life and can therefore be known only by faith."[8] But if the term "historical," as E. Pousset likewise notes, "can also apply to anything which happened" (ibid.), then we can say that "at least it is historically demonstrable that the apostles were convinced that they had 'seen' Jesus and that they conclude on the basis of this seeing that Jesus had risen" (H. Ebert, *Die Krise des Osterglaubens*, 312) and that "Jesus' resurrection is therefore probably historical" (J. J. Smith, loc. cit.).

In the matter of the "empty tomb," two things stand out. It is not pure legend as R. Bultmann said, nor can it be demonstrated to be a fact of the historical order as easily as J. M. Hervé thought. But with Pere Benoit we can say: "the tradition of the finding of the empty tomb is of great value; it is not a suspect and late invention; it is a primitive datum which can really, with the subsequent apparitions, justify and ground the Christian faith" (loc. cit.).

More decisive than the empty tomb are the "appearances." For the fact of these appearances "and their essential content are indisputable, though the place and number and sequence of the appearances are uncertain" (W. Bulst, loc. cit.). When we add to them the radical change, the unshakable certainty and readiness for sacrifice that they produced in the apostles and the effect they had on the conversion of the Gentiles and the establishment of the Church, they simply cannot be explained as purely subjective visions. There had to be some "objectivity" to them that can only be adequately explained by some kind of objective resurrection of Jesus from the dead.

Jesus' resurrection was not a simple "resuscitation," it was a "transformational" resurrection. Jesus did not rise in precisely the same material, spatial body that He had before He died. Nor did He rise in a completely new material, spatial body of the same kind that He had before He died. He did not rise in a body simply belonging to this spatial-temporal world. But He did rise in a real body that was a corporeal reality and to some extent in identity and continuity with His former body. He arose in a real body "that was not subject to the usual limitations of our space-time world" (Schmitt, loc. cit.).

And it was Jesus who appeared to the apostles in this "risen body," the same Jesus they had known before He died. He was the same Jesus but different. The same in personal identity and mind and will and soul, but different in body. The Apostles did not immediately recognize Him, it is true. But He was the same Jesus and He could and did identify Himself to the satisfaction of the apostles who had known Him before He died, and even to the satisfaction of Paul who had been an opponent of Christ and had not known Him before He died.

And so the New Testament shows us, if we come to it with open minds, that Jesus' resurrection was a real though eschatological event, that it was assured by credible witnesses and that it solidly justifies and grounds our traditional Christian faith.

The Church

Creeds and Councils of the Church solemnly affirm this biblical belief in the resurrection of Jesus to be a fundamental truth of the Christian faith. The resurrection of Jesus in His glorified body is posited in all the professions of faith from the beginning (DS 11, 12; 44; 72; 76; 125: 801; 852; 1338; 1862). The resurrection of Jesus, as Karl Rahner notes, is the central theme of faith itself (1 Cor 15:17ff.), in that it is the perfect accomplishment of God's saving action for the world and for man. . . . All this involves an absolute mystery of faith in the strict sense. The resurrection has both a Christological and a soteriological aspect. Christologically, Jesus with His whole, and therefore His corporeal, reality rose to perfect fulfillment in glory and immortality (in contradistinction to bringing back a dead man to life). This was properly His because of His passion and death, which produced this concrete fulfillment by intrinsic necessity. Since Jesus' death and resurrection form a single event, the phases of which are inseparably interconnected (Lk 24:26, 46; Rm 4:25; 6:4ff.), it is not a mythical expression but the actual truth, when Scripture and tradition view the resurrection as the objective acceptance of Jesus' sacrificial death, which belongs to the essence of the sacrifice itself. Soteriologically, Jesus' resurrection is not only in the ideal order an "exemplary cause" of the *resurrection of all*, but objectively is the beginning of the transfiguration of the world as an ontologically interconnected occurrence.... And his return will only be the disclosure of this relation to the world attained in his resurrection (*Sacramentum Mundi 5*, 331-333).

GENERAL RESURRECTION AT THE END OF THE WORLD

Just as the Christian creeds professed a belief in the resurrection of Jesus, so they professed a belief in the resurrection of men at the end of the world. This doctrine was held by the Eastern and the Western Church, by Catholics and by Protestants. Fathers and theologians defended it against pagans and Gnostics and Manicheans, against the Albigenses and Cathari, against Materialists and Rationalists. Unbelievers often derided this resurrection as ridiculous and as scientifically impossible, as a product of wishful thinking. But it remained one of the distinctive marks of Christians. Until recent times. For not long ago Dr. Schubert Ogden wrote: "But what I must refuse to accept, precisely as a Christian theologian, is that belief in our subjective existence after death is in some way a necessary article of Christian belief" (*The Reality of God and Other Essays*, p. 230).

For most Christians today, however, the resurrection of the dead seems still to be an article of faith. Adventists, Mormons, Lutherans generally believe in a literal resurrection of the dead. While Baptists do not seem to maintain a literal resurrection of the body, they do hold that a man's distinct identity and personality will always exist. Episcopalians, Methodists, Presbyterians seem to agree substantially that there will be a resurrection of the dead in a spiritual body that will be continuous with but not identical to the body laid in the grave. Eastern Orthodox Christians believe in the resurrection of the body and that the resurrected bodies will be like that of our Lord after His resurrection. Roman Catholics generally believe that all the dead will rise again with their bodies on the Last Day. Some liberal Protestants deny the resurrection of the flesh but hold that our personal identity persists in a different kind of body. The more radical of these say the soul need not wait till Judgment Day for its new organism: at death it receives "that body that shall be." Thus they can abandon the whole apparatus of the general resurrection and the last judgment.

Many, many questions have been raised about the resurrection of the dead at the end of the world. But today there is a preliminary question that must be considered. In our study of the interim state of man we noted a tendency among a few Protestant and Catholic theologians to posit an immediate resurrection at death, based largely on the assumption that the soul cannot exist without a body. And so at death, it is said, the soul receives a "new embodiment" that fits it for ongoing existence and activity in the interim state. J. M. Shaw posited such an immediate resurrection at death but in such a way as apparently to do away with an interim state and with a resurrection at the end of the world. Russell Aldwinckle also posited an immediate "embodiment" or "resurrection at death," but in his view this embodiment is only an 'interim embodiment' and so does not eliminate the general resurrection at the end of the world. Among Catholic theologians Ladislas Boros stands out, for he too opts for an interim state of immediate but initial resurrection at death, followed at the end of time by a final and complete resurrection in a transfigured universe.

What is to be said of these views? If we measure their acceptability by their compatibility with the traditional dogma of a general resurrection at the end of the world, then the positions of R. Aldwinckle and L. Boros are acceptable, that of J. M. Shaw is not. For both Aldwinckle and Boros admit a general resurrection at the end of the world and try to harmonize it with their "immediate resurrection at death." Shaw does not. That a general resurrection at the end of the world is a dogma, is a part of the traditional faith of the Church, seems to be beyond doubt. For we read in the Apostles' Creed, "I believe . . . in the resurrection of the body, and life everlasting" (DS 30); in the Niceno-Constantinopolitan Creed, "We expect the resurrection of the dead and the life of the world to come" (DS 150); in the Athanasian Creed, "At his coming, all men are to arise with their own bodies, and they are to give an account of their lives" (DS 76). The Fourth Lateran Council declared, "He (Christ) will come at the end of the world; He will judge the living and the dead; and He will reward all, both the lost and the elect, according to their works. And all these will rise with their own bodies which they now have so that they may receive according to their works . . . the wicked a perpetual punishment with the devil; the good, eternal glory with Christ" (DS 801). And we find the same profession in Lyons II (DS 854) and in the Benedictine Constitution (DS 1002).

But today the question and the attack turn largely on Sacred Scripture. Does Scripture really teach a general resurrection at the end of the world? In the past, of course, it was generally *assumed* to teach this. But was this assumption largely the consequence of the dogmatic pronouncements? Did not theologians turn to Scripture merely to find there the general resurrection they were looking for, and so of course find it there? Today if we look at the Scripture merely in its own light, will we find there a resurrection of the dead at the end of time, and a general resurrection that involves all men, the wicked as well as the good? Perhaps we should add that we are concerned with resurrection not "as the restoration of a deceased person to the conditions of the present life," but as "the conferring upon the deceased of a new and permanent form of life."

Old Testament

Does the Old Testament tell us there will be a general resurrection of all men at the end of the world? The simplest answer seems to be: No. Some of the very late books of the Old Testament tell of a resurrection of the *righteous*, but of a general resurrection of all men at the end of time they say nothing explicitly. And whether they even point in that direction is very debatable.

The Old Testament tells us that at the prayers of Elijah (1 K 17:17-24) and of Elisha (2 K 4:18-37) Yahweh restored "to the conditions of the present life" two children who had died. But they tell us little of a resurrection that confers "upon the deceased a new and permanent form of life." Most of the Old Testament is silent about an afterlife in any form. Until quite late there is no word about a resurrection of the body for the dead but only about a shadowy existence in Sheol. The first clear affirmation of a resurrection of the dead is found in *Daniel* where we read that "many of those who sleep in the land of the dust shall awake, some to everlasting life, others to everlasting reproach and horror" (12:2-3), (cf. JBC 26:34). P. P. Saydon says of this passage, "the doctrine of the resurrection and the last judgment is clearly stated, though still in an undeveloped form . . . Although the universal resurrection is not explicitly asserted, it is at least implied in the eschatological outlook of the prophet" (*A Catholic Commentary on Holy Scripture*, Thomas Nelson & Sons, p. 642). Josef Schmid, however, says of this passage that it is "distinguished . . . by the fact that not only just but also impious will rise again." But he adds, "There is no thought of a general resurrection" (*Sacramentum Mundi*, 5, 335). In 2 Maccabees we read, "the King of the world will raise us up. . . . Ours is the better choice, to meet death at men's hands, yet relying on God's promise that we shall be raised up by him, whereas for you there can be no resurrection, no new life" (7:9, 14). Of this passage J. Schmid notes that "once again there is no mention of a general resurrection even of the Israelites, and for the impious there is none" (loc. cit.) T. Corbishley, S.J., however, thinks that 7:14 "does not imply that there would be no resurrection of the wicked, but only that there would be no resurrection to the life of happiness but to eternal death" (*A Catholic Commentary on Holy Scripture*, p. 720). Whatever the author of this passage may have had in mind, it is clear that he did not *affirm* a belief in a general resurrection of all men at the end of time. J. Schmid adds, however, that "after the Maccabean period the belief in the resurrection prevailed in Palestinian Judaism. . . . And mainly through the influence of the Pharisees it became the general national belief and a dogma which was incorporated into the *Shemone Esre* (2nd Benediction) to be recited daily by every Jew. But the resurrection was . . . rejected by the Sadducees . . . and by Hellenistic Judaism . . . Judaism never reached agreement whether all men or only some will rise again. . . . The oldest testimony to the view that all men, just and impious, Jews and pagans, will rise again, is the *Ethiopic Book of Enoch* . . . The teaching of most rabbis from the earliest Tannaite period onwards was and remained that *all* the dead are resurrected. With the destruction of Jerusalem, Sadduceeism disappeared from Jewish history and the Pharisee rabbis . . . imposed their own doctrine as alone valid and as binding on all. . . . Modern Reform Judaism has abandoned the doctrine of the resurrection of the body and replaced it by belief in immortality" (loc. cit.).

New Testament

Does the New Testament teach a general resurrection of all men at the end of the world? The answer definitely seems to be: Yes. It is true that most of the New Testament texts about the resurrection of the dead deal with the resurrection of the Christian. But there are also texts in the Synoptics, Acts, Paul and John that affirm or imply a general resurrection of all men.

The *Synoptic* writers clearly indicate there will be a resurrection of the dead at the end of the world, and they imply that this will be a general resurrection of all men in what they say about the judgment of all men.

To bolster their denial of the resurrection of the dead, the Sadducees offered Jesus what they considered an insoluble problem for a resurrectionist, that of a woman who had successively married seven brothers: "At the resurrection, therefore, of which of the seven will she be the wife?" Involved in their denial of the resurrection was a misunderstanding of it as a mere prolongation of the conditions of this life. In His reply Jesus not only affirmed the resurrection and refuted their denial of it by an appeal to the Torah and to the power of God but also exposed their misunderstanding of it by declaring that in the resurrection the dead would be transformed into sons of the resurrection who like angels would be unable to die any more: "You err because you know neither the Scriptures nor the power of God. For at the resurrection they will neither marry nor be given in marriage, but will be as angels of God in heaven. But as to the resurrection of the dead have you not read what was spoken to you by God.... He is not the God of the dead but of the living" (Mt 22:28ff; Lk 20:27-38). Here the resurrection of the dead is explicitly affirmed. And implicitly, it would seem, also the resurrection of all men, since no restriction is indicated.

But still more clearly is a general resurrection of all men implied in "final judgment" passages. For at this judgment all men will be judged, not only the righteous but also the impious. And visibly judged so that all can see who are being judged. A "risen body" seems obviously postulated for such a visible judgment. Two such passages stand out in the Synoptics. The first is: "Woe to thee, Corozain, woe to thee, Bethsaida! For if in Tyre and Sidon had been worked the miracles that have been worked in you, they would have repented long ago, sitting in sackcloth and ashes. But it will be more tolerable for Tyre and Sidon at the judgment than for you" (Lk 10:13, 14). The more famous passage is this: "When the Son of Man shall come in His majesty . . . He will sit on the throne of His glory; and before Him will be gathered all the nations, and He will separate them one from another . . . and He will set the sheep on His right hand, but the goats on the left. Then the king will say to those on his right hand, 'Come, blessed of my Father, take possession of the kingdom . . .' Then He will say to those on his left hand, 'Depart from me, accursed ones, into the everlasting fire' " (Mt 25:31-41). D. M. Stanley, in his comment on this passage, correctly notes: "the judgment, exercised over the wicked as well as the just, presupposes the general resurrection."[9]

Paul is generally considered a major witness to the resurrection of the dead. It has been said that little of consequence has ever been added to what he wrote about the resurrection in his letters to the Thessalonians and the Corinthians. Belief in a future resurrection was a basic part of his missionary message. At Thessalonica members of the Church had wondered whether some of their number who had died would share in the paraousia. Paul wrote to them not to grieve: "for since we believe that Jesus died and rose again, even so, through Jesus, God will bring with Him those who have fallen asleep. . . . For the Lord Himself will descend from heaven with a cry of command, with the archangel's call, and with the sound of the trumpet of God. And the dead in Christ will rise first" (1 Th 4:13-16). Among the Corinthians, Paul learned, there were some who said: "there is no resurrection of the dead" (1 Cor 15:12). So he set about answering them and "proving" to them that there was a resurrection of the dead because Christ had been raised from the dead. "For I delivered to you as of first importance what I also received, that Christ died for our sins in accordance with the Scriptures, that He was buried, that He was raised on the third day in accordance with the Scriptures, and that He appeared to Cephas, then to the twelve. Then He appeared to more than five hundred brethren at one time, most of whom are still alive, though some have fallen asleep. Then He appeared to James, then to all the apostles. Last of all, as to one untimely born, He appeared also to me. . . . Now if Christ is preached as raised from the dead, how can some of you say that there is no resurrection of the dead? But if there is no resurrection of the dead, then Christ has not been raised. . . . For if the dead are not raised, then Christ has not been raised. If Christ has not been raised, your faith is futile and you are still in your sins. . . . But in fact Christ has been raised from the dead, the first fruits of those who have fallen asleep. For as by a man came death, by a man has come also the resurrection of the dead. For as in Adam all die, so also in Christ shall all be made alive" (1 Cor 15:3-22).

Thus for Paul the resurrection of Jesus is the principle of the resurrection of the Christian to the eternal life of glory. The Father who raised Jesus will also raise the Christian (2 Cor 4:14). Those who die with Christ will live with Him (2 Tm 2:11). Christ is the first of the risen. Men will rise in Him as they died in Adam. This resurrection is not a return to the conditions of the present life, but to a life of the spirit, the life already possessed by the risen Jesus and communicated from Him to those who believe in Him (J. L. McKenzie, op. cit., 731-734). Obviously Paul is most concerned with the resurrection of the Christians, for those who die with Christ will live with Him. And if it is true that he makes no explicit statement of a general resurrection at the end of the world, yet he comes very close to this when he writes "as in Adam all die, so also in Christ shall all be made alive." He also implies a general resurrection of all when he speaks of a universal judgment of good and bad alike (1 Cor 6:2f.; 2 Cor 5:10; Rm 2:6; 2 Th 1:5-10), for such a resurrection of all must precede collective judgment of all.

There are still other testimonies to a general resurrection in the New Testament, some implicit, some more explicit. *John's* Gospel tells us: "the hour is coming in which all who are in the tombs shall hear the voice of the Son of God. And they who have done good shall come forth unto resurrection of life; but they who have done evil unto resurrection of judgment" (5:28-29). W. Leonard says of this passage that it "evokes the thought of the general resurrection. . . . It is quite clear . . . that not faith alone but works rooted in faith shall decide the resurrection of men to life rather than to the judgment of condemnation reserved for those who have done evil things" (*A Catholic Commentary on Holy Scripture*, 990). And Bruce Vawter writes: "The final judgment will be the consummation of Christ's work: The just will rise to eternal life and the evil to damnation, each being judged according to his works" (JBC 63:85). In *Acts* there is an explicit testimony to the general resurrection, where Paul says: "having a hope in God which these men also look for, that there is to be a resurrection of the just and the unjust" (24:15). N. M. Flanagan says of this passage: "that hope is now a reality, through the resurrection of Christ, a resurrection which makes certain the resurrection of all men" (*New Testament Reading Guide, Acts*, 92). And C. S. Dessain adds: "This seems to be the only reference in St. Paul to the resurrection of the unjust" (*A Catholic Commentary on Holy Scripture*, 1042). Two passages in the book of

Revelation clearly imply a general resurrection: "Behold He is coming with the clouds, and every eye will see Him, every one who pierced Him; and all the tribes of the earth will wail on account of Him. Even so. Amen" (1:7); and Rv 20:11-12, which tells of the universal judgment and general resurrection that mark the end of this world (cf. JBC 64:87).

Early Church Fathers

Did the Early Church Fathers find in Sacred Scripture solid testimony for a general resurrection of all men at the end of the world? Did they expect such a resurrection? One of their dominant expectations clearly seems to have been that of the resurrection of the dead. The Didache sees the resurrection of the dead preceding the parousia, and apparently limited to the righteous. But the normal teaching was that good and bad alike would rise. Athenagoras argued that a resurrection is logically demanded by the fact that man is a complete being made of body and soul and has an end assigned him by God that is plainly unattainable in this world: hence a future life is necessary in which body and soul must participate. Irenaeus, Tertullian and Hippolytus strongly defended the resurrection of the body against the Gnostics, basing their proof to some extent on reason but mostly on the evidence of Scripture. Origen believed in the spirituality and immortality of the soul but strongly defended the resurrection of the body against the pagans. For the later Fathers, both Greek and Latin, the resurrection was an unquestioned article of the Church's faith: they assumed that it would be universal, including all men, good and bad alike. Most of them avoided speculation about it but merely affirmed the traditional dogma and defended it by appeals to the divine omnipotence. The early Creeds and Ecumenical Councils canonized the testimony of Scripture and the teaching of the Fathers.[10]

WHAT DOES THE GENERAL RESURRECTION MEAN AND IMPLY?

"Whenever the New Testament mentions the resurrection," notes Josef Schmid, "it speaks of the 'resurrection of the dead,' never of 'resurrection of the body' (of the flesh), which is not found until 2 Clement, 9, 1 and Justin, Dialogue 80, 5. What is always meant, therefore, is the whole man" (loc. cit. p. 339). If we look to the early Creeds of the Church, we find "resurrection of the body" in the Apostles' Creed (DS 30), but "resurrection of the dead" in the Niceno-Constantinopolitan Creed (DS 150). Lateran IV, Lyons II and the Benedictine Constitution all say men will rise "with their own bodies" (DS 801, 854, 1002). Karl Rahner declares that "resurrection means the termination and perfection of the *whole man* before God, which gives him eternal life" (*Theological Investigations*, II, 203ff.). Similarly J. Ratzinger writes that "the awakening of the dead (not of bodies) of which Scripture speaks, is thus concerned with the salvation of the one undivided man, not just with the fate of one-half of man . . . So the idea of immortality denoted in the Bible by the word 'resurrection' is an immortality of the 'person,' of the one creation man" (loc. cit.). Today, then, these theologians say that resurrection of the dead means the "whole man," and like most other theologians today they put their stress on this "wholeness," and in the process seem to down-grade a basic implication of the general resurrection at the end of the world, namely that this implies and involves a *naturally immortal soul in every man.*

In the light of all the criticism that has in recent years been hurled against the existence of an immaterial soul, and most especially against the existence of a naturally immortal soul, this affirmation will very likely seem to many a rather stupid return to the psychology of the Dark Ages. And yet if we really believe in a general resurrection of all men, wicked as well as good, it is a very logical—and necessary—affirmation. A great deal has been written in recent years on the question of resurrection of the body vs. immortality of the soul, and on the question of the language of resurrection vs. the language of immortality. A number of theologians such as O. Cullmann, H. Thielicke, P. Benoit, have opted for resurrection rather than immortality. They have rejected not so much the soul itself, but the soul that by its very nature is immortal. They consider a naturally immortal soul a part of a Greek dualistic view of man that is out of harmony with the unitary man of the Bible and of modern psychology. On the other side, A. Winklhofer maintains the traditional naturally immortal soul, while R. Aldwinckle opts for immortality in an "embodied" form. In the question of language, N. Pittenger seems to think that the language of resurrection preserves more adequately than the language of immortality the idea that we survive death with the full integrity of our humanity, so that our total experience in the body here and now is somehow preserved in the life beyond. On the other hand, H. Wheeler Robinson opted for immortality, despite his long standing preoccupation with the Hebrew Scriptures. For him the term 'immortality' is preferable to 'resurrection,' because our whole life of thought points to the immortality of the soul and its values rather than to the resurrection of the body. Whatever may be said of these preferences, it seems to me that it is not a question of the language of immortality *or* the language of resurrection, but of *both*, of immortality and of resurrection. Our whole life of thought points both to the immortality of the soul and its values and to the resurrection of the body and its values.

But what is of primary importance is not the question of *language*, but the question of the *reality* of immortality of the soul and of the *reality* of the resurrection of the body. Dr. Cullmann's book, *Immortality of the Soul or Resurrection of the Body*, indicates this. And in the light of all we have said earlier, it should be clear that the disjunction must be removed, and that we must hold both the immortality of the soul and the resurrection of the body. We must hold to a resurrection of the body at the end of the world, for this is a basic teaching of Scripture and of the Church. And if we wish to take adequate account of the scriptural, credal, and conciliar teaching of the Church on a general resurrection, we must hold not only an immortal soul but a naturally immortal soul. No other explanation of the biblical and ecclesial teaching is at all adequate. The biblical and psychological view that man is a unitary being is correct as far as it goes, but it does not go far enough. It may be true that "the Hebrews did not conceive of man as

constituted of a material body and a spiritual soul" (JBC 34:12).
But neither did they conceive of an afterlfe for every man
in an everlasting heaven or hell. Their view of the afterlife was
woefully inadequate. So was their view of man. They were poor
eschatologists. They were equally poor psychologists. This is not
to blame them, but simply to evaluate them. They were men of
their times, subject to all the eschatological and psychological
limitations of those times.

But today we have a fuller view of eschatology and a fuller
view of man. And to explain either pilgrim man or eschatological
(i.e. after-death) man adequately, we must posit in every man
a mortal body and an immortal soul. This does not mean the
Platonic view of a pre-existent soul incarcerated in a confining
body. But it does mean there is and must be in man an immaterial
soul, no matter what some modern psychologists may say to the
contrary. Grant that man is a unitary being: he is also a unitary
being that is at the same time material and immaterial. No one
has or can give an adequate explanation of all that man is and
does without giving him an immaterial soul, and an immaterial
soul that is the ultimate principle of his unity, his personal continuity, his activity, his "self-ness," his "person."

If man is more than a body, then he must have a soul, such
a soul. If he is a unity of mind and body, then he must have
such a soul as principle of this unity. If he is a supra-material
being, then he must have a supra-material soul as principle of
this supra-material being. If man has immaterial activities, then
he must have an immaterial soul as principle of these immaterial
activities. If man is an enduring "I", an enduring "self", an enduring "person", aware of his freedom and of his responsibility,
then he must have an immaterial soul as a principle of this enduring "person." There is no other adequate explanation of all
that man is or does.

And if man has an immaterial soul, then this soul must be
immortal, as the Fifth Lateran Council declared (DS 1440).
It may be very "modern" to say that at death, since man is a
unitary being, "the whole man dies," body and soul. But this is
simply not true, at least not adequately true. For if all men live

on after death then the whole man does not die, but only his body. His soul does not die. It is not mortal as the body is. *I*, the total I, do not die. If the same person lives on in the interim state that lived in the pilgrim state, then the whole man, the whole person, the whole I does not die. And the soul that is the principle of that person does not die. And if every man is destined by God to live forever, then his soul must also be destined to live forever and thus to be immortal. If man will never die, if this person, this self will never die, then neither will his soul, the principle of his "person," his "self," his unity and continuity and immaterial activity. And both the New Testament and the Creeds of the Church and the dogmatic Councils of the Church have consistently taught down the centuries that man is destined to live forever—either in heaven or in hell. If we accept this teaching, then an immortal soul clearly seems to be a necessary implication of this teaching and of this belief.

And not just an immortal soul, but a *naturally immortal soul,* seems to be a necessary implication of this teaching and of this belief, that man will live forever. For if God has destined every man to live forever, then he also destined him to have a soul that could and would live forever. If God has destined every man to live forever, then He has built into every man a capacity to live forever. And He has built this capacity not into man's body which dies, but into his soul that does not die. By its very God-given nature a man's soul is immortal, and can and will live forever. An evolutionary origin and development of man can easily be harmonized with this natural immortality. Only natural immortality will adequately explain every man's destiny to live forever. Gift-immortality, pneuma-immortality, an immortality that is contingent on a special love-relationship or faith-relationship with God, will not apply to the wicked, to those who die in grave sin, to those who condemn themselves to live forever without God in hell. J. Ratzinger adds another perspective to this view when he presents his "dialogic immortality."[11] "Having a spiritual soul," he writes, "means precisely being willed, known and loved by God in a special way; it means being a creature called by God to an eternal dialogue and therefore capable of its own part of knowing God and of replying to Him. . . . What we call in substantialist language 'having a soul', will be described in more historical, actual language as 'being God's partner in a dialogue.' This does not mean that talk of the soul is false (as is sometimes asserted today by a one-sided and uncritical biblical approach); in one respect it is indeed even necessary in order to describe the whole of what is involved here. But on the other hand it also needs to be complemented if we are not to fall back into a dualistic conception which cannot do justice to the dialogic and personalistic view of the Bible. . . . So when we say that man's immortality is based on his dialogic relationship with God, whose love alone bestows eternity, we are not claiming a special destiny for the pious but emphasizing the essential immortality of man as man."

The "risen body" has fascinated men down the years. What kind of body will it be? Will it be the same as the pilgrim body or different? "Every orthodox thinker," says J. T. Addison, "from Paul to today has declared the resurrection body is the same as the earthly body and yet different. But each has tended to emphasize the one truth or the other—either to insist on the identity or to dwell on the change. St. Paul is clearly of the latter group— he is concerned with the contrast between the body that was buried and the body that will rise" (op. cit. 145 ff.). Paul's answer has been called the noblest, boldest, most convincing ever formulated. What is Paul's answer? Long ago the Corinthians were disturbed about the resurrection. "How are the dead raised," they asked, "with what kind of body do they come?" (1 Cor 15:34). Paul's answer was rather blunt. "You foolish man. What you sow does not come to life unless it dies. And what you sow is not the body which is to be, but a bare kernel, perhaps of wheat or of some other grain. But God gives it a body as he has chosen, and to each kind of seed its own body. . . . So it is with the resurrection of the dead. What is sown is perishable, what is raised is imperishable. It is sown in dishonor, it is raised in glory. It is sown in weakness, it is raised in power. It is sown a physical body, it is raised a spiritual body. . . . I tell you this, brethren: flesh and blood cannot inherit the kingdom of God, nor does the perishable inherit the imperishable. Lo, I tell you a mystery. We shall not all sleep, but we shall all be changed. For this perishable nature must put on the imperishable, and this mortal nature must put on immortality" (1 Cor 15:36-53).

If Paul's answer is the noblest, boldest, most convincing ever formulated, it may also well be the most mysterious. For scholars and exegetes have pondered it down the years, discussed it, analyzed it in itself and in its relations to other parts of Pauline doctrine, and they have regularly disagreed about its precise meaning and implications. Paul has indeed told us a *mystery*. Is there a *corporeal identity* between the earthly and the risen body? Or is there perhaps just an identity of person? These are basic questions that have agitated men for a long, long time. And men are still divided in their answers.

G. C. Berkouwer writes: "that Paul was not driving at proving the identity of the resurrected body to the earthly body that is sown is evident from his mention of the great variety of 'flesh' and the difference in glory between celestial and terrestrial bodies. The one flesh or body can become visible reality in many different forms."[12] L. Audet says "the risen body will not be numerically the one left in the grave, for the risen body will have different constitutives and will have no blood and no flesh. But the same ego will remain identical in transit from one kind of body to another. For while psyche and sarx pass away, the person continues in virtue of the pneuma."[13] P. Althaus rejects any continuity between our present body and the resurrection-body, claiming that "according to Paul, the present body of flesh must vanish to make place for something of a completely different substance" (*Die Letzen Dinge*, pp. 125-6).

On the other side J. T. Addison writes: "The new body will be not only different from the old, but the same. The old has not been annihilated to give place to a new creation. Between the two there is an organic connection, a real continuity. It is out of the fleshly, by a miracle of God, that the spiritual will grow, even as the full ear grows out of the seed. Through all the changes that are to be, *some germ of bodily identity* will be preserved" (op. cit.). And J. A. Schep declares that "there is an essential continuity and organic relation between that which dissolves in the earth and that which God causes to sprout forth from it."[14]

Corporeal identity of some sort seems beyond doubt to be the teaching of the Church. For we are told by the Athanasian Creed that "all men will rise with their own bodies" (DS 76), by Lateran IV that "all these will rise with their own bodies which they now have" (DS 801), by Lyons II that "all men appear before the judgment seat of Christ with their own bodies" (DS 854), by the Benedictine Constitution that "all men will appear with their bodies" (DS 1002). Hence, most theologians view corporeal identity as "a truth of faith" (cf. Hervé, loc. cit.), although one says "this is a point that is not a formal dogma of the Church...but a doctrine almost universally admitted and professed."

Is corporeal identity also the teaching of St. Paul? It seems to be. For he says: "*this* perishable nature must put on the imperishable and *this* mortal nature must put on immortality" (1 Cor 15:53). J. Schmid declares that for Paul "just as the body of the risen Lord is identical with his earthly body, so also the Christians' heavenly bodies are identical with their earthly ones. That is already implied in the concept of resurrection, but it is also confirmed by the image of the kernel of wheat (1 Cor 15:36-38) and the idea of transfiguration" (loc. cit. 339). If there is an essential continuity and organic relation between the seed that dies and the wheat that rises from it, then so should there be, according to Paul, an essential continuity and organic relation between the pilgrim body that dies and the resurrected body. If something of the wheat seed goes into the wheat plant, then something of the pilgrim body should go into the risen body. If the resurrection of Christ is a model of the resurrection of the Christian, then we can say with W. Pannenberg that "there is a continuity between the old and the new body: it is precisely the earthly mortal body which is transformed into a new mode of existence, an immortal spiritual body" (*Grundzuge der Christologie*, 1964).

But what does corporeal identity mean? Does it mean an

identity of matter? So that there will be, must be in the risen body some of the matter that was in the earthly body? Paul says "it is sown a physical body, it is raised a spiritual body" (loc. cit.). What does he mean by a "spiritual body"? A body of "spirit"? And if it is a "body of spirit," can it be a material body, can it even be a body? E. Käsemann seems to think that Paul teaches that the resurrection body is a spirit-body. But most interpreters say, and correctly, that he does not teach this. "Spiritual body," says W. Rees, does not mean "a body made of spirit, an immaterial body (which would be a contradiction), but a material body perfectly fitted to be the instrument of a soul elevated and transfigured by union with God, in short, a body like our Lord's body after His resurrection" (*A Catholic Commentary on Holy Scripture*, 1097). G. C. Berkouwer declares that "the spiritual body is contrasted to the physical (and) involves a perspective concerning reality that is wholly dominated by the Spirit, the pneuma" (op. cit., 191-192). R. Kugelman writes that "the risen body will be pneumatikon, the perfect instrument of man's pneuma . . . and perfectly docile to the divine spirit. The model of this 'spiritual body' is the risen body of Christ" (JBC 51:86). X. Leon-Dufour says simply: "the body of earthly misery and sinfulness will be transformed . . . into a 'spiritual body'. . . one not subject to decay" (op. cit. 42). And long ago St. Thomas Aquinas wrote: "the body will not become spirit, as some heretics think: no, man will remain composed of body and of spirit. The glorious body is spiritual, i.e. entirely subject to spirit" (*Suppl.* q. 83, a. 1). Summing up all of this we can say simply that the risen body will be a "spiritual body" and this does not mean that it will be a body made of spirit.

But does this mean that this "spiritual body" will be in some sense, a material body? And if it will be a material body in some sense, will some or all of its matter be the same matter that was in the pilgrim body? To the first question, will the "spiritual body" in some sense be a material body, many interpreters say, and say correctly, that it will be in some sense material. When "St. Paul calls the risen body a 'spiritual body,' says C. Davis, "it means that the risen body is transformed and penetrated with the spirit. To us, spiritual means immaterial, but that is not what Paul had in mind. Paul teaches that the risen bodies are brought within the divine sphere and share the divine qualities of power, glory, splendor, holiness. In the resurrection of Christ we have the exemplar and cause of our own. The risen body was clearly a body in the sense of a tangible and extended reality. Attempts to overspiritualize the risen body, to volatilize away its materiality, always come up against the experience of the apostles that the risen Christ had a true human body" (*Theology Digest*, Spring, 1960, 99ff.).

If we cannot "volatilize away" the materiality of the risen body, what can we say about this materiality? Will it be the same as that of the pilgrim body and yet different? The answer would be simpler if we could only define matter. But we cannot. We can say a great deal about matter, about its laws of change and movement, its mass, charges, valences, its molecules, atoms and electrons. . . . We can say a great deal about the physical, chemical and biological properties of pilgrim man's matter. But we cannot define matter, we cannot define just what belongs to its essence. Yet if the risen body of Christ was a "tangible and extended reality," a body that could eat and drink, that had the solidity and denseness of reality that we associate with matter, then it would seem clear that it involved matter, and essentially the same matter as the pilgrim body of Christ. And then our own risen bodies will also involve matter, and essentially the same matter as our pilgrim bodies. But the materiality of our risen bodies, like that of the risen body of Christ, will be relatively different from that of our pilgrim bodies, different in its relations to spirit and to space and to time. For some theologians the difference will lie largely in this: that in the pilgrim body matter tends rather strongly to resist the self-expression of spirit but in the risen body matter will be wide open to and an apt instrument of spirit. For other theologians the difference lies largely in matter's relation to space. The matter of the risen body will be less limited spatially, less bound by the laws of three-dimensional space, more open to hyperspace or space of four dimensions. For still other theologians the difference lies rather in matter's relation to time, for in the risen body matter will have a new time dimension, a dimension of time raised to the power of eternity so that it can support risen human life throughout eternity.

If, then, the risen body will be in some sense 'material,' does this mean that some or all of its matter must come from the earthly body? W. Rees writes that "on the question how far the risen body will be materially identical with the body that dies, theologians differ: the majority teach that some particles at least will be common to both, but others (e.g. Billot) hold this is not necessary" (*A Catholic Commentary on Holy Scripture*, loc. cit.). The minority opinion is interesting. "For the Thomist," wrote C. Davis, "nothing else is required for the identity of the body than the identity of the soul or form. The soul immediately informs prime matter. As soon as the soul takes over and informs a certain quantity of matter, this becomes the self-same identical body previously possessed" (loc. cit.). Thus material identity of the elements is not required to explain the resurrection of the body. Formal identity is quite enough to safeguard and properly expound the dogma of the resurrection, and this formal identity is had by the identity of the soul or form. Thus, according to Billot, "God can make a resurrected body that would not possess a single atom of the matter its body possessed before death" (*De Novissimis*, 136).

But the majority opinion seems more solid, for "Scripture connects our resurrection so closely with that of Christ that some connection between the actual matter of our earthly body and that of our risen body is no doubt to be admitted" (Arendzen, op. cit. 90). But these theologians think that there is sufficient material identity, sufficient identity of matter, if *some* of the material parts which belonged to the earthly body be present in the body at the resurrection. All the parts need not be present. For just as a human body always remains the same in spite of the constant changing of its constituent matter, so it is enough for resurrectional identity if a relatively small share of the amount of matter in the earthly body is contained in the body after the resurrection. Thus there is no real difficulty against the Christian belief in the resurrection if the same parts of matter may have successively belonged to several bodies.

A. Winklhofer, however, wants to specify this common matter still further. So he has recourse to something like a "corporeal seed." Thus he writes, "the earthly body continues to exist in its substance, for even in our lifetime there is present always an enduring substance of the human body, as the essential element that remains and is unaffected by cell-changes and constant replacement of matter and is unaltered through all the developments from youth to age. This continues in existence and immediately after death is preserved supernaturally and given a new mode of being. Thus there remains supernaturally something of our body, a 'seed' from which can issue a complete human body of a new nature when reunited with the soul filled with the glory of Christ and the fire of the Holy Spirit, the giver of life" (op. cit. 218ff.). What is to be thought of Winklhofer's 'corporeal seed'? Evidence for it in the empirical order seems non-existent, unless we give some credence to the affirmation that all men have an "aura" or an "astral body" or a "double."[15] But Winklhofer's inferential evidence from psychology has some weight, and is perhaps backed up by some implications of Paul's thought.

If we move into still deeper waters, we face the question whether the risen body will not only be a material body somehow but also be a body of *"flesh and blood"?* Paul says that "flesh and blood cannot inherit the kingdom of God" (1 Cor 15:50). But what does he mean by this? That the risen body will not be a body of flesh and blood? Some scholars maintain just this. L. Audet wrote that "the new body will be even of different constitutives; it will have no blood, no flesh even . . . 'Soul' (psyche) passes away no less than 'flesh' (sarx); person continues but solely in virtue of the pneuma" (loc. cit. 6ff.). And R. J. Campbell says "the Church's doctrine of corporeal resurrection means that the human body will be 'corporeal'? Yes. Flesh and blood? No. Scripture is emphatic about that. Flesh and blood cannot inherit the kingdom of God: neither doth incorruption inherit corruption."[16]

Against this view J. A. Schep maintains that "Paul proclaims

the dead bodies of believers will be raised in the *flesh*, but with
a great change by the power of God. For by 'flesh and blood'
he means (and the New Testament) the whole man in his weak,
perishable, corruptible human nature. And hence 'man' as he is
now, a frail, earthbound perishable creature, cannot have a place
in God's glorious heavenly kingdom: his human nature must first
be changed so he will be able to live in a world completely different from the present world."[17] J. L. McKenzie writes that Paul's
statement that "flesh and blood" cannot inherit the kingdom of
God is . . . not a denial of the resurrection of the body, which Paul
is at pains to assert, but an affirmation that the risen body cannot
be a body of flesh, understanding flesh as the subject of sin. It
must become a "spiritual body" (op. cit. 282). And W. Rees notes
that "flesh and blood" here means "human nature in its present
frail state. There must be a change to make this material body
everlasting" (loc. cit. 1098). Further, if "the model of this 'spiritual body' is the risen body of Christ" (JBC 51:86), then our risen
body will be a body of flesh, of sinless flesh. For the risen Christ
said to His Apostles: "See my hands and feet, that it is I myself.
Feel me and see; for a spirit does not have flesh and bones, as you
see I have" (Lk 24:38ff.). Commenting on this R. Ginns writes:
"His glorified body retained all its physical reality, including its
tangibility and its normal organs, as is shown by his eating the
proferred food" (*A Catholic Commentary on Holy Scripture,*
970). And if we turn to John's Gospel we read: "And after eight
days his disciples were again inside, and Thomas with them. Jesus
came, the doors being closed, and stood in their midst, and said,
'Peace be to you.' Then he said to Thomas, 'Bring here thy finger
and see my hands and bring thy hand, and put it into my side;
and be not unbelieving, but believing.' Thomas answered and said
to him, 'My Lord and my God' " (Jn 20:24-28). It seems clear
then that if the risen body of Christ was a body of flesh and blood,
so will our risen bodies be bodies of flesh and blood.

   Will our risen bodies be able to eat and drink, to assimilate
food, to exercise the vegetative life fully? J. Pohle wrote that "of
the bodily functions all those that pertain to the vegetative life
will cease in the other world. Nutrition and propagation are in-

compatible with the final state." For St. Paul says "Food is for the stomach and the stomach for food—and God will destroy both the one and the other" (1 Cor 6:13). And commentators conclude from this that stomach and food are "merely transitory things, which one day will cease."[18] JBC adds that "eating and drinking belong to mortal life in this world and will have no place in the life of glory" (51:32).

But V. de Broglie offers an interesting argument for ascribing to the glorified body the power of eating and even the full exercise of vegetative life. "Vegetative life," he writes, "essentially consists in the active assimilation and deassimilation of elements that are variously furnished to the living organism . . . not only by eating and drinking but also by respiration, circulation of the blood, etc. Will there be no vegetative life in the blessed? No respiration? No circulation of the blood? And yet a real flesh and blood man? With real, living cells? blood but no circulation? lungs but no respiration? Would the glorified body be really the same as before? Even the same kind of body as before? Does the fact that there will be no generative operations, prove or imply that there will be no vegetative operations of any kind? If there will be no vegetative operations in the blessed, then why will they have senses of taste and smell? For taste is ordered to eating and drinking, and smell to respiration. . . . If these senses are removed, what happens to the integrity of the human body? If the senses remain—but completely inoperative . . . unusable . . . why? Why such merely ornamental monuments of a previous life? If the blessed have the same kind of body, why not the same kind of vegetative life? Sacred Scripture (Lk 24:43; Ac 1:4; 10:41) all seem to indicate that Christ's eating actions after His resurrection were the same as before—involving ordinary assimilation of the food, not its miraculous disappearance. . . ." And so he concludes that "it does not seem to be prohibited to hold the view that says the bodies of the blessed will exercise true vegetative life, even to the extent of true eating and assimilation of food, if this should be desired, though it is not at all needed."[19]

One last question concerns special qualities or gifts that God will give to risen bodies. Paul says of the risen body, "it is sown a physical body, it is raised a spiritual body" (1 Cor 15:44). And if 'spiritual body' means a body that is perfectly docile to the spirit, to the pneuma, as it definitely seems to, then the risen body of the *blessed* will be perfectly dominated by the spirit. What form will this dominance take or effect? Many theologians envisaged four special effects of this dominance, four special supernatural qualities of the risen bodies of the blessed, qualities that seem to them to be implied in 1 Cor 15:42-44 and other passages of the New Testament. They called these qualities impassibility, splendor, subtility, agility. In virtue of its impassibility the risen body would be immortal and no longer susceptible to suffering, sickness, death, or to any bodily evil whatever. It would be immune to pain, frailty, hunger, thirst, weariness, exhaustion. It would have no need to eat, drink, or sleep. By its splendor the risen body would "shine as the sun" (Mt 13:43). It would have perfect bodily beauty and its own special light which could be suspended by the blessed at will. The radiance of the soul would irradiate the body as light within it irradiates a crystal. Subtility would make the risen body perfectly docile to the spirit and give it a share in many of the powers and privileges of the spirit. Very likely it would give it the power to compenetrate other bodies. By its agility the risen body of the blessed would be able to move easily from place to place, perhaps from planet to planet, from star to star, with the speed of thought. And thus the wide expanse of the universe, the remotest recesses of the starry skies would be accessible to the risen bodies of the blessed.

Will the risen bodies of the *wicked* enjoy these special qualities? The answer seems to be: No. For these qualities derive from the dominance of the *indwelling Spirit*, and the wicked are not indwelt by the Spirit nor are they docile to the Spirit. And so the risen bodies of the wicked will not enjoy the impassibility, the splendor, the subtility, the agility that the blessed will enjoy. They will not be immune to pain and suffering. But they will be immortal and incorruptible, because these qualities pertain to their final state. And if their immortality and incorruptibility involve a non-necessity of eating, drinking, sleeping, then they will not need to eat, drink, sleep, even though they have material bodies of

250 EVERLASTING LIFE AFTER DEATH

flesh and blood, that are fitted to their final state. Their risen bodies will not be glorious, will not "shine like the sun": that seems clear. It seems likely that they will have a very limited ability to move from place to place, a very limited access to the wide expanse of the universe, and that they will find the transfigured universe hostile to them, for it will be fitted for those who love God. For the rest we can only wonder and speculate. And we will speculate a bit more in our last chapter.

Notes for Chapter 10

1. H. Cornelis, O.P., "The Resurrection of the Body and Primitive Conceptions of the Last Things," **The Resurrection of the Body,** (Notre Dame, Fides, 1964), pp. 30-92.
2. **Manuale Theologiae Dogmaticae, I,** Parisiis, Apud Berche & Pagis, ed., 1957, pp. 184-194.
3. **Kirche Unterwegs,** (Freiburg, Olten, 1966), p. 120.
4. "Resurrection Faith Today," **Theological Studies,** Sept., 1969, p. 415.
5. "The Resurrection of Jesus and Historical Criticism," **Theology Digest,** Summer, 1969, pp. 110-113.
6. **Passion et Resurrection du Seigneur,** (Paris, 1966), p. 295.
7. "The Origin of Resurrection Belief," **Theology Digest,** Summer, 1975, pp. 136-139.
8. "La Resurrection," **Nouv. Rev. Theol.,** 91, 10, 1969, pp. 1009-1049.
9. **New Testament Reading Guide, The Gospel of St. Matthew,** (Collegeville, The Liturgical Press, 1960), p. 80.
10. J. N. D. Kelly, **Early Christian Doctrines,** (London, Adam & Charles Black, 1965), pp. 466-479.
11. **Introduction to Christianity,** (New York, Herder & Herder, 1970), pp. 269-273.
12. **The Return of Christ,** (Grand Rapids, Mich., W. B. Erdmans, 1972), p. 189.
13. "What Is the Risen 'Spiritual Body',?" **Theology Digest,** Spring, 1973. pp. 4-6.
14. **The Nature of the Resurrection Body,** (Grand Rapids, Mich., W. B. Erdmans, 1964).

15. Cf. Gerda Walter, "The Human Aura," **Tomorrow,** 2:81-87, 1954; S. Ostrander & L. Schroeder, **op. cit.,** "Kirlian Photography— Pictures of the Aura," pp. 200ff.; N. O. Jacobson, M.D., **Life without Death,** (New York, Dell, 1971), pp. 150ff. "Etheric Double," p. 288; Andrija Puharich, **Beyond Telepathy,** (Garden City, N. Y., Doubleday Anchor, 1973), "Aura," pp. 243-245, "Doubling of the Personality," pp. 103ff.; Ducasse, **op. cit.,** "Projection of the Double," p. 9.

16. **The Life of the World to Come,** (London, Londman & Green, 1948), p. 186.

17. The Nature of the Resurrection Body, (Grand Rapids, Mich., W. B. Eerdmans, 1964), p. 188.

18. C. J. Peifer, OSB., **New Testament Reading Guide, First Corinthians,** (Collegeville, Liturgical Press), p. 25.

19. **De Fine Ultimo,** (Paris, Beauchesne et Ses Fils, 1948), p. 282.

Chapter 11
Will There Be a Parousia of Christ at the End of the World?

At the end of the world the dead will rise again. And the cosmic Christ will come to judge all men and to indicate whether they are worthy or unworthy to live with Him in His transfigured cosmos. Lateran IV expressed it this way: Christ "will come at the end of the world; he will judge the living and the dead; and he will reward all, both the lost and the elect, according to their works" (DS 801). At His Incarnation He came into our world, emptied of His glory and majesty. At the end of the world He will come again in glory and majesty as Lord of History, Redeemer and Lord of the Cosmos, to consummate an eternal kingdom that will transcend our space-time limitations. Will he also come *before* the end of the world to establish a *millennial kingdom* on earth, in which He will reign?

MILLENNIALISM

There is a strange and mysterious passage in the Book of Revelation, that has challenged the minds of men down the centuries. It reads like this: "Then I saw an angel coming down from heaven, holding in his hand the key of the bottomless pit and a great chain. And he seized the dragon, that ancient serpent, who is the Devil and Satan, and bound him for a thousand years, and threw him into the pit, and shut it and sealed it over him, that he should deceive nations no more, till the thousand years were ended. After that he must be loosed for a little while. Then I saw thrones, and seated on them were those to whom judgment was committed. Also I saw the souls of those who had been beheaded for their testimony to Jesus and for the Word of God, and who had not worshipped the beast or its image and had not received its mark on their foreheads or their hands. They came to life, and reigned with Christ a thousand years. The rest of the dead did not come to life until the thousand years were ended. This is the first resurrection. Blessed and holy is he who shares in the first resurrection. Over such the second death has no power, but they shall be priests of God and of Christ, and they shall reign with him a thousand years" (Rv 20:1-6).

"They shall reign with him a thousand years"

These are the words that have intrigued men over the years. Those who looked forward expectantly to this millennial kingdom on earth toward the end of the world came to be called Millennialists (or Chiliasts). Some of them expected it to be a kingdom of sensible and carnal pleasures, such as Cerinthians, Ebionites, Marcionists, Apollinarists. Others looked forward to purer, higher delights in this earthly kingdom, such as Papias, Tertullian, Lactantius and St. Irenaeus. In recent times many Protestants have espoused Millennialism in one form or another. (Most of what follows is based on L. Boettner's excellent study, *The Millennium*, The Presbyterian and Reformed Publishing Co., Philadelphia, 1958). Mormons, Adventists, Jehovah's Witnesses have been strong Millennialists.

Some Millennialists have believed that Christ will return before the Millennium, and these are called Pre-Millennialists. They hold there will be a Tribulation and a Rapture, but they divide into two groups over the question whether the Rapture comes after or before the Tribulation. Those who hold that the Rapture comes after the Tribulation maintain "that the Christians who constitute the Church go through the Tribulation and are exposed to its afflictions: at the end of it Christ comes with great power and glory to raise the righteous dead and to *rapture* the saints; these are caught up to meet Him in the air but almost immediately return with Him as He comes to destroy the forces of Antichrist in the battle of Armageddon and to establish His kingdom . . ."

These Premillennialists hold "that the coming of Christ will be preceded by certain recognizable signs, such as the preaching of the Gospel to all nations, the apostasy, wars, famines, earthquakes, the appearance of the Antichrist or the Man of Sin, and the Great Tribulation" (ibid.).

Those who think that the Rapture comes before the Tribulation hold "that Christ may come at any moment without warning signs: at His coming the righteous dead are raised and together with the living saints are caught away in a secret Rapture to meet the Lord in the air, where they remain for a period of seven years. During that time the Antichrist rules on the earth and the dreadful woes spoken of in the Book of Revelation (chs. 4-19), fall on the inhabitants of the earth. At the end of that period Christ and the saints return to earth, Antichrist and his forces, who are persecuting the Jews and have them shut up in Jerusalem, will be destroyed in the battle of Armageddon, and the millennial kingdom will be set up on earth. The Jews are to be converted at the mere sight of their Messiah and, as the Lord's 'brethren,' are to have a very prominent and favored place in His kingdom" (ibid.).

Post-Millennialists hold "that Christ will return after the Millennium. They maintain that the Kingdom of God is now being extended in the world through the preaching of the Gospel and the saving work of the Holy Spirit in such a way that the world will eventually be Christianized. The return of Christ will occur at the close of a long period of righteousness and peace (the Millennium). The Kingdom of God is the product of the supernatural working of the Holy Spirit in connection with the preaching of the Gospel, and not the result of a natural evolutionary process by which mankind will be improved. The Millennium is a golden age of spiritual prosperity during the Church age. It is an indefinitely long period, perhaps much longer than one thousand years, during which the world will enjoy a state of righteousness and peace. Not every person will be a Christian nor will all sin be abolished but evil in its many forms eventually will be reduced to negligible proportions so that Christian principles will be the rule and not the exception, and Christ will return to a truly

Christianized world. Christ's second coming will be followed immediately by the general resurrection, the general judgment, and the introduction of heaven and hell in their fullness" (ibid.).

There are also many Protestant A-Millennialists, for Amillennialism is "the official view of the Missouri Church Synod Lutheran Church, of the Christian Reformed Church, of the Orthodox Presbyterian Church and of the Reformed Presbyterian Church" (ibid.). They maintain that the Bible does not predict a millennial period of world-wide peace and righteousness before the end of the world. It rather seems to indicate that there will be a parallel and contemporaneous development of good and evil, of God's kingdom and Satan's kingdom, until the second coming of Christ. At Christ's second coming there will be a general resurrection and judgment, and the institution of an eternal and perfect Kingdom of God in which there will be no sin, suffering and death.

Catholics generally have been A-Millennialists. Long ago Augustine interpreted this passage of Rv 20 of a "spiritual millennium." For him the "first resurrection" refers "to the transition from the death of sin to life in faith and takes place in baptism and in the effects of grace. The imprisonment of Satan is the defeat undergone by the prince of this world when the human race was redeemed by Christ. The kingdom of Christ is the Church in the world: its members reign along with the Lord, since they already possess on earth some of the glories of the heavenly kingship (cf. Ep 1:14). This kingdom has a symbolic duration of a thousand years, a period that makes a perfect number. The liberation of the fiend in the last days symbolizes the last persecution stirred up by Satan against the Church. The 'second resurrection' is the resurrection of the body at the end of the world. The first was a spiritual, the second a bodily resurrection" (E. Bettencourt, *Sacramentum Mundi* 4, 43-44). After Augustine Millennialism was quite abandoned, and the symbolic interpretation of the millennium usually prevailed. But there were attempts to explain the text as "a prophecy of concrete events. The most successful was that of Joachim of Fiore (d. c. 1200), who attributed a reign of a thousand years to the Holy Spirit and calculated that the reign of God would come in 1260" (ibid.). In the light of today's

Pentecostal movement, some seem to be reconsidering this view of Joachim of Fiore.

In 1944 the Holy Office declared that "the system of mitigated Millennialiarianism, which teaches that Christ the Lord will come visibly to this earth to rule . . ." cannot be safely taught (DS 3839). A recent manualist declared that "subtle millennialism is at least false and temerarious, and without foundation in Scripture, since the New Testament gives no intermediate period between the resurrection of the dead and the second coming of Christ: both will happen on the 'last day' " (Jn 5:28, 29; 6:39ff.; 12:48; 1 Th 4:15ff.; 1 Cor 15: 52; Mt 13:49; 25:31-46; Ac 1:11) (Hervé IV, 523). JBC declares that "nothing in the preceding chapters (of Rv, not even 5:10), would lead us to suspect that such a reign might be forthcoming. Besides, an intermediate reign of Christ seems foreign to the New Testament taken as a whole. . . . What is the meaning of this borrowing from Jewish eschatology? No satisfactory explanation has yet been devised. Among many interpretations of the passage, Augustine's has been most widely accepted" (64:83-84).

What do we conclude? That even if no satisfactory explanation of this passage has been found as yet, its explanation in terms of a millennial kingdom of Christ on earth before the end of the world is to be rejected. For Millennialism lacks an adequate foundation in Scripture. It is completely absent from the teaching of Jesus. There is only a single reference to it in Rv 20 (cf. Aldwinckle, op. cit. 146). There is nothing in the preceding chapters that would lead us to suspect that such a reign might be forthcoming (JBC) and no indication in the New Testament of such an intermediate period between the resurrection of the dead and the second coming of Christ (Hervé, loc. cit.).

PAROUSIA

Will there really be a "second coming" of Christ in glory at the end of the world? A basic Christian Creed, that of Nicea-Constantinople, says: "He is going to come again in glory to judge the living and the dead" (DS 150). That has been the faith of most Christians over the years. But there have always been men who denied there would be such a "Second Coming," such a "Parousia." Some have said the early Church imagined this Second Coming and inserted it in the Scriptures. Christ, they say, never spoke of a Second Coming, but only of the inauguration of His reign in which men's hearts would be possessed by th' boundless love of God. Harnack rejected the idea of the Secoi.d Coming, as merely a part of the environmental husk that Jesus used to convey the true kernel of the eternal gospel of the fatherhood of God, the brotherhood of man, the infinite value of the soul, and the ethic of love. For Albert Schweitzer Jesus was not the incarnate Son of God but a Jewish apocalyptic preacher who came to warn his people that God's judgment was about to fall on them, that the end of the world was at hand and that human history was about to end in a great apocalyptic conflagration. This end, however, did not occur. History did not end. The kingdom of God did not come. Jesus died on the cross with a cry of frustration: "My God, my God, why hast thou forsaken me"? (Mt 27:46). In short, Jesus was a deluded Jewish fanatic who died a martyr to his own fanciful delusions. For Rudolf Bultmann the parousia is a 'myth.' Eternal life is the life I receive now. Judgment is the crisis in which I stand now. The end of time is the Kairos in which the issue of life and death is being decided. The eschaton does not lie in the future of man's history but it is the time God gives me now as an opportunity to decide for authentic existence.

REALITY OF THE PAROUSIA

Human reason can not demonstrate that there will be, must be, such a Second Coming of Christ at the end of the world to judge the living and the dead. Only divine revelation can tell us whether such a Parousia is part of God's salvific design for mankind. Can we find such a revelation in Sacred Scripture?

Old Testament

If we view the parousia against the background of Old Testament thought, two elements of this thought stand out rather prominently, the coming of the "Day of the Lord" and the coming of the "Son of Man." There was a belief in the Old Testament that Yahweh is the Lord of history, the Lord who directs the course of man's history. And the "Day of the Lord" was an expression to indicate His solemn intervention in the course of that history. At first the "Day of the Lord" applied only to Israel. Gradually it was extended to the whole world, as the "Day" on which Yahweh would manifest Himself in His power and glory. This "Day" would mark the definitive victory of God over His enemies. In Daniel (9:26; 11:27; 12:13) it is the "end of the world" (cf. X. Leon-Dufour, op. cit., 89ff.). In the New Testament the "Day of the Lord" became the day of Christ, the day of the "Son of Man." The "Day" when Jesus, glorified under the aspect of the "Son of Man," would come at the end of time (Lk 17:24ff.) in glory as judge. On that "Day of God" (2 P 3:12) the heavens would be destroyed and elements melted in flames to be replaced by a new heaven and a new earth" (J. L. McKenzie, op. cit., 181).

But "the Old Testament conception which lies at the root of the New Testament Parousia" is the coming of the *"Son of Man"* (Dn 7:13ff.). In Daniel the coming of this "son of Man" is "the last act of world history, the erection of the reign of God and the subjection of all hostile powers" (McKenzie, op. cit., 638). If we read the passage in Daniel we find that it is wrapped in mystery: "I gazed into the visions of the night. And I saw, coming on the clouds of heaven, one like the son of man. He came to the one of great age and was led into his presence. On him was conferred sovereignty and kingship, and men of all peoples, nations and languages became his servants. His sovereignty is an eternal sovereignty which shall never pass away, nor will his empire be destroyed. ... And sovereignty and kingship, and the splendours of all the kingdoms under heaven, will be given to the people of the saints of the Most High. His sovereignty is an eternal sovereignty and every empire will serve and obey him" (Dn 7:13-14, 27).

Who or what is this "one like a son of man?" Interpreters

differ. "The son of man is not a real individual but a figure of speech. However, because in Daniel the thought of 'kingdom' often shifts imperceptibly into that of 'king,' the concept of the 'son of man' eventually shifted from a figure of speech for the theocratic kingdom into a term for the messianic king himself. This change appears in Enoch, written a century or two before the time of Christ" (JBC 26:28). X. Leon-Dufour declares that in the parables of Enoch "a mysterious being is held in reserve for the end of time. Then he will sit upon his throne of glory; universal judge, savior, and avenger of the just who will live in his presence after the resurrection. He has some of the features of the royal Messiah and of the Servant of Yahweh . . . but there is no question of his suffering and he has not an earthly origin. . . . Belief in this heavenly savior ready to reveal himself prepares the way for the gospel use of the expression 'Son of Man'" (op. cit. 493-4). The Jerusalem Bible notes that "here in Daniel the expression signifies a man who is mysteriously more than human. That it indicates an individual is attested by early Jewish aprocryphal writings (Enoch, 2 Esd) inspired by this passage, as also by rabbinical tradition from the 2nd to the 9th centuries, and most particularly by Jesus who applies it to Himself (Mt 8:20). That it has a collective sense also is deduced from v. 18 (and v. 22) where the 'son of man' and 'the saints of the Most High' seem more or less identified. But the collective (and equally messianic) sense is an extension of the individual sense: the 'son of man' being leader, representative and exemplar of the 'saints of the Most High.' It was with this in mind that St. Ephraim believed that the prophecy applied first to the Jews . . . but beyond this, and perfectly, to Jesus" (1437). P. P. Saydon adds that "Catholic exegesis has always recognized the Messias as the king described by the title 'Son of Man'" (*A Catholic Commentary on Holy Scripture*, 635).

New Testament

The word 'parousia' is used of the Son of Man or of Christ

in the Synoptics only in Matthew (24:3, 27, 37, 39), but in Mark and Luke Jesus speaks of the Son of Man as 'coming' (Mk 14: 62; Lk 18:8). The word also occurs in James (5:7, 8), 2 P (1:16; 3:4, 12) 1 Jn (2:28), and of course in Paul. Instead of parousia Paul at times uses the word "Revelation" or "Unveiling" (1 Cor 1:7; 2 Th 1:7).

In the *Synoptic* Gospels "the parousia is described as the coming of the Son of Man in glory (the glory of the Father) with the angels (Mt 16:27; Mk 8:38; Lk 9:26), as a coming on the clouds with power and glory (Mt 24:30; Mk 13:26; Lk 21:27). This parousia will be preceded by signs in the heavens, the departure of the heavenly bodies from their courses (Mt 24:29; Mk 13:24; Lk 21:25-7), and this coming will be like a flash of lightning (Mt 24:27; Lk 17:24). In this coming the Son of Man is enthroned at the right hand of God and receives judicial power over all men (Mt 13:41 etc.; Mk 14:62; Lk 22:69)" (J. L. McKenzie, op. cit. 638). It is noteworthy that in these Gospels this title 'Son of Man' is used only by Jesus, and this has led most scholars to conclude that the title was original with Jesus Himself. Whence did He derive this title? P. P. Saydon says simply: "there can be no doubt that Christ derived this title from Daniel 7:13, and interpreted it in a Messianic sense by appropriating the prerogatives and functions of the heavenly being that appeared to Daniel in human form. . . . Thus Christ will be a king and will sit at the right hand of God and will come in the clouds and judge all men" (loc. cit. 635). Sometimes Jesus does not "identify Himself explicitly with the Son of Man (Mt 16:27; 24:30), but elsewhere it is clear that He is speaking of Himself" (Mt 8:20; 11:19; 16:13; X. Leon-Dufour, op. cit. 494). Why did He choose this title? "It is possible that He had chosen the expression because of its ambiguity: susceptible as it was of a commonplace meaning (the 'man that I am'), it contained also a clear allusion to the Jewish apocalyptic" (ibid). These Synoptic parousiac passages do not all say clearly and explicitly that the parousia will be *at the end of the world*, but this implication is clear in many and explicit in some.

The *Pauline* concept of the parousia is substantially identical with that of the Synoptics. It is "the day of our Lord Jesus Christ" (1 Cor 1:8), when "the Lord himself will descend from heaven with a cry of command, with the archangel's call, and with the sound of the trumpet of God. And the dead in Christ will rise first" (1 Th 4:16). "He comes on that day to be glorified in his saints, and to be marveled at in all who have believed" (1 Th 1:10). "Then comes the end, when he delivers the kingdom to God the Father after destroying every rule and every authority and power" (1 Cor 15:24). "The day of the Lord will come like a thief in the night" (1 Th 5:2). Whence did Paul derive this belief in a future coming of Jesus? The traditional view has been that Paul was reproducing the teaching of Jesus Himself, who said that He would return in glory. But another view holds that the Pauline parousia cannot be traced to the Old Testament idea of the Messiah, nor to the expectation of the apocalyptic writers, nor to the teaching of Jesus, nor to the current conception of the Messiah. It came rather from the early Christians who applied to Jesus Old Testament passages which were originally written about Yahweh and spoke of a "coming" or manifestation of Yahweh. Probably there are elements of truth in both views.

In the *Catholic epistles* we find much the same conception of the parousia, though less frequently (Jm 5:7-9; 1 P 1:7; 4:13). 2 P offers us a rather vivid account of it: "But the day of the Lord will come like a thief, and then the heavens will pass away with a loud noise, and the elements will be dissolved with fire, and the earth and the works that are upon it will be burned up" (2 P 3:10).

The parousia is not entirely absent from the *Johannine* writings. "The Johannine texts on the Son of Man show in their way all the aspects of the theme which we have noted in the Synoptics. The glorious aspect: it is as Son of Man that the Son of God will on the last day exercise the power of judging (Jn 5:26-29). Then the angels will be seen ascending and descending on Him (1:51) and this final glorification will make known His heavenly origin (3:13), since 'He will ascend up to where He was before'" (6:62) (X. Leon-Dufour, op. cit. 494).

1 Jn 2:28 mentions it and elsewhere in 1 Jn the doctrine of the parousia seems to be clearly assumed. The book of Revelation supposes rather than inculcates the doctrine. At the end of the book we hear "The Spirit and Bride, say, 'Come'. . . . He who testifies to these things says, 'Surely I am coming soon.' Amen. Come, Lord Jesus" (Rv 22:17, 20). "This cry," it has been said, "takes up again an Aramaic prayer of the Church in its early days: '*Marana tha*' (cf. 1 Cor 16:22). Christian hope will never find better expression, because it is in essence only the ardent desire of a love which hungers for the presence of the Lord" (X. Leon-Dufour, op. cit., 212-213).

TIME OF THE PAROUSIA

This is one of the more difficult questions for New Testament scholars. Did Jesus, did Paul, does the New Testament tell us when the parousia will occur and bring man's history to an end? As might be expected, scholars differ widely in their answers. Some seem convinced that Jesus and Paul and the early Church generally expected an imminent parousia, others incline to doubt this or deny it. So we look first at Jesus, then at Paul, then at the New Testament generally, and ask if they tell us when the parousia will occur.

Jesus

Did Jesus expect an imminent parousia? Did He say the parousia was imminent? Did He know when it would take place? Catholic scholars give us variant answers. One firmly maintains that there are many assertions to show that Jesus did not anticipate an imminent parousia, such as Mt 24:14, 21, 31; Lk 21:24. What is more, the parables of the return suggest a long absence of the Lord (Mt 24:48; 25:5; 25:19), and so do the parables of gradual growth of the kingdom of God on earth (Mt 13:24-33). True, there are also passages that indicate that He expected an imminent parousia but these are not to be taken literally but rather as indicating a revelation of His power. Another also contends that Jesus did not expect an imminent parousia, i.e. an imminent end and judgment of the world, but he explains Jesus' expectation a bit differently. What He did expect at His death was a great event (perhaps the destruction of Jerusalem) and an outburst of pneumatic power (at Pentecost?) that would mark the beginning of a new era in human history, the era of Christianity. Thus Jesus had *two ends* in mind: one imminent but pneumatic—at Pentecost, the other remote and cosmological—at the end of the world.[1]

Klaus Berger, on the other hand, maintains that Jesus did expect an imminent parousia: "an imminent expectation is the only possible form of eschatological hope that can be attributed to Jesus." "It is now taken for granted," he writes, "that the message of Jesus was concerned with the expectation of the Kingdom of God in the future, very close at hand, an expectation shared with apocalyptic and already voiced in the Old Testament" (*Sacramentum Mundi* 4, 342-344).

B. M. Nolan thinks that Jesus probably hoped for a speedy parousia. "Jesus," he writes, "had at least a vague idea of an interval between his death and the end of the world. He identified himself with the son of man, who was active on earth, would suffer and rise, and be revealed in future glory. But whether that revelation in glory referred to the parousia or to the coming of the Kingdom in many non-definitive but climactic events such as the exaltation of Christ, the Pentecostal outpouring of the Spirit, the Gentile mission and the destruction of Jerusalem, is not certain. The two contradictory verses, Mk 13:30 and 32 indirectly reveal that Jesus himself had no schedule for the future: he only knew that he would be the final judge. As a dedicated prophet in an apocalyptic climate, he probably hoped for a speedy parousia, but he preserved a reverent agnosticism about its exact date."[2]

R. E. Brown also inclines to think that Jesus thought and spoke of an imminent parousia. "There are many texts," he writes, "that imply an interval between Jesus' death and the parousia," e.g. references to a church or community life, a mission of the disciples to Israel or beyond, the growth parables, the orders to baptize and to commemorate Jesus in the Eucharist. But how long an interval? He notes three types of sayings that seem quite distinct. "Two famous passages in Mk indicate the parousia will come in the lifetime of Jesus' hearers (Mk 13:30; 9:1). The eschatological discourses (Mk 13, Mt 24-25, Lk 21), indicate a delayed parousia in terms of the signs that will precede the coming of the Son of Man, e. g. false messiahs, persecution, war, and cosmic cataclysms (cf. Mt 24:48; 25:5, 19). Another group of sayings insists that the time of the parousia cannot be foretold (Mt 24:42-44; Lk 12:39-40; Mt 24:50; Lk 12:46; Mt 25:13; Lk 17:20-21; Mk 13:32)." "Which is the more original strain in Jesus' teaching?" he asks. And his answer is interesting. "The New Testament Epistles give independent evidence of the confusion that reigned in the first century thought about the Parousia (cf. 1 Th with 2 Th 1; Cor 15 with 2 Cor 5; 1 P 4:7 with 2 P 3:4-11). Could such confusion have arisen if Jesus both knew about the indefinite delay of the parousia and expressed himself clearly on the subject? One is almost forced to take at face value the admission of Mk 13:32 that Jesus did not know when the parousia would take place." Then he adds: "Is it totally inconceivable that, since Jesus did not know when the parousia would occur, he tended to think and say that it would occur soon? That God would make Jesus victorious and would eventually establish His own reign was a basic conviction of Jesus' life and mission. Could Catholic theologians hold not only that knowledge of the parousia was not an essential of Jesus' mission, but also that Jesus was not protected from the confused views of his era about the time of the parousia?"[3]

What can we conclude? That it seems rather clear that Jesus did not know just when the parousiac end of the world would occur. Perhaps He did envision two parousiac outbursts of power, one pneumatic shortly after His death, the other cosmic at the end of the world. But that He thought the parousiac end of the world would come soon is not certain.

Paul

Did Paul think the parousia was imminent? Once again inter-

preters disagree. C. P. Ceroke writes that an "analysis of 1 Th
4:12-18 makes it impossible to avoid the conclusion that both
Paul and the Thessalonians had in view a proximate parousia.
But in 2 Th 2:1-12 (written about 6 months after 1 Th) Paul
in effect denied that the parousia is imminent" ("Parousia in
the Bible," NCE, 10, 1034). On the other hand Bruce Vawter
declares that "quite as in 1 Th, Paul (in 2 Th 2:1ff.) neither
affirms nor denies the imminence of the parousia. What he denies
is that the day of the Lord has actually begun ... since it is well
known that certain events must first occur, and these have not
yet occurred."[4] And X. Leon-Dufour writes: "In correcting
their illusions Paul never says he fosters the hope of being alive
at the time" (1 Th 4:17) (op. cit. 92). Once again, what can we
conclude from all this? That it seems rather clear that Paul did
not know just when the parousiac end of the world would come.
And that he did not say it would come in the remote future,
nor did he affirm or deny that it would come "soon." Perhaps
he hoped for a while that it would, but the way he engaged in
such widespread missionary activity so quickly would seem to
indicate that an imminent parousia was hardly the driving moti-
vation of his life and activity.

New Testament

If we turn to the New Testament as a whole, does it say
the parousia will come quickly? unexpectedly? at an unknown
date? Will it be preceded by definite signs?

C. P. Ceroke (loc. cit.) says that "a number of texts seem
to suggest with all desired clarity that the parousia is an imminent event (Mt 10:23; 24:34; Mk 13:30; Lk 21:32; 1 Th 4:13ff;
1 P 4:7; Rv 3:11; 22:20)." E. Pax writes that "there is no doubt
that a great number of early Christians (Mk 9:1; 13:30; 1 P 4:7;
Rv 1:3), including for a time even Paul (Rm 13:11; 1 Th 4:15ff.;
1 Cor 7:26) hoped for an early parousia. But the fact that its
evident delay did not lead to any crisis of faith . . . is proof
enough that there can be no question of a so-called postpone-

ment of the parousia. Rather the early Christians concentrated on that which was essential—the ascension on which the Christian life was based and which was to be realized and lived out daily with the support of the Holy Spirit. The interval between epiphany and parousia is thus occupied with the formation of the Christian" (*Sacramentum Verbi* 2, 633-8).

And J. L. McKenzie adds with his usual good balance: "The parousia was never described by Jesus as an event which was in the remote future; and to be altogether accurate the attitude of the early Church should be described as a hope and an expectation that the parousia was near rather than a firm conviction that it was near. Many critics have defined the early Church as an 'eschatological community' which did nothing except live in common awaiting the parousia. The Church had no awareness of its mission, these critics say, until it was necessary to renounce the hope that the end was near. This conception can scarcely be combined with the evangelistic work of the apostles, particularly of Paul and his associates; the community which extended itself through so much of the Roman world was not an eschatological group withdrawn from the world. And this movement occurred while the hope that the parousia was near was still strong, as one can see in the Synoptic Gospels and the epistles of Paul" (op. cit. 640).

To sum it up, then, the New Testament did not say the parousia would be very remote nor did it say definitely that it would come quickly. It did say that the precise time of the parousia was unknown (Mt 24:36; Mk 13:32; Ac 1:7; 1 Tm 6: 14-15) but that it would come unexpectedly (Mt 24:27; 1 Th 5:2) and would be preceded by "signs" (2 Th 2:3; Mt 24:14; Lk 21:25-27).

Today

What do men say today? Will the parousia come soon or will it be a long, long time in coming? Adventists and many Pentecostals think it will come very soon. Recently there have appeared two very interesting speculations about the time of the parousia, one arguing that it will be very, very remote, the other suggesting that man has it in his power to hasten the parousia.

R. *Pendergast* says he is "uncomfortable with the assertions one sometimes hears in charismatic groups that the second coming of the Lord is imminent." His reading of the 'signs of the times' suggests the contrary. For "to one who believes that God is the author of nature and the master of history, the signs of the times indicate clearly that His design is far from complete." "If the parousia is to be the decisive culmination of *cosmic* history, and not of the earth alone," then the end is not at all imminent since the culmination of cosmic history is very remote. It has taken the cosmos 10 billion years to produce man, and on this time-scale "the history of the human race is quite short." Is it likely "that after so lengthy a prelude, the drama of human existence should end so soon?"

The human race is still in its adolescence. It is still very far from scientific maturity. It is very far from political maturity in which all men cooperate for the planetary common good. It is far from space-travel maturity. It is very far from evangelizing maturity, for it is very far from the proclamation of the Good News to the entire universe. "Can the universal history centered around Christ have reached its maturity, if the influence of the central figure still affects only a small part of the cosmos?". . . "Modern theories of planet formation make it likely that the universe contains an unimaginable number of planets suitable for intelligent life, and the theory of evolution suggests that intelligent life has evolved on a significant fraction of them . . . It becomes clear that all intelligent beings are to be united into one through the Son of God who died to save all, who is the center of the whole creation". . . . "We and our whole solar system may have vanished long before history has run its course. But, in any event, the consummation of universal history . . . will not occur before the Good News has been spread far beyond Earth, whether by us or by others" (*America*, March 30, 1974).

A. *Fritsch, S.J.*, presents a view that "sees modern man hastening the Day of the Second Coming through his work of unification of the world community for the sake of a renewal of the cosmos. . . . The first Advent was preceded by preparation: the earth matured in billions of years to the point where the Word could burst forth. The second Advent must be prepared for by the cosmatization of man, a maturation in working and living together as a cosmic family. The first Advent sets the initiation of the whole process of cosmatization which will terminate in the Second Advent . . . We continue from the force of habit to think of the parousia whereby the Kingdom of God is to be consummated on earth, as an event of a purely catastrophic nature, that is to say, liable to come about at any moment in history, irrespective of any definite state of mankind. But why should we not assume, in accordance with the latest scientific view of mankind in a state of Anthropogenesis, that the parousiac spark can, of physical and organic necessity, only be kindled between heaven and mankind which has biologically reached a certain critical evolutionary point of collective maturity? The active expectation of a new Earth should stimulate and catalyze our activity in this world, making man discern those tasks most necessary at this moment which will precondition the earth for its fulfillment in the parousia. Once seeing that technological application is part of total Christification, the believer can move from a generalized desire for activism to specific social involvement, in full confidence that such a plunge into earthly problems is truly salvific . . . One can visualize the whole sequence of cosmic movement as a Christification: the processive Incarnation; the cosmic forces converging on the person of Christ (1st Advent); the scattering of the Word to the world, of carrying Christ to others; the beginning of the process of drawing all men together as one unity through cosmatization (processive eschatology); the making of Christ visible in his full glory—the Second Coming" (*Theology of Earth*, 107).

SIGNS OF THE PAROUSIA

The New Testament seems to offer a number of 'signs' that

will precede the parousia and enable men to know that the parousia is not far off. And those who down the centuries have expected an early parousia, have made much of these signs. Some have believed that these signs were so clearly being verified in their time that the parousiac end of the world must be close at hand. But they were disappointed. Today, too, there are once again many who think that those signs are being verified and that the parousia therefore must be close at hand. What are these signs? A number have been singled out: prodigies in heaven and on earth, a great apostasy, the preaching of the Gospel to all nations, the conversion of the Jews, the coming of Antichrist.

Matthew 24 seems to indicate many of these: "Tell us . . . what will be the sign of your coming and of the close of the age? And Jesus answered them . . . many will come in my name, saying, 'I am the Christ' and they will lead many astray . . . nation will rise against nation . . . and there will be famines and earthquakes in various places . . . then there will be great tribulation, such as has not been from the beginning of the world until now. . . Immediately after the tribulation of those days the sun will be darkened, and the moon will not give its light, and the stars will fall from heaven. . . . And this Gospel of the kingdom will be preached throughout the whole world, as a testimony to all nations; and then the end will come" (cf. Lk 18:8; 21:5-7; Mk 13:1-4). Lk 18:8 seems to indicate a great apostasy: "When the Son of man comes, will he find faith on earth?" Rm 11:25f. seems to tell of the conversion of the Jews: "I want you to understand this mystery, brethren: a hardening has come upon part of Israel, until the full number of the Gentiles come in, and so all Israel will be saved." 2 Th tells us of Antichrist: "Let no one deceive you in any way; for that day will not come, unless the rebellion comes first, and the man of lawlessness is revealed, the son of perdition" (2:3ff.). So does 1 Jn: "Children, it is the last hour and as you have heard that antichrist is coming, so now many antichrists have come; therefore we know that it is the last hour. . . . This is the antichrist, he who denies the Father and the Son" (2:18,22).

Are these clear-cut signs of an imminent parousia at the end of the world? Are they meant to foretell events so spectacular they will capture attention and indicate that the end of the world is at hand? Down the centuries interpreters have disagreed over these signs and they still disagree today.

D. M. Stanley thinks the Matthean signs refer to the ruin of the Temple at Jerusalem. "Actually," he writes, "the catastrophe means the end of the Old Testament world and the liberation of Christianity from Judaism. Jesus refuses to reveal 'when' this will happen, but he does foretell 'signs,' realized in the years before A.D. 70. A series of pseudo-messiahs will appear. There will be talk of wars . . . In the years before A.D. 70 the young Church will meet a series of crises: martyrdom, apostasy, loss of first fervor of fraternal love. Yet patient endurance will triumph. The Gospel will be preached to pagans, throughout the Mediterranean world, as Paul already testifies in A.D. 58 (Rm 10:18)."

A New Catechism gives a very different but very interesting interpretation of the "signs" presented to men by prophets, evangelists and apocalyptic seers down the years. It does not see these signs as a picture of the destruction of Jerusalem. It does not see them as a description of the course of events that will precede and mark out the end of the world. Rather it sees these signs as giving us a general sense of the course of history and its consummation, affirming that whatever happens, God moves to His triumph in all things. "They depict in extremely vivid colors the calamities and miseries of all ages, the horrors of war, even catastrophes on a cosmic scale. And we hear at the same time the message that even then—and above all, then—God remains faithful. 'Now when these things begin to take place, look up and raise your heads, because your redemption is drawing near' (Lk 21:28). This is the statement which the horrifying pictures of the prophets, the evangelists and the apocalyptic seers make, for all ages" (Herder and Herder, N. Y., 1967, 478).

The "*salvation* (conversion?) *of all Israel*" mentioned in Rom 11:25 has long fascinated interpreters. Does Paul mean there will be a conversion of all Jews toward the end of the world—and this will be a sign that the parousia is at hand? Interpreters once again disagree. J. A. Fitzmyer says that "in Paul's view of the divine plan of salvation . . . the conversion of Israel will take place, when the pleroma (fullness) of the Gentiles has come in." Then he asks a question without answering it: "Does Paul mean by pleroma all the Gentiles there are?" (JBC 53:114). A. Theissen goes a step further: "The time will come when the present problem of Israel's exclusion from the salvation of the Messiah will cease to exist because of her conversion, which will follow upon the conversion of the Gentiles. . . . 'Fullness' (pleroma of the Gentiles, need not be pressed so as to mean every individual, nor, 'all Israel' " (*A Catholic Commentary on Holy Scripture*, 1072, 1073). B. M. Ahern says: "Israel's hardening of heart is only partial and temporary, to last only until the Gentile community has entered the kingdom. When this has come about, then Israel shall be saved, for Isaias foretold that the Messiah would bring it salvation and forgiveness of sin. Hence the very fact that Israel needs forgiveness certifies that the prophecy will be fulfilled."[5] But G. C. Berkouwer goes much further in his treatment of the "mystery of Rm 11:25." "Many have concluded," he writes, that "what Paul meant by 'Israel'. . . was not the nation of Israel, but the totality of those to be saved, both Jews and Gentiles, the believers, the true, spiritual Israel . . . the church as the new Israel. . . . But . . . H. M. Matter correctly observes that the 'spiritual Israel' interpretation cannot be harmonized with Paul's train of thought . . . Many have concluded that undoubtedly the real content of the mystery of Rm 11:25 is that *in the end of time all Israel* will be saved . . . On this view 'all Israel' means 'Judaism at the last day'. . . Understood in this sense, Israel's repentance is clearly taken as a *sign*. But . . . can this really be Paul's meaning? . . . Is there not good reason to suppose that Paul was not referring to what we think of as the future (the last generation) but was thinking of his own time as the last days?" (op. cit. 345, 346, 347).

What must we conclude from these variant interpretations? Since neither the time of Israel's conversion, nor the nature and extent of it can be clearly determined, it can hardly qualify or function as a "sign" that the parousia is at hand.

Of all the "signs" of the parousia of Christ, the most tantalizing, the most discussed, the most mysterious, is that which is called the *Antichrist,* the "man of sin," the "man of lawlessness," the "son of perdition." Throughout Christian history men have tried to identify this Antichrist with this historical figure or that, with this anti-christian movement or that. Not long ago Jeanne Dixon, our American "prophetess," declared that Antichrist was born in the Near East on February 5, 1962, and "will reach the pinnacle of his power in 1999, when a terrible holocaust will shock the world's peoples into a true renewal . . . His life will parallel that of Jesus—even to his sudden appearance on the world scene when he is about thirty."[8]

Will there be a "parousia" of Antichrist that will precede and announce the parousia of Christ? Will there be one Antichrist or many? Is Antichrist at work now?

If we turn to *John* there is not one antichrist, there are many: "so now many antichrists have come; therefore we know that it is the last hour." For whoever denies that Jesus is the Christ, whoever denies the Father and the Son (1 Jn 2:18, 22), whoever does not confess Jesus come in the flesh (I Jn 4:3; 2 Jn 7), that one is the deceiver, the antichrist. Thus "John clearly alludes to heretics and apostates," one commentator writes, "among whom the apostasy announced by Jesus and predicted by Paul is taking place. The eschatology is therefore present reality; but the current drama of faith must be understood in relation to a much larger horizon, that which the Apocalypse fully describes" (X. Leon-Dufour, op. cit., 17-18). *Paul,* however, seems to speak of a single eschatological "Antichrist," for he writes: "that day will not come, unless the rebellion comes first, and the man of lawlessness is revealed, the son of perdition . . . And you know what is restraining him now so that he may be revealed in his time. For the mystery of lawlessness is already at work; only he who now restrains it will do so until he is out of the way. Then the lawless one will be revealed, and the Lord Jesus will slay him with the breath of his mouth and destroy him by His appearing and His coming. The coming of the lawless one by the activity of Satan will be with all power and with pretended signs and wonders, and with all wicked deception for those who are to perish, because they refused to love the truth and so be saved" (2 Th 2:3-10).

Hundreds of attempts have been made to determine "what is restraining him now so that he may be revealed in his time" (2 Th 2:6). Apparently Paul and the Thessalonians knew who or what this restraining power was, but we do not. Some have suggested that this "restrainer" was the Roman Empire, or the sum total of the preachers of the Gospel, or the Archangel, St. Michael (cf. Rv 12:7-9; 20:1-3, 7), or the prayer of the Church, or a divine decree, or the Holy Spirit. But none of these suggestions have been found very satisfactory. One wonders why no one has suggested that the pope or the papacy might be the "restrainer."

Those who think Antichrist is an individual have often tried to identify him with some historical figure. Once it was Nero who was identified as antichrist. The number 666, "the number of the beast" (Rv 13:18), has been found to be the sum of the numerical values of the letters of the name "Nero Caesar," written in Hebrew characters (*Nun* 50, plus *resh* 200, plus *waw* 6, plus *nun* 50, plus *qoph* 100, plus *samekh* 60, plus *resh* 200). "But," writes G. C. Berkower, "there is nothing resembling unanimity about the interpretation of the number 666, and it appears extremely difficult to arrive at a conclusive answer" (op. cit. 280-281). Later on individual popes or the papacy itself were thought by many to be the antichrist, and by the Reformers. But "this opinion is abandoned by respectable Protestant exegesis today" (JBC 48:32).

Many, if not most modern commentators, seem to view Paul's Antichrist as a collectivity rather than as an individual: "most modern commentators consider him to be a mere personification of the evil forces that will, it seems, get the upper hand at the end of the world" (Dom B. Orchard, *A Catholic Commentary on Holy Scripture*, 1140, 1141). J. L. McKenzie writes that "there are good reasons for doubting the long established opinion that he signifies a real historical eschatological figure . . . Antichrist is rather a personification of the powers of evil which occasionally focus in some individual person and can be expected to do so again. The consummate wickedness of Antichrist is depicted in traits which suggest diabolical malice; but this is a poetic emphasis upon his malice rather than an indication that Antichrist is diabolically possessed or still less that he is a diabolical incarnation" (op. cit. 35-6). JBC says that "though Paul appears to speak of a single eschatological 'antichrist,' his meaning is not certain, especially in view of the fact that his descriptive language is largely borrowed from Old Testament types (Ezk 28:2; Dn 11:36). The Antichrist figure of the *Syn* and *Ap* certainly implies a collectivity of persons" (JBC 62:15).

But even if most modern commentators consider antichrist a collectivity of persons or a personification of the powers of evil, other commentators think the evidence for this is not so strong as to preclude the possibility or even the probability that antichrist is a single person. Dom B. Orchard notes that "the teaching of St. Paul on the antichrist is quite compatible with his being a single person, and the manner in which all the Sacred Books from Daniel to Apocalypse speak of him, as a man incarnating all the forces of evil and as the false counterpart of Christ Himself in the last days of the world, does not permit us to lay aside as improbable the view that the Antichrist is indeed an individual" (*A Catholic Commentary on Holy Scripture*, 1141). And Bruce Vawter writes that although Antichrist usually "is represented in the New Testament as a series or a collectivity rather than a single individual (yet) in 2 Th Paul seems to be thinking of a single person, who would, therefore, epitomize the antichristian spirit, who would be Satan's instrument par excellence In this case, as a single individual, he is obviously an eschatological figure, that is to say, one who belongs to the last times, immediately preceding the parousia. It would be idle, therefore, to try to identify him with any known historical person." He adds very appositely, however, that "on the other hand, Paul has insisted that 'the mystery of iniquity is already at work.' Thus, whether or not he was speaking of a single man of sin in the preceding verses, he would agree with 1 Jn that 'many antichrists have arisen.' Always and in every age the Church and the Christian are confronted by those who usurp the place of God and delude many through their ability to offer a specious substitute for the Gospel complete with 'powers and signs and lying wonders.' Throughout history these antichrists have been many: we may think of Caesaro-papism, the Enlightenment, and, more recently, the omnipotent State and omnipotent Science. Paul's words of warning and consolation are, therefore, equally appropriate for us today as in the perspective for which he originally intended them" (*New Testament Reading Guide*, op. cit. 57-60).

What must we conclude about all these 'signs' of the parousia of Christ? After hundreds of years of study and discussion, interpreters are far from agreed on just what these "signs" mean and whether they are strictly eschatological signs that will immediately precede the end of the world. Obviously, then, these "events" can hardly serve as adequate signs of an imminent parousia. They can hardly—either singly or collectively—qualify or function as signs that the parousia of Christ is definitely close at hand. H. Schlier summed it up very simply when he wrote: "There are indeed signs of the coming end, but they are always ambiguous. One cannot note the presence of God's time and substantiate it as he can other events. Nor is it your business to know the time or the hour which the Father in his power has set" (Ac 1:7).[7] And yet, although these signs are ambiguous, and though they only give us a general sense of the course of history and its consummation, should there at any time be a convergence of these sign-events, those who note these events and their convergence and their conformity to the New Testament signs of the parousia of Christ would be well advised to "wonder" whether the parousia of Christ might not be approaching and so prepare themselves for it by closer union with Christ and His Church. Then when the parousiac Christ comes "like a flash of lightning," they will be ready.

SIGNIFICANCE OF THE PAROUSIA

What does this parousia of Christ signify? What is its deeper meaning? Why should there be such a parousia? What role does it play in God's salvific plan? If we say that Christ is already present, what do we mean when we say He will come again at the end of the world? These and many other similar questions men have been asking down the years. And they have been giving quite different answers. One of the simplest is the credal answer: "He is going to come again in glory to judge the living and the dead" (DS 150). This we shall ponder in our next chapter. Another answer is that He will come again to establish the "new heaven and the new earth." This we shall consider in our last chapter. Two other answers interest us now.

One sees the parousia as marking the "end of human history." For K. Rahner "the parousia, as understood in theology, is the permanent blessed presence of Christ in the manifest finality of the history of the world and of salvation which is perfected and ended in the destiny of Jesus Christ. It is the fullness and the ending of the history of man and the world with the glorified humanity of Christ—now directly manifest in his glory—in God" (*Sacramentum Mundi* 4, 345).

Russell Aldwinckle says that the parousia "will be a real event . . . in that the parousia brings to an end the long process of historical development. It will not be a historical event in the sense that the parousia will inaugurate another historical epoch within the limits of this present spacetime process. . . . The parousia is not literal in the sense that a new historical utopia on earth will be established which modern historians and scientists can examine with the methods they have devised for the exploration of this present world. It is literal in the sense that the union of Christ with His people at the end of history will be a meeting between a real Christ and a real community of persons" (op. cit. 128).

For A. Winklhofer "it is this coming and nothing else that brings history to its fulfillment. It gives all history its meaning, and its course is understandable only in view of it. This second coming not only seals and certifies an end, but causes it, and this in order to bring about a fulfillment which consists in a mysterious transformation of the entire creation and particularly of man. . . . It is an event visible to all men in every part of the earth, clearly and unmistakably one in which Christ is at work. The Lord has no need of any announcement in the press, by television or radio. He will just be there, as he always was mystically there, and will fill with his tremendous presence the whole creation, heaven and earth, to the furthest star of our expanding universe" (op. cit. pp. 164ff.).

The other, and closely related answer, is that of S. J. Duffy. "In the New Testament perspective," according to him, "all converges upon the parousia: judgment, retribution, consummation of life inaugurated by Christ's resurrection, definitive constitution of His kingdom . . . the parousia is (the) final event of salvation history. The glorious return of Christ and the ensemble of eschatological events He will then effect mark the consummation of God's redemptive plan. . . The parousia . . . a reality already at the heart of the present world . . . will harvest in final, perfect form what already is (1 Jn 3:2). This in no way implies that the parousia brings with it nothing new. Christ's emergence from His secret presence in the Church, His resurrection of the dead, His definitive judgment and situation of each person within the divine plan, His transfiguration of non-rational creation, His enthronement as center of creation, all are new events giving the personal eschata, death and particular judgment, their full significance. Yet these final events now exist hiddenly in Christ's kingdom, as Christ Himself lives hiddenly in glory to be manifested only at His return (Col 3:1-4). Hence the parousia is not simply another item in an array of last things. As God's final loving intervention it is the plenitude of Redemption, the crowning triumph of Christ as Savior" ("Parousia in Theology," NCE 10, 1037-9).

Notes for Chapter 11

1. F. G. Glasson, **The Second Advent,** (London, Epworth Press, 1947).

2. "The Meaning of the Parousia Today," **Theology Digest,** v. XVIII, 1970, pp. 151-152.

3. "How Much Did Jesus Know?", **Theology Digest,** v. XVII, 1969, pp. 44-47.

4. **New Testament Guide, 1, 2 Thessalonians,** (Collegeville, Liturgical Press), p. 57.

5. **New Testament Reading Guide, Galatians and Romans,** pp. 76-77.

6. Cf. R. Woods, **The Occult Revolution,** (New York, Herder & Herder, 1967), pp. 165ff.

7. "The End of Time," **Theology Digest,** Fall, 1969, p. 203.

Chapter 12
Will There Be a General Judgment of All Men at the End of the World?

How long man's history will continue, we do not know. Its end may still be billions of years away. But its end will come. Man's pilgrim state will be over. Man's final number will be achieved. Man's history will be at an end. Man's final state of trans-temporal and trans-spatial existence will begin. What will happen then? Our scientists and our philosophers can only speculate. They do not know. Only God knows. And God has told us something about this end and this beginning. In the words of the Creeds and Councils of Christ's Church: "the dead will rise. And Christ will come again in glory." To do what? "To judge the living and the dead" (DS 150). To judge all men. That is what God has planned. That is what Christ will do.

This can seem very strange to some. God "desires all men to be saved" (1 Tm 2:4). So He sends His Son to be their Savior. And this Son, His Word, was made flesh and dwelt among us, lived, suffered and died for men. And He will come again at the end of the world to judge them! He came to justify them by His grace. He will come again to judge them according to the works they have done in their pilgrim state, according to the way they have responded to His love and His grace! So that those who have done good deeds will go into eternal life; those who have done evil will go into everlasting fire (DS 76)! This can seem very strange indeed. For the dead will already have been judged at their death—and most likely by this same Christ—in the judgment of each individual which we call the particular judgment. Will all men be judged again at the end of the world—and by Christ their Savior? And if they will be, is this general judgment of all men the main purpose of Christ's Second Coming? Or one of its essential purposes? How will this general judgment differ from the particular judgment? And why should there be such a judgment at all? These are some of the many questions that men have asked about this general judgment. To try to answer them we turn first to Sacred Scripture.

Old Testament

The Old Testament, of course, does not tell us that Christ will be the judge of all men at the end of the world. But prophets often warn of the Day of Yahweh on which God will judge the sinful. Thus Jeremiah writes that "Yahweh roars from on high, He makes His voice heard from His holy dwelling place . . . The sound reaches all the inhabitants of the earth, to the far ends of the world. For Yahweh is indicting the nations, arraigning all flesh for judgment; the wicked he abandons to the sword—it is Yahweh who speaks" (25:30-31). Some of the Psalms present Yahweh as judge of the world and of nations: "See, Yahweh is enthroned for ever, He sets up His throne for judgment; He is going to judge the world with justice, and pronounce a true verdict on the nations" (Ps 9:7). But the idea of a great judgment of all the nations is more characteristic of apocalyptic literature than of the Old Testament. But Daniel tells us: "Thrones were set in place and one of great age took his seat. . . . A thousand thousand waited on him, ten thousand times ten thousand stood before him. A court was held and the books were opened" (7:9, 10). And in Joel we read: "Let the nations rouse themselves, let them march to the Valley of Jehoshaphat, for I am going to sit in judgment there on all the nations round. . . . Host on host in the Valley of Decision. For the day of Yahweh is near in the Valley of Decision" (4:12, 14).

New Testament

The New Testament tells us of a twofold judgment, one historical and the other eschatological, one that is already present and one that is to come at the glorious return of Christ, one that is in history and another that is outside history and ends history.

In the *Synoptic Gospels* Matthew and Luke mention the judgment more frequently than Mark and judgment often means condemnation: "They will receive the greater condemnation" (Mk 12:40; cf. Mt 23:33; Lk 20:47). Matthew and Luke speak of the "day of judgment": "But I tell you, it shall be more tolerable on the day of judgment for Tyre and Sidon than for you. . . . But I tell you that it shall be more tolerable on the day of judgment for the land of Sodom than for you" (Mt 11: 22, 24; cf. Mt 10:15; Lk 10:12-15). Everyone will be judged, we are told, according to the way he has judged his neighbor: "judge not, that you be not judged. For with the judgment you pronounce you will be judged, and the measure you give will be the measure you get" (Mt 7:1-2); or according to the love or indifference he has shown to others (Mt 25:31-46). Though the scene so vividly described in Mt 25:31-46 has little resemblance to a judgment scene and no words suggesting judgment, it is usually called the "last judgment." And rightly so. For the reality of "judgment" is obviously and also necessarily implied. If the separation of the sheep and goats is not a "judgment," what is it? If the distinction of "blessed" and "cursed" is not a judgment, what is it?

Paul assumes that the idea of judgment is familiar to his readers, and he often mentions it, especially in his Letter to the Romans. He speaks of a past judgment—in the sense of a condemnation of all men because of one man's trespass: "for the judgment following one trespass brought condemnation, but the free gift following many trespasses brings justification. . . . Then as one man's trespass led to condemnation for all men, so one man's act of righteousness leads to acquittal and life for all men" (Rm 5:16, 18). But Paul speaks not only of a judgment of condemnation and acquittal in the past (and perhaps in the present). He also says there will be a judgment of judicial decision at the end of the world. And he uses some rather strong words about it: "by your hard and impenitent heart you are storing up wrath for yourself on the day of wrath when God's righteous judgment will be revealed. For he will render to every man according to his works . . . on that day when, according to my Gospel, God judges the secrets of men by Christ Jesus" (Rm 2:5-6, 16). The judgment is generally associated with the parousia of Christ, and sometimes in very vivid terms: "This is evidence of the righteous judgment of God, that you be made worthy of the kingdom of God, for which you are suffering— since indeed God deems it just to repay with affliction those who afflict you . . . when the Lord Jesus is revealed from heaven with His mighty angels in flaming fire, inflicting vengeance on those who do not know God and upon those who do not obey the Gospel of our Lord Jesus. They shall suffer the punishment of eternal destruction and exclusion from the presence of the Lord and from the glory of His might" (2 Th 1:5-9). Who and what will be judged on that day of judgment? All men. "The living and the dead" is the way we read it in 2 Tm 4:1, an expression that was incorporated into the early creeds and emphasizes the universality of the divine judgment. In Rm 2:5-6 we read that "on the day of wrath when God's righteous judgment will be revealed . . . He will render to every man according to his works." In 2 Cor 5:10 we are told that "we must all appear before the judgment seat of Christ so that each one may receive good or evil, according to what he has done in the body." It is not surprising then that JBC declares that "the New Testament insists upon the universality of the judgment" (Mt 25:32; Jn 5:28f.; 2 Tm 4:1; 1 P 4:5), (JBC 64:87).

What will be the norm and object of this judgment? X. Leon-Dufour writes: "For those who claim to know it, the norm will be the Mosaic Law (Rm 2:12); those who have not known the Law of Moses will be judged by the natural law (Rm 2:14f.); but those who have accepted the Gospel will be judged by the law of liberty (Jm 2:12). But ill fortune awaits him who shall have judged his neighbor (Rm 2:1ff.) for he will be judged with the same severity with which he judged others (Rm 14:10ff.; Jm 2:13)." As objects of this judgment we note slander (Rm 3:8), violation of the vow of virginity (1 Tm 5:12), the Judaizers who disturb the Galatians (Gal 5:12), those who do not believe the truth (2 Th 2:12), those who disobey public authority (Rm 13:2), hard and impenitent hearts and the secrets of men (Rm 2:5-6, 16). Thus Paul, even though he puts a very heavy emphasis on grace and justification by grace, still clings fast "to the assertion that at the end men are judged 'by their works' and no one can escape giving an account of the way he has lived his life. There is a freedom which is not cancelled out even by grace and indeed is brought by it face to face with itself" (J. Ratzinger, op. cit. 247ff.).

Who will be the judge on the last day? In his letter to the Romans Paul calls God the judge quite often: "the judgment of God" (Rm 2:2, 3); "God's righteous judgment" (Rm 2:5); "God judges" (Rm 2:16); "God judges the world" (Rm 3:6). But in 2 Tm 4:1 we read: "Christ Jesus who is to judge the living and the dead." But in 1 Cor Paul writes: "It is the Lord who judges me. Therefore do not pronounce judgment before the time, before the Lord comes, who will bring to light the things now hidden in darkness and will disclose the purposes of the heart" (1 Cor 4:4). Will God, then, be the judge or Christ? Both, Paul seems to say: "God judges the secrets of men by Christ Jesus" (Rm 2:16).

In John's Gospel judgment is twofold, in the present, and in the future. But the heavier stress is on judgment in the present, during the time of Jesus. Judgment is present from the moment the Father sends the Son into the world: "For God sent the Son into the world, not to condemn the world, but that the world might be saved through Him. He who believes in Him is not condemned; he who does not believe is condemned already, because he has not believed in the name of the only Son of God. And this is the judgment, that the light has come into the world, and men loved darkness rather than light, because their deeds were evil" (Jn 3:17-19). Each one is judged according to his attitude toward Jesus: "Truly, truly, I say to you, he who hears my word and believes Him who sent me, has eternal life; he does not come into judgment, but has passed from death to life" (Jn 5:24). This judgment in the present, what is it, then? It seems to be "rejection of faith in Jesus Christ" (J. L. McKenzie, op. cit. 468). It seems to be "not so much a divine sentence as a revelation of the secret of human hearts. . . . Since the time of Christ the judgment is an accomplished fact, continually present, of which there is awaited only the final consummation" (X. Leon-Dufour, op. cit. 243).

But there is also a future judgment on the last day, as John is well aware. For he writes: "He who rejects me and does not receive my sayings has a judge; the word that I have spoken will be his judge on the last day" (Jn 12:4, 8). And again: "For the Father . . . has given Him (the Son) authority to execute judgment, because He is the Son of man. Do not marvel at this; for the hour is coming when all who are in the tombs will hear His voice and come forth, those who have done good, to the resurrection of life, and those who have done evil, to the resurrection of judgment" (Jn 5:26-29).

Who is the judge for John? Jesus or the Father? Or both? In Jn 12:47 Jesus says, "I did not come to judge the world but to save the world." And in Jn 8:15 he says, "I judge no one." But Jesus also says: "the Father judges no one, but has given all judgment to the Son . . . and has given him authority to execute the judgment, because he is the Son of man" (Jn 5:22, 27). And yet elsewhere Jesus does seem to say or imply that the Father is the judge, for he says, "I do not seek my own glory; there is One who seeks it and he will be the judge" (Jn 8:50). Thus John, like Paul, seems to say that the judge is both the Father and the Son, or as John writes it of Jesus: "it is not I alone that judge, but I and he who sent me."

Other books of the New Testament also tell of the last judgment. In Heb 6:2 we are told of an "eternal judgment," which is interpreted as "the general judgment after the resurrection of the body, which fixes the destiny of each one for ever and is therefore called 'eternal' " (W. Leonard, *A Catholic Commentary on Holy Scripture*, 1164). 2 Peter says, "the heavens and earth that now exist have been stored up for fire, being kept until the day of judgment and destruction of ungodly men" (3:7). The Book of Revelation tells of the last judgment in very vivid terms:

"The nations raged, but thy wrath came, and the time for the dead to be judged, for rewarding thy servants, the prophets and saints, and those who fear thy name, both small and great, and for destroying the destroyers of the earth" (11:18). It declares that the dead will be judged by what they had done: "And I saw the dead, great and small, standing before the throne, and books were opened. Also another book was opened, which is the book of life. And the dead were judged by what was written in the books, by what they had done. And the sea gave up the dead in it, Death and Hades gave up the dead in them, and all were judged by what they had done" (20:12-13).

Early Church

If we turn to the Early Church we find many of the Fathers and writers testifying to the last judgment. We need merely mention Tertullian, Hippolytus, Cyprian, Basil, Chrysostom (cf. Hervé, op. cit. 536), Athanasius, Gregory Nazianzen (J. N. D. Kelly, op. cit. 480). "But it is Augustine, as usual, who best represents the balanced thought of the West. God's judgment, he affirms, is a permanent feature of history, but since the fact of it is not always obvious God must have a day on which His combined wisdom and righteousness will be vindicated before every eye. For confirmation of this, and to fill in the picture, he turns to the New and the Old Testaments. Both teach that the judgment belongs to Christ (at) His triumphal advent at the end of time. All mankind, the righteous as well as the sinners, will be subjected to this judgment" (J. N. D. Kelly, op. cit., 481-2).

Who will be judged? Basically, all men, the fallen angels, the world. For in 1 Cor 6:2, 3 we read: "Do you not know that the saints will judge the world? . . . Do you not know that we are to judge angels'," And W. Rees, commenting on this passage says: "Saints means Christians and 'angels' means 'fallen angels'," and he adds: "the redeemed will be judged but will also be judges" (op. cit. 1088). R. Kugelman writes: "the saints share in Christ's royal power and will participate in his judgment of the world" (JBC 51:30). That all men will be judged seems very clear for we read that before Christ "will be gathered all the nations" (Mt 25:32), that "he will render to every man according to his works" (Rm 2:6), that "Christ Jesus... is to judge the living and the dead" (2 Tm 4:1), and that "we must all appear before the judgment seat of Christ" (2 Cor 5:10). But certain men or types of men are singled out. Hebrews tells us, "God will judge the immoral and adulterous" (13:4). Mt says those who judge others will be judged: "for with the judgment you pronounce you will be judged" (7:2). In James we read that "judgment is without mercy to one who has shown no mercy" (2:13) and that "we who teach shall be judged with greater strictness" (3:1). 2 Peter stresses the unrighteous and "especially those who indulge in the lust of defiling passion and despise authority" (2:9-10). And he also points to the fallen angels: "God did not spare the angels when they sinned, but cast them into hell and committed them to pits of nether gloom to be kept until the judgment" (2:4).

What will be the *Norm* of judgment? In the Gospel of Matthew it seems to be the love or indifference one has shown to others, and basically to Christ: "I was hungry and you gave me no food. Truly, I say to you, as you did it not to one of the least of these, you did it not to me" (Mt 25:42,45). For Paul, "the norm will be the Mosaic Law for those who claim to know it ... those who have not known it will be judged by the natural law" (X. Leon-Dufour, op. cit. 243). The norm is also a man's knowledge of God and his obedience to the Gospel of our Lord Jesus (2 Th 1:5-9), and basically the "works" a man has done, what a man "has done in the body" (Rm 2:5-6; 2 Cor 5:10). For John, it is Christ and His word, i.e. a man's attitude toward Christ: "He who rejects me and does not receive my sayings has a judge: the word that I have spoken will be his judge on the last day" (Jn 12:4,8).

Christ, then, is the norm of judgment, the object of decision. Men will be judged by their explicit or implicit acceptance or rejection of Christ. G. C. Berkouwer writes: "the judgment... is concentrated in Christ Himself: it is not an unveiling of all things in general, but of one's relationship to Christ in particular".... "From this it is evident that the central decision of life, namely for Christ or against Him, is the crucial factor and circumscribes life in its entirety" (op. cit., 158, 161). R. Guardini spells this out more fully: "What will be the standard of judgment? Love, the love that is aroused by compassion for man's need. What is here in question is the first and greatest commandment and the second that is like it. How will this standard of love be applied? ... Man will be judged according to his relationship to Christ.... Every intimation of truth, however fragmentary, is also the beginning of a knowledge of Christ. Similarly, any charitable action is directed toward Christ, and reaches him in the end. The doer need have no thought of Christ, need not even know Christ or have heard of Him. Yet what is done is done to Christ, for Christ has placed Himself, as it were, behind each man to lend final weight to each individual being" (op. cit., 94-97)

Just *where* the last judgment will take place we do not know. The valley of Jehoshaphat has often been suggested, because Joel wrote: "I am going to gather all the nations and take them down to the Valley of Jehoshaphat, for I am going to sit in judgment there" (4:2, 12). A very ancient tradition identified this valley with part of the Kidron valley, but this tradition "has no foundation. The name (Jehoshaphat) is symbolic, not geographical, signifying the place where Yahweh judges" (J. L. McKenzie, op. cit. 418). J. P. Arendzen has written that the place of judgment will be "somewhere on earth, but since risen bodies are not subject to laws of earthly gravity, they may rise as in a vast amphitheatre, encircling the throne of the Judge placed in the height of the heavens" (op. cit., 84).

Just *how* the last judgment will take place we do not know. It seems clear, however, today, that the apocalyptic details we find in Rv 17-20, such as "the judgment of the great harlot," "the beast with seven heads and ten horns that carries her" and the rider on "a white horse" and the "thrones" of those to whom judgment was committed, "a great white throne," the "book of life," need not be taken literally. "It is false," writes one commentator, "exegesis to insist upon apocalyptic details to the extent that the reality of the judgment itself becomes impossible to grasp" (J. L. McKenzie, op. cit. 469). Just what real details lie embedded in this imagery is impossible to define.

Why will there be a general judgment is a two-pronged question: (1) why should there be a general judgment if there has already been a definitive particular judgment at death? (2) why should there be a general judgment at all? Theologians have come up with answers that show substantial agreement but different emphasis.

K. Rahner's direct answer is simple enough: "It may be said that the particular or personal judgment is primarily concerned with the destiny of the individual insofar as he is not just an element in the collectivity of mankind. The general judgment speaks of the fact that mankind and its history as a collective unity, comes under God's judgment." Unfortunately he then proceeds to obscure this simple answer by discussing in a very unsatisfactory way the question of the "time interval" between the two judgments. "Very great prudence is needed," he writes, when speaking of the "time" of the "intermediate state between particular and general judgment" (for) "it is certain that this interval cannot be regarded as a continuation of time as we know it." This is obvious enough. But then he goes on: "Is it right, for instance, to imagine that the particular judgment on a person who dies today is separated from the general judgment by a length of time which runs in this world from now to the end of history?" (*Sacramentum Mundi* 3, 275). Of course it is right, and not only right but necessary from our point of view "to imagine that the particular judgment on a person who dies today is separated from the general judgment by a length of time which runs in this world from now to the end of history." For the particular judgment of many persons has taken place and the end of the world and the general judgment have not taken place, and very likely will not take place for a long, long *time*. And even from the viewpoint of the dead it also seems "right" to speak of such an "interval." If they go to purgatory there is a "before and after" as regards their purification and maturation, and a "before and after" as regards their entry into heaven. If they go to hell or heaven, their active conscious life and activity must involve not only duration of existence but also succession of activities, of thoughts, of volitions before the end of the world and their general judgment. How else can these persons be truly alive?

To the question, "What need is there of a general judgment, if each soul is judged at death?" J. P. Arendzen gives a direct answer: a general judgment is needed for an open display of God's justice and of Christ's triumph. "It is meet and just," he writes, "that previous to the entry of the host of the redeemed into the eternal celestial city where they will abide forever in the full completion of their manhood, there should be an *open display* of the whole human race to vindicate the justice of the ways of God and the triumph of Christ, who came to redeem them. Human eyes and ears should see the judge and hear the sentence and the human race gathered together should acclaim the Divine decree that will settle all things. It is meet and just that Christ, who came in lowliness in the days of Bethlehem, and who was raised on Golgotha on the Cross of shame, should revisit the earth in great power and majesty, coming on the clouds of heaven. Then all men shall see God's age-long plan fulfilled and bear witness that it is well done" (op. cit. 80-81). A. Winklhofer adds another dimension. "The sentence of the particular judgment," he writes, "is already definitive and is not reversed. But a man's acts are not limited to the time of his life on earth. Ripples go on and on. His acts, both good and bad, are always having some effect, certain consequences. An ordinary person often has more influence on history than many gifted persons . . . v. g. insignificant parents of illustrious children. Thus after the particular judgment there is a continuous accumulation of new effects from each man's life, with social and historical ramifications for good or ill. Christ's kingdom, previously present in the Church in a hidden manner, now radiates its splendor over the whole creation. The Last Judgment is of its nature a Theodicy, a justification of God in the sight of all creatures. God now shows his hand, lifts the veil from all the mystery of history, the mystery of evil and of free will. He shows how in creating free beings he created adversaries, irrevocably against him. Now is made clear that God's design for his creation was always going forward, in spite of the opposition and forces of hell and of Antichrist. God was always in control" (op. cit. 195-200).

J. H. Wright (NCE 8, 30ff.) adds an interesting and comprehensive summation of many of the implications of the general judgment. He sees the general judgment as one aspect of a single consummating divine intervention, as a victory and a purification, as a public divine revelation, as the definitive establishment of the heavenly society.

He sees Christ coming and executing judgment in the act of raising men from the dead, some to a resurrection of life, others to a resurrection of judgment, and in this act of judging, which is at once Christ's Second Coming and the cause of mankind's resurrection, he sees "fallen angels and condemned men ... compelled by the inner consequences of their rebellion to glorify the power and wisdom and goodness of God in the justice of their punishment."

He sees the judgment as "a purification for those who are alive at the coming of Christ but are not perfectly prepared for heaven. For them ... the purification of purgatory is here accomplished" (1 Cor 3:10-15).

He sees the general judgment as "a public divine intervention making known to all the justice of God's judgment ... for the glory and joy of the saved and for the shame and sorrow of the lost."

He sees the judgment as "the revelation of the forgiven, secret sins of the just," a revelation that will not embarrass them since it will also manifest their sorrow and penance and their "humble acceptance of God's forgiveness." But one cannot but wonder about this. Will there really be such a revelation of the forgiven, secret sins of the just? Is this really necessary? Is this really compatible with the love and compassion and complete forgiveness of Christ? Must there, will there be a revelation of every sin of the just? Even of every sin of the wicked?

He sees at the general judgment Christ bringing to fulfilment the commission He received from the Father at the Incarnation "to redeem fallen humanity, to head a new race of men
vivified by the Holy Spirit" and "to establish an eternal kingdom
where God's love may enrich forever those He has made His
sons."

He sees the general judgment as definitively establishing
what God had primarily intended, "the heavenly society" and
"family of persons joined to the persons of the Holy Trinity
and to one another in everlasting knowledge, love and joy."

He sees that then the "action of Christ in subduing all enemies
is at last brought to a close by this act of power and justice
and love" as He delivers the kingdom to God the Father, for
then all things are "subject to Christ and Christ is subject to
the Father" and then "there will begin the everlasting kingdom
of the Father, where God is all in all" (1 Cor 15:24-28).

Could we say all this a bit differently? Long ago God
dreamed a dream of men and now He wants all men to know
how much of His dream has come true. He dreamed of having
billions of adopted sons and daughters, made in His own image
and likeness. He would build them an immense world of planets,
stars, galaxies, super-galaxies. And turn it over to them so that
they might build a better world of things and men. A world
in which they would come to love Him and one another more
and more. He wanted them to love Him, but He did not want
a forced love, He wanted a freely-given love. And so He would
gift them with freedom, immense freedom, freedom even to
say No to Him and His wish and will. He knew there was a
risk in this, but He so much wanted their freely-given love,
that He would take the risk. And so He built them a cosmos
and watched it slowly unfold and develop until it was ready
for man. Then man came forth and went to work building
what he considered a better world. But in the process he chose
to walk his own road, not the road God had hoped he would
walk. And so man brought into his world sin and sorrow and
pain and suffering and death. But God so loved this world of
men that He sent His only begotten Son into their world to

show them the way back to God, to show them how to be and to live as God's adoptive sons. This Son of God came into their world as the Christ, as the Word made flesh. He lived with them, taught them, suffered and died for them, rose from the dead and ascended into heaven. He called them to be one with Him in love of God and of one another, and sent into every man His enabling grace often during his lifetime and especially at death, so that everyone might be saved and achieve eternal life and happiness in the kingdom of God.

That was God's dream, His hope. And now He wanted all mankind to know His dream and His hope, how He had destined all of them for the everlasting joys of heaven. He wanted them to know how their world had begun, grown and developed. How man had come into it and chose to turn away from God's plan and walk his own road, that brought him sin and sorrow and pain and suffering and death. He wanted them to know why He had sent His Son to redeem them and His Spirit to sanctify them. He wanted them to know what Christ had done for them by His life, suffering, death, resurrection and ascension, and how His grace and His love had gone out to them over and over again. He wanted them to know how the Holy Spirit had "worked" in their minds and hearts to draw them to faith and hope and love of God and one another so that all might be "one in Him" with the Father and through the Spirit. He wanted them to know how much God had loved them all and graced them all and called them all freely to open themselves to a saving love of God and one another. Called them all freely in death to make a final, irrevocable, fundamental option for or against God, for or against Christ, a final choice of eternal union with God or eternal separation from God. He wanted all men to see that He had made them free to accept or reject His love for all eternity, and He would abide by their free choice. If they chose Him they would have Him for all eternity, and that would be heaven. If they chose themselves they would have themselves for all eternity, and that would be hell. To make all mankind know this and see this will be the last "work" of Christ the Judge before He hands over the kingdom to the Father.

Chapter 13
Will There Be a New Creation at the End of the World?

Men have always speculated about an end to this world of ours. About the goal of man's history. Rudolf Bultmann has maintained that as historians "we cannot claim to know the end and goal of history." This may be true, depending on his view and definition of history. But as Christians we do claim to know the end and goal of history. Its goal is the redemption, the salvation, the Christification of man. Its end will come at 'the end of time' when Christ comes again to judge the living and the dead. Then man's pilgrim state will come to an end. Then empirical man's history will come to an end. But man himself will not come to an end. He will go on living forever and forever. That is what we read in Sacred Scripture. That is what the Church teaches us by her creeds and councils, her Fathers and theologians. When will man's pilgrim state end? At the parousia, when Christ comes again—at the end of the world.

Will this world really come to an end? The entire cosmos of galaxies and supergalaxies, of which our solar system is but a tiny part, and our planet earth just a speck? Or will it be only planet earth that comes to an end? And if this world 'comes to an end', does this mean it will be annihilated and replaced by an altogether 'new world'? Or changed and transformed so as to befit 'terminal man'? Many such questions have engaged the minds of many men over the centuries. And their answers have varied widely. But only God can tell us what will happen when Christ comes again. Scientists, historians, philoso-

phers can speculate. Only God can tell us. Has He? Possibly
a deeper, longer study of God's creation and man's history may
give us hints of the answer. But it is in the Bible that we are
much more likely to find God's answer to these questions,
if He has given any answer so far. So we turn to the Sacred
Scriptures.

Old Testament

The Old Testament seems to say the "world" will vanish,
but by "world" it seems to mean only the "visible universe" and
by "vanish" only "change." In Ps 102 we read: "Aeons ago, you
laid earth's foundations, the heavens are the works of your hands;
all will vanish, though you remain, all wear out like a garment,
like clothes that need changing you will change them; but yourself, you never change and your years are unending" (25-27).
Commenting on this JBC merely says: "God is eternal, outlasting
'earth' and 'heavens,' which he changes 'like clothing,' when
it is worn out" (35: 118). J. L. McKenzie states that "when the
visible universe is mentioned in a single phrase it is 'heaven and
earth'; but this phrase does not mean 'world.'. . . The Greek
word *kosmos* for world appears in the Old Testament only in
late Greek books, and its use shows the influence of Greek usage"
(op. cit. 942). In Isaiah we are told: "Now I create new heavens
and a new earth, and the past will not be remembered"; and
"as the new heavens and the new earth I shall make will endure
before me—it is Yahweh who speaks—so will your race and name
endure" (65:17; 66:22). In his commentary E. Powers says that
"The New Heaven and the New Earth indicate a transformation
of the universe in which wickedness and oppression will be
replaced by righteousness and happiness. Past evils shall be for-
gotten. . . . The Messianic kingdom here depicted is material
rather than spiritual. The picture is incomplete" (*A Catholic
Commentary on Holy Scripture*, 573). And F. L. Moriarty
writes: "A panorama of joy, with the whole universe sharing
man's redemption, now extends before us . . . very plainly the
achievement is God's, and he and Israel are united in common

joy. The world will not be destroyed but transformed into 'new heavens and a new earth,' a phrase familiar in apocryphal literature" (JBC 22:67).

New Testament

The New Testament also tells us that this 'world' of ours will pass away and that there will then be a "new heaven and a new earth." But interpreters are not agreed on just what this 'passing away' and this 'renovation' will mean.

In *Matthew's Gospel* we often find Jesus declaring there will be an end of the world. Thus in Matthew 13 we read: "He who sows the good seed is the Son of man; the field is the world, and the good seed means the sons of the kingdom; the weeds are the sons of the evil one, and the enemy who sowed them is the devil; the harvest is at the close of the age, and the reapers are the angels. Just as the weeds are gathered and burned with fire, so will it be at the close of the age" (13:37-39). And again: "So it will be at the close of the age. The angels will come out and separate the evil from the righteous, and throw them into the furnace of fire" (13:49-50). And: "lo, I am with you always to the close of the age" (28:20). The "close of the age" means the "end of the world."

Paul tells us "the form of this world is passing away" (1 Cor 7:31), and "then comes the end, when He delivers the kingdom to God the Father after destroying every rule and every authority and power.... When all things are subjected to Him, then the Son Himself will also be subject to Him who put all things under Him, that God may be everything to everyone" (1 Cor 15:24, 28). This beautiful but enigmatic passage is packed with meaning. Commenting on it, R. Kugelman writes: "then comes the end: the consummation of time when Christ, having completed His redemptive mission and brought all the elect to the glory of His resurrection, manifests his total victory over the evil spirits. Then, having completed His work, He hands over to His Father the royal authority that was conferred on him as Savior of the world and Head of the Church.... Since His glorious resurrection Christ reigns in glory; He is the Lord. At His parousia, His royal majesty will be manifested to all. . . . With the resurrection of the dead at the end of time Christ's victory will be complete. With the completion of Christ's redemptive mission, God the Father will be manifested as the first principle of all life, and the final end of all creation and of salvation history" (JBC 51:84). Paul says "the form of this world is passing away," but he does not say this world will be annihilated at the end of time. Rather he says, or implies, that all creation will be renewed, for he writes that "the creation waits with eager longing for the revealing of the sons of God . . . because the creation itself will be set free from its bondage to decay and obtain the glorious liberty of the children of God" (Rm 8:19,21). J. A. Fitzmyer commenting on this writes: "Paul seems to say that . . . redeemed humanity will live in peace with God in a world transformed by His Spirit. For Paul the created physical universe is not to be a mere spectator of man's triumphant glory and freedom, but is to share in it. When the children of God are finally revealed in glory, death will have no more dominion over them, and the material world will also be emancipated from this 'last enemy' " (JBC 53:87). From what will creation be set free? From the disturbance of its harmony, according to A. Theissen, so that it will come to "fullness of harmony and order" and share "the glory of the children of God" (*A Catholic Commentary on Holy Scripture*, 1065).

The Second Letter of Peter says "the day of the Lord will come like a thief, and then the heavens will pass away with a loud noise, and the elements will be dissolved with fire, and the earth and the works that are upon it will be burned up" (3:10). Does this mean the utter destruction of the "heavens"? According to T. W. Leahy, "the 'heavens' may signify the heavenly bodies, perhaps including the angelic powers connected with them." But he adds: "Although the image of fire is often mentioned in the Old Testament and the New Testament in connection with the day of the Lord, 2 P 3:7-13 is the only scriptural passage asserting a final conflagration by which the universe will be destroyed that day. The idea of a final conflagration was, however, widespread at the time of the composition of 2 P. . . . Originating in Persia, the idea spread to the Greco-Roman world and into Jewish apocalyptic, whence it influenced Christian thought. . . . In none of these cases of biblical expression, therefore, does the acceptance in faith of the revealed truths of salvation history necessarily involve acceptance of the scientific validity of the imagery involved" (JBC 65:20).

In the *Book of Revelation* we read that: "then I saw a new heaven and a new earth; for the first heaven and the first earth had passéd away, and the sea was no more. And I saw the holy city, the new Jerusalem, coming down out of heaven from God, prepared as a bride adorned for her husband; and I heard a great voice from the throne saying, 'Behold the dwelling of God is with men. He will dwell with them, and they shall be His people, and God Himself will be with them; He will wipe away every tear from their eyes, and death shall be no more, neither shall there be mourning nor crying nor pain any more, for the former things have passed away'." In his commentary on this passage, J. L. D'Aragon writes: "creation must be renewed or refashioned in order to befit redeemed humanity (Is 65:17; 66:22) . . . brutal power and violence (of the sea) are incompatible with the peace of the world to come. . . . God is the Architect and Builder of the holy city. . . . The intimacy that the first man enjoyed in paradise and that Israel experienced in the desert and Temple is now granted to all members of the people of God forever. . . . The former world disappears, with all those repulsive characteristics that gave it the appearance of a creation enslaved to sin" (JBC 64:88).

When we ponder these scriptural passages two main questions come quickly to mind. The first is: does the end of the world mean the end of the entire universe or only of part of it? We are so used to considering the world as the cosmos, as the entire universe, that we almost take for granted that the Bible views it in the same way. When we profess that God is the creator of heaven and earth we mean that He has created the entire universe, the cosmos, the world. And so when we think of the end of the world, we mean just that: the end of the entire universe. But does the Bible mean that? J. L. McKenzie says: "When the visible universe is mentioned in a single phrase it is 'heaven and earth'; but this phrase does not mean 'world' " (op. cit. 942). And again: "heaven and earth are the comprehensive biblical designations of the biblical universe" (ibid. 208). Viewed this way, the end of the world would mean the end of our visible universe, the end of planet earth and its atmospheric environment and perhaps the sun, moon, stars, planets that are visible to us. U. Simon in pondering a "world cataclysm," believes it more reasonable to confine the notion of cataclysm to the world over which man has control. He thinks that "whereas the pre-scientific theologian could hold quite happily that the trumpets would sound and the whole universe quaver and melt in the final catastrophe, no such view can now be maintained. Instead it must be asserted that it is extremely improbable that a universe of these dimensions will be affected one way or another by human affairs. If the earth, for example, were to suffer total destruction, either by natural means (collision or destruction) or by human means (weapons so powerfully destructive that nothing can survive) it is less than probable that such a catastrophe would cause physical effects beyond this planet. Again if mankind succeeded in establishing posts on other planets of the solar system, it might take its genius for destruction thither but again not beyond. Thus it follows that the old fantasy which dreamt of a world cataclysm can no longer be entertained.... Since the Universe is not a piece of clockwork which God has left to its own devices, but rather the Creation which he sustains with His Word and His Spirit, it is both more reasonable and in line with true eschatology to confine the notion of cataclysm to the world over which man has control" (*The End is Not Yet*, 15, 16).

What is to be said of U. Simon's view? To earth-bound and planet-bound man, it seems very reasonable that a final cataclysm should go only as far as man's influence has gone. But if the whole world was created for man, why should it not partake of his destiny, the glory of the children of God, as Paul seems to say (Rm 8:19-22)? If pilgrim man is destined to carry the Good News to the outermost limits of the universe before the parousia, as some think, why should not the entire universe share in the glory and freedom that will come to man at the end of the world? Many of the interpreters of the Old Testament and of the New Testament read it that way. E. Powers says "new heaven and new earth indicate a transformation of the *universe*." F. L. Moriarty writes of "the whole universe sharing man's redemption." J. A. Fitzmyer sees Paul envisioning "the created physical universe." And A. Winklhofer writes: "since 'heaven and earth' is the usual scriptural expression for the whole universe, there is good reason for accepting a transformation of the whole, including all the galactic systems. This is the universe, a whole system of matter and fields of energy in continuous development, of which our own galaxy apparently forms an insignificant part, that will undergo decay and then renewal, fulfilment and rebirth" (op. cit. 245).

The second question is this: does the end of the world mean its annihilation (and re-creation) or merely its transformation? J. L. D'Aragon writes that "biblical understanding of the relationship between this corrupt world and the future era is divided. The best attested school of thought holds that the present creation will be entirely destroyed (Ps 102:26; Is 51:6; Mk 13:31; Ac 3:21; 2 P 3:7, 10-12) and that a new heaven and a new earth will replace it; on the other hand the New Testament also speaks of the liberation (Rm 8:21) and the renewal (Mt 19:28) of creation" (JBC 64:87).

Today the second view, transformation and not annihilation, seems to be growing stronger and stronger. Those who hold it think that the biblical passages should be construed as 'change-passages', not as 'annihilation-passages', if they are taken in a fuller biblical context. Ps 102:25-26, they claim, seems strongly to say "change," not "annihilation." E. Powers in his comment on Is 65:17; 66:22 says "new heaven and new earth" indicate a transformation of the universe (*A Catholic Commentary on Holy Scripture*, 573). J. A. Fitzmyer in his comment on Rm 8:19-21 says the world will be "transformed by his Spirit". . . and

"the created physical universe ... the material world will be
emancipated from death ... and share the glory of the children
of God" (JBC 53:87). And F. L. Moriarty in his comment on
the Isaian passages says "The world will not be destroyed but
transformed into 'new heavens and a new earth' " (JBC 22:67).
Three commentators on the Catholic epistles say the same thing,
namely "by 'perished' is meant 'changed,' not 'annihilated' " (Eat-
on); "the universe will not be entirely destroyed in its substance, but transformed. It will be purified by fire and rendered
worthy of the just who will inhabit it" (Maunoury); "nature
is not destroyed, but transformed into a new world. The change
is greater than that of the deluge, which is its type" (Chaine).

M. E. Williams writes that "It would be rash ... to read into
some of the Biblical accounts, 2 Peter for example, a reference
to a vast nuclear explosion. For the Christian belief in the end
of the world is not a belief in the total annihilation of matter
and the survival of purely spiritual realities. Today the theologians tend to explain the end in terms of a gradual transformation rather than a discontinuity between this world and the
world to come. One has to be careful not to interpret the biblical language too literally ... 2 P 3:10-13 (did not intend) to
give an exact physical description of the changes that will take
place in the material universe ... but to convey religious truths
in the most effective way. 2 Peter speaks of a change and transformation of the world rather than annihilation. ... It is reasonable to suppose that the world will remain in some changed form
as the connatural surrounding of risen man, as it is today the
connatural surrounding of mortal man" (*New Catholic Encyclopedia* 5, 339).

A. Winklhofer likewise sees the end-change as one of transformation and not annihilation, but in his estimate this transformation will take place suddenly and catastrophically. "Since
'heaven and earth' is the usual scriptural expression for the whole
universe, there is good reason," he thinks, "for accepting a
transformation of the whole, including all the galactic systems.
... This world will pass away because of God's will to transform it, and its passing takes the form of a catastrophic event

that happens suddenly and overwhelms man and the world with unimaginable force. What seems to be utter destruction is in reality regeneration, which results in a new form, a 'new heaven and a new earth.' The entire universe, this enormous sphere of action of the human mind, becomes directly accessible to man's new senses in its entire being, in all its relationships, in all its intelligible content. It becomes comprehensible in its highest aspects, and it reflects the countenance of the Trinity … and particularly the countenance of the Son, the model and archetype from the beginning of all things in heaven and earth. The fire of God, the splendour of his glory, will blaze over the creation, making it utterly transparent to the sight of man. All these things happen together: the Lord's second coming, the general judgment, the resurrection of the body and the renewal of all things. It is vain to look for any temporal or logical renewal sequence" (op. cit. 248-252).

Early Church Writers

If we turn to the Early Church Writers we find that some of them were "annihilationists" or "destructionists," others were "transformationists." 1 Clement said heaven and earth will melt away like lead melting in a furnace (16:3). Hermas said the present world must perish by blood and fire and the cosmic order must be transformed to become fit for God's elect (Vis. 4:3; 1:3). Ps. Barnabas taught that "the Son of God would appear at the beginning of the seventh millennium and reign with the just until a new universe was called into existence at the commencement of the eighth" (15:4-9). Tertullian said the day of the Lord will not come until the earth is destroyed (*De anim.* 55-8). For Origen there will be a successive cycle of worlds, with the infinity of rational creatures passing through different phases of existence, higher and lower, according as from time to time they choose good or evil. On the other hand Irenaeus and Hippolytus teach that the world is to be dissolved but not annihilated (*Adv. Haer.* 5:36, 1; *Philos.* 1:3). Gregory of Nazianzus and Didymus declared that the world will be renewed (*Orat.*

21 in *Laudem S. Athan.* 25; in Ps 101:28). Jerome often declares that the end of heaven and earth will not be its destruction but its change into something better (In Is 51:6; 65:17f.; In Ps 101:26, 27). And Augustine writes in the same vein (*De Civ. Dei* 20:14). So did Gregory the Great. And so did Thomas Aquinas and medieval theology generally.

Church's Magisterium

In the past the Church's Magisterium has said little about the end of the world and its new creation. Pius II in 1459 condemned the view that the world would be naturally destroyed and ended by the heat of the sun consuming the humidity of the land and the air in such a way that the elements are set on fire (DS 1361). More recently, *Vatican II* seems to favor the 'transformation' view. In *Lumen Gentium* it described the Church as a pilgrim Church, imperfect and changing, which "will attain its full perfection only in the glory of heaven. Then there will come the time of the restoration of all things. Then the human race as well as the entire world will be perfectly re-established in Christ" (Abbott, op. cit., n. 1; n. 48). In its Pastoral Constitution on the *Church in the Modern World* it stated that "the expectation of a new earth must not weaken but rather stimulate our concern for cultivating this one. For after we have obeyed the Lord and in His Spirit nurtured on earth the values of human dignity, brotherhood and freedom, and indeed all the good fruits of our nature and enterprise, we will find them again but freed of stain, burnished, and transfigured. This will be so when Christ hands over to the Father a kingdom, eternal and universal, a kingdom of truth and life, of holiness and grace, of justice, love, peace" (ibid. 38-9).

CONCLUSION

If we try to sum up all the evidence of Scripture, Fathers and Church, what will the end of the world be? The Old Testament tells us that at the end of the world the world will not be destroyed but transformed into "new heavens and a new earth" with the whole universe sharing man's redemption. The New Testament also says this "world" of ours will "pass away" and then there will be a "new heaven and a new earth." By "world" it seems to mean our entire cosmos, not just planet earth, and by "new heavens and a new earth" it seems to mean a "new cosmos," not just planet earth. And by "pass away" it does not seem to mean that the world will be annihilated but rather that it will be transformed from its present condition to a condition that will befit terminal man. But whether this transformation will take place gradually or suddenly and catastrophically is not clear. To the early Church writers it was clear that the world would come to an end and some seemed to think this would mean its annihilation. But the more influential Fathers opted for a transformation of the world into something better and Vatican II also seems to favor this transformationist view. Today the view that at the end this universe will be transformed, not annihilated, seems to be definitely in the ascendency. This view has a solid biblical and patristic foundation. It fits readily into an evolutionary view of the universe. One of its strongest proponents was Teilhard de Chardin who wrote: "However possible it is that some catastrophic disaster will end the world, we have 'higher reasons' for being sure that this will not happen."[1] What, then, will we have at the end? We will have "blessed" and "damned," heaven and hell, the kingdom of God and of Christ, the "new heavens and the new earth," the New Jerusalem.

There will be a *heaven* of everlasting joy and happiness. God's abode, where His Majesty will be most resplendent. Where His infinite light and vision, love and joy will be shared by all the citizens of heaven, the blessed angels and saints. The heaven to which Christ ascended and where He sits at the "right hand of the Father," participating in the kingly power of God. A heaven "higher than all the rest which are called heavens... holier than all which are called holies."[2] To this heaven pilgrim man looked forward in hope for a home which God would build him there (2 Cor 5:1-5). Here he would find his inheritance (1 P 1:4), his reward (Mt 5:12) and his treasure (Mt

6:20). Here he would find throughout eternity bliss and peace, life and love, joy and happiness in an ineffable degree. He would find the total fulfilment of his spiritual and bodily nature. He would enjoy the company of the Risen Christ and His Blessed Mother and all the holy angels and saints. Two of the intertestamental books tried to describe this heaven in the material terms of their time and culture. The *Book of Enoch* wrote of a heaven with a wall built of crystals, a ceiling like the path of stars, a house built of flames of fire, a lofty throne on which sat the Great Glory and his raiment shone more brightly than the sun. The *Secrets of Enoch* said the eternal abode of the righteous was a celestial paradise with the tree of life from whose roots four streams flowed with milk, honey, wine and oil.

The New Testament spoke of heaven in more spiritual terms quite often, but at times it also used material terms. Jesus spoke of eternal dwellings and described the happiness of heaven both as a wedding feast and as eternal life. John stressed eternal life, a life that begins here through faith, love and baptism and reaches its consummation in heaven. The deepest aspect of this heaven for Paul is the immediate vision of God that it brings to the blessed. But he adds that "there are things which no eye ever saw and ear ever heard and which never occurred to the human mind, which God has provided for those who love Him" (1 Cor 2:9).

Many theologians have stressed a heaven of everlasting happiness as constituted by eternal companionship with Christ. To some extent this must be true for Paul very much wanted to make his "home with the Lord" (2 Cor 5:7). And obviously to be in the company of Christ, to see Him face-to-face and talk and walk with Him, when we have so long and so deeply desired to see directly the God-Man, the One who lived, suffered, died for us, and rose from the dead to immortal life that we might have life and have it more abundantly, this must mean an ineffable joy and love and happiness. To know, love, see Him directly, and to be known, loved, seen directly by Him, must mean incomprehensible joy. To be thus with Christ is undoubtedly a real aspect of heaven as we envision it. But it hardly constitutes the essence of heaven as we envision it. For we are already "with Christ" here on earth through faith and baptism and the Eucharist, but we are not "in heaven." The Apostles and His Mother saw Him face-to-face, walked and talked with Him, loved Him and were in intimate fellowship with Him, and were seen and loved by Him in turn while He and they were on earth, but they were not then 'in heaven.' Heaven must be much more than "being with Christ" as the Apostles and His Mother were, if it is not to run the risk of eternal boredom.

What is to be said of the "*kingdom of God*" in the final state of man? "In the Synoptic Gospels the term kingdom of God is frequently used to designate the central theme of the mission of Jesus ... and there can be little doubt that it goes back to Jesus Himself" (J. L. McKenzie, op. cit., 479). This kingdom is presented there both as a present reality and as a future reality. As a future reality it is intimately connected with the end of this world and the beginning of the next and with the heaven of everlasting happiness. Interpreters view it as a kingdom of glory that marks God's ultimate victory over evil in all its forms and phases, that affects the whole of man and his social existence, that brings him a new heaven and a new earth. But there remain some questions about this eternal kingdom.

Will this eternal kingdom be the kingdom of God or the kingdom of Christ? That is what some theologians have been asking (Berkouwer, op. cit. 426ff.). For Paul wrote to the Corinthians: "There comes the end, when He delivers the kingdom to God the Father after destroying every rule and every authority and power. For He must reign until He has put all His enemies under His feet.... When all things are subjected to Him, then the Son Himself will also be subjected to Him who put all things under Him, that God may be everything to every one" (1 Cor 15:24-28). He seems to mean that "our Lord's office of redeemer and Messiah ... ceases when all the redeemed are gathered. A mediator is no longer needed" (W. Rees, *A Catholic Commentary on Holy Scripture*, 1097). For "then God Himself will be in direct contact with all of redeemed creation."[3] Then "the Incarnate Son, the Savior of redeemed humanity, will render to His Father—homage—together with all redeemed creation (and) with the completion of Christ's redemptive mission, God the Father will be manifested as the first principle of all life and the final end of all creation and of salvation history" (R. Kugelman, JBC 51:84).

Does this mean that the *kingdom of Christ* then comes to an end? It seems to. And Oscar Cullmann says it does: this passage shows that the kingdom of Christ lasts only until the parousia, but the kingdom of God goes on forever (cf. Berkouwer, op. cit. 426ff.). The kingdom of Christ comes to an end, he thinks, because its work is done and a mediator, a redeemer, a kingly Messiah is no longer needed. So Christ hands back to the Father the Messianic authority and kingship the Father had given Him. And henceforth there is only the eternal kingdom of God. Cullmann's conclusion seems valid. But it rests heavily, if not exclusively, on this one passage of 1 Cor. There are other passages in Sacred Scripture that seem to say quite as clearly that the kingdom of Christ will have no end. Isaiah wrote: "Wide is his dominion in a peace that has no end, for the throne of David and for his royal power" (Is 9:7). Luke says: "he will reign over the house of Jacob for ever; and of his kingdom there will be no end" (1:33). And in 2 Peter we read: "there will be richly provided for you an entrance into the eternal kingdom of our Lord and Savior Jesus Christ" (2 P 1:11). The Nicene-Constantinople Creed seems to adopt the Lukan phrase when it professes that "he ascended into heaven, sits at the right hand of the Father, and is going to come again in glory to judge the living and the dead. His reign will have no end" (DS 150).

Can we reconcile these two opposed views? Probably we can. At the parousia the messianic kingdom of Christ comes to an end, for there are no more men to be redeemed. But Christ as messianic and divine king goes on reigning forever in the eternal kingdom of the Father, Son and Holy Spirit. For "then I looked and I heard around the throne and the living creatures and the elders the voice of many angels, numbering myriads and thousands of thousands, saying with a loud voice, 'Worthy is the Lamb who was slain, to receive power and wealth and wisdom and might and honor and glory and blessing.' And I heard every creature in heaven and on earth and under the earth and in the sea, and all therein, saying: 'To Him who sits upon the throne and to the Lamb be blessing and honor and glory and might for ever and ever.' And the four living creatures said, 'Amen,' and the elders fell down and worshipped" (Rv 5:11-14).

What is the *essence of heaven?* The essence of the everlasting happiness of the blessed lies not in their eternal companionship with Christ and the angels and saints, not in their membership in the eternal kingdom of God, but in their beatific vision, love and enjoyment of the triune God. For the three divine persons have an infinitely perfect vision and love and enjoyment of the divine essence and of one another. And in this infinite knowing, loving and enjoying lies the very life of the triune God, the very essence of their endless and infinite happiness. If the blessed are to be endlessly and supremely happy, then, they must share in the very life of the triune God, in the divine life that makes Them endlessly and infinitely happy.

Heaven then means a completely new dimension of human life and human love, a divine dimension that penetrates every corner of man's spiritual nature and extends its glory to his risen body. It means a life and a love and an enjoyment that will fulfil all our heavenly desires, and the reaches of our spiritual nature and our glorified souls and bodies. There we will know God as He knows Himself. And we will be loved by God in turn with an ineffable and ever creative love that will go on throughout eternity. God made us for Himself, so that we might find our life and our rest in Him. In the beatific vision of the triune God we will find our eternal life and rest. Long ago St. Augustine said it beautifully: "Thou hast made us for Thyself, O God, and our hearts are restless till they rest in Thee." In the beatific vision, love and enjoyment of God we will find our eternal life and rest and fulfillment. What is more, whatever we go, whatever we do, we will have this beatific vision and love and enjoyment for they will be rooted in the very depths of our spiritual nature, in the very core of our spiritual and glorified being. Once we receive them they will be ours throughout eternity. We cannot lose them. They are not tied to any particular "place." If we are in heaven in the company of the Risen Lord and the angels and Saints, we shall have them there. If we travel to and through our "new heaven and our new earth," we shall have them with us and in us always. Wherever we go in the cosmos, whatever we do there, we shall always have in us the beatific vision, love and enjoyment of the divine essence and persons and be utterly impeccable and supremely happy.

And there will be a *New Heaven and a New Earth*. Those who have the beatific vision of the triune God enjoy it wherever they are, wherever they go. And at the end of the world they can go to the "new heavens and the new earth" that God makes for His glorified sons and daughters. There was a rather widespread thought in years gone by that they would live and love only in heaven, in the company of the Risen Lord, His Mother, the angels and the saints. This thought is hardly acceptable today unless "heaven" takes on a much wider meaning. For if God is going to make for these glorified sons and daughters a "new heaven and a new earth," He obviously expects them to use them.

And this "new heaven and new earth" will not be just planet earth and its telluric atmosphere, but the entire cosmos with all its galactic systems so transformed by God as to fit the final condition of his glorified sons and daughters. For at the end of the world this entire universe will be emancipated from death and will share the glory of the children of God. The entire universe, according to A. Winklhofer, will become "directly accessible to man's new sense in its entire being, in all its relationships, in all its intelligible content." It will reflect the countenance of the Trinity and particularly the countenance of the Son, the model and archetype from the beginning of all things in heaven and earth. The fire of God, the splendor of

His glory, will blaze over the creation, making it utterly transparent to the sight of man (loc. cit.).

What will happen to planet earth? Will it and its atmosphere continue to exist? Will it still have mountains and valleys
and plains, fields and meadows, rivers and lakes and seas and
oceans? Breathtaking dawns and glorious sunsets and moonbeams
dancing on its waters at night? Its whispering and roaring winds,
its springtime rains and its winter snows? Will it continue to
have plants and animals, forests, gardens, flowers, fruit-trees,
birds and fish and animals of all kinds? Some theologians seem
to say No. Glorified sons and daughters of God will have no
need of all this. They will be intent on higher things. They
will find their joys in a scale of beings higher than all material
creatures. Plants and animals were needed by pilgrim man. But
glorious man has no need for them. So why should they be
there? Let the dead past bury its dead.

But most likely they are wrong. For planet earth was the
dwelling place of the Incarnate Son of God, of the Word made
flesh, of the Redeemer of mankind and of the world. He was
born at Bethlehem, He lived at Nazareth, He walked the roads
of Palestine, loved its hills and valleys, its flowers and trees,
the birds of the air, the fish of the rivers and seas, the sheep
that browsed on the hillsides. Will He permit all this to be
just a memory? Will He not want it to go on throughout
eternity but transformed so as to befit glorified men? Will
He not want it to be the same and yet different, just as His
risen body is the same and yet different? If plants and animals
shared in man's fall, will He not want them to share in man's
redemption and glory? If plants and animals were meant to be
man's companions and joy in the past, why not in the future?
What would planet earth be without them? Will they be corruptible as they are now? Or will they be incorruptible? They
will be whichever He thinks best for us.

What will *glorified cosmic sons and daughters of God* be
in their "new heavens and new earth," in their transfigured
cosmos? They will be the same persons they were in their pilgrim

EVERLASTING LIFE AFTER DEATH

and interim state and yet different. With the same minds and wills and souls they had in these states, and yet different. For now they have *glorified* souls and glorified bodies. But still bodies that are still somehow 'material bodies,' somehow bodies of flesh and blood and bones (Lk 28:34-43). So that they will be able to see and to hear and to taste and to touch and to feel, to walk and run and dance and talk and sing. They will not be subject to time and space limits in the way they were as pilgrims. Neither will they be angels. They will be human beings, but human beings with glorified souls and glorified bodies.

They will have what we have called "paranormal" powers. They will have telepathic powers by which they will be able to communicate thoughts and desires and feelings to one another at a distance, independently of channels of sense and notwithstanding intervening material obstacles. They will have clairvoyant powers by which they will be able to perceive objects and scenes and forms that are distant in space and time and not accessible to their organs of sense. They will have precognitive powers by which they can have advance knowledge of future occurrences that are proximate or remote in time and space. They will have retrocognitive powers by which they can know past objects and achievements that were very remote in time and space. They will have psycho-kinetic powers by which they can affect and move and most likely transform matter even at a distance by the simple concentration and application of their mental and volitive powers. They will have projective powers by which although they are bodily in one place they can project 'themselves' to other and even very distant places and see and hear things and persons over there. And very likely they will have still other powers, paranormal powers, perhaps paranormal linguistic powers, perhaps other paranormal communicatory powers, of which we are not yet aware.

Their glorified bodies will have qualities that they did not have in their pilgrim state. They will be impassible and immortal, no longer susceptible to suffering, sickness, death, to pain or hunger or thirst or weariness or exhaustion. They will be resplendent, beautiful and radiant with the glory light of their souls irradiating their bodies. They will be subtile, perfectly docile to the Spirit and able to compenetrate other bodies and matter at will. They will be agile, able to move easily from place to place, perhaps from planet to planet and from one part of the cosmos to another—with the speed of thought. And so the wide reaches of the cosmos will be quite accessible to them.

What will these glorified human beings be able to do in their transfigured universe, on their transfigured earth? The simplest answer seems to be: whatever they wish. For according to an old theological dictum heaven will mean the satisfaction of every rational desire. And their transfigured cosmos will obviously be an 'extension of heaven,' wide open to whatever use the glorified men will wish to put it. It will be theirs to use and develop into an ever better and better universe. There will be no conflicts, no enmities, no hatred, no wars, no property bounds, no segregation, no discrimination. There will be abundant space and abundant opportunity for everyone to do whatever he wishes and wherever he wishes. Charity will no longer be a "law" imposed on men: it will be part of the very essence of glorified men. Their beatific vision will make it impossible for them to be uncharitable, envious, jealous, avaricious, unjust.

Will these glorified men be able to grow in perfection and make progress of various kinds? In our study of heaven we noted that an older theology often spoke of a static heaven of eternal rest and immobility and immutability, modelled on its concept of the immobility and immutability of God. In this view the blessed would be immutably and eternally happy and perfect. They could not grow in perfection, they could not grow in happiness, they could not make further progress in knowing, loving, doing, achieving. Perhaps these older theologians did not quite mean this or mean it in just this way, but they often left this impression. As mobility, mutability, imperfection characterized pilgrim men, so immobility, immutability, perfection would characterize glorified men eternally.

But a more recent theology is moving in the direction of a more "dynamic heaven," a heaven that admits growth and progress in perfection throughout eternity. Is such a theological view compatible with the essential teaching of Sacred Scripture and of the Church? It seems to many of us that it is. If it makes a basic distinction that was part of traditional theology. A distinction between *essential* beatitude and *accidental* beatitude or between *essential* perfection and *accidental* perfection, or between the happiness and perfection of the beatific vision and the human perfection of other aspects of glorified men. Thus there would still be immobility (on the more strictly divine level of the beatific vision) and mobility on the more human level. There would still be immutability on one level, but also mutability on another level. There would still be immutable perfection on one level, and increase of perfection on other levels. There would still be the unchanging duration of the beatific vision on one level, but change and succession on other levels. There would still be "eternity" on the "divine" level, "temporality" on other levels. There would be no end to their beatific vision, no change in it, no succession, no growth in perfection: it would always remain an eternal, timeless act of vision, love, joy, union, possession, that would completely fill each man's cup of perfectibility and happiness on this "divine" level. But men would still be men, albeit with glorified souls and glorified bodies. They would still have human minds and human wills and on this level they could grow in knowledge and love and achievement, they could make progress and increase in perfection. Surely a God of ever-creative love would want this. Surely an ever-building God would want to go on building His glorified children into ever richer sons of men. If God by His gift of the beatific vision grants glorified men a share in His divine contemplative and amative life, would He not also grant them a share in His creative, His building life, so that they could go on through all eternity as co-creators with Him of an ever better world in which they could endlessly grow in perfection, in achievement, in happiness on the "glorified human" level?

What kind of progress will men be able to make in their glorified state? Some theologians say they will be able to make *moral* progress. This may be correct, depending on their understanding of moral progress. But moral progress cannot mean progress toward greater sinlessness, for there will be no sin in glorified man. Nor can moral progress mean increase in "grace," in "merit," in "degree of glory," unless they are prepared to abandon the traditional doctrine that a man's "grace" and "merit' in death are the measure of his "glory" after death, a doctrine that has a very solid foundation. Nor can moral progress mean an increase in their essential love of God, for this is proportioned to their degree of grace, merit, glory. But moral growth can mean, it seems, an increase in one's knowledge and appreciation of God's ongoing creative love and its effects, for this need not involve an increase in one's degree of grace, merit and glory. And moral growth can mean an increase and expansion of one's love of neighbor, so that this love goes on extending itself to more and more persons in more and more ways throughout eternity, for this too need not involve an increase in one's degree of grace, merit and glory. Other meanings of moral growth need to be very carefully pondered.

Where would this moral growth take place? In the heaven of God? Or in the transfigured universe that is an extension of this heaven? Probably in both. But mostly in the transfigured universe. For God will make this transfigured universe precisely for glorified men, to give them endless opportunities for growth and progress throughout eternity. In it they will be able to 'see' God's ongoing creative love at work and 'see' its effects, and grow in their appreciation of His ongoing creative love. In it they will be able to see other glorified men doing thousands of things, manifesting their love of God and of neighbors in a thousand ways, and thus be able to expand their love of neighbor more and more.

What other kinds of progress might glorified men make in their transfigured universe? They could use their minds to grow in knowledge—both speculative and practical. They could learn more, grow more in any area of knowledge that interested them. In Science. In Art. In Philosophy. In Theology. In Languages. In Music. In Astronomy. In Cosmology. In Anthropology. In Sculpture. In History. In Geography. In Literature. In Engineering. In Sociology. And so on and on.

They could have Halls of Science, of Art, of Literature, Mathematics, where all man's achievements of the past would be on record, where they could study these, absorb them, and be drawn to expand them further and further in innumerable directions. They could have Halls of Music where they could see and study all the great achievements men have made in composition, in instrumentation, in orchestration, in singing . . . and be drawn to expand these, one in this way, another in that way. They could have Halls of Psychology where they could see how far man has gone in his study of the psychology of man and where they can go further and further in this study. They could have Halls of Parapsychology where they could see what powers men had and have in this area, to what extent man used them in the past, and how they can further use and expand these powers in endless ways. They could have Halls of Physics, where they can see how far man has gone in his study of matter and energy and nuclear fusion and fission and where he can go further and further. They could have Halls of Cosmology where they can see what man has learned about the cosmos, its origin and development, its laws and its powers and its limits, and where man can deepen his knowledge and utilization and control of this incredibly great universe. They could have Halls of Philosophy where they can see what the great philosophers of the past have done in this area and be drawn to develop a higher, deeper, wider philosophy that can encompass more and more of the transfigured universe of men and things. They can have Halls of Travel, of Interplanetary Travel, of Interstellar Travel, Intergalactic Travel, where they can see what progress man has made in these areas and be drawn to make ever greater progress. And so on and on (cf. A. Borgia, op. cit.).

What else can glorified men do in their transfigured universe? They can visit or dwell in *New Jerusalem*. One of the most fascinating and tantalizing glimpses of the end of the world that the Apocalyptist offers us is his description of the New Jerusalem in the 21st and 22nd chapters of the Book of Revelation: "in the Spirit he carried me away to a great high mountain, and showed me the holy city Jerusalem, coming down out of heaven from God, prepared as a bride adorned for her husband; and I heard a great voice from the throne saying, 'Behold the dwelling of God is with men. He will dwell with them, and they shall be his people.'. . . It had a great high wall with twelve gates. . . . The city lies four-square, its length the same as its breadth; and he measured the city with his rod, twelve thousand stadia. . . . And I saw no temple in the city, for its temple is the Lord God the Almighty and the Lamb. And the city has no need of sun or moon to shine upon it, for the glory of God is its light, and its lamp is the Lamb. . . . Then he showed me the river of the water of life, bright as crystal, flowing from the throne of God and of the Lamb through the middle of the street of the city; also on either side of the river, the tree of life with its twelve kinds of fruit, yielding its fruit each month. . . . And night shall be no more; they need no light of lamp or sun, for the Lord God will be their light, and they shall reign for ever and ever. . . . Behold the dwelling of God is with men . . . he will wipe away every tear from their eyes, and death shall be no more, neither shall there be mourning nor crying, nor pain anymore, for the former things have passed away" (Rv 21:1ff.-22:1ff.).

Interpreters have been differently impressed by this picture of the "New Jerusalem." One is impressed by its light, one by its river of life, another by its tree of life with its twelve kinds of fruit, another by its coming down from heaven as a bride adorned for her husband, another by the throne of God and of the Lamb, another by its relation to man's initial Eden. One was impressed by its size and population. "Did you ever think about the size of the city?", he asked. "It's astounding . . . an area of 2,250,000 square miles. (And) in the matter of population . . . it's even more wonderful still. . . . On the basis of the number of people to the square mile in the city of London, the population of the City Foursquare comes out at a hundred thousand millions" (W. M. Smith, op. cit. 246-7).

Some commentators have identified this New Jerusalem with the millennial kingdom, others with heaven itself. But W. M. Smith has stated that since "it is seen coming down from heaven" it "is not to be identified with heaven," and "since it belongs to the state of perfect renovation and eternity," it is not to be identified with the millennium. Rather it is a part of "a new heaven and new earth" (ibid. 240ff.).

There is glorious imagery and symbolism here. But it is impossible to determine just what reality underlies this imagery. But we can speculate, and in our speculation we can ponder its possible connection with Old Jerusalem. "Old Jerusalem" has a central position in Luke and Acts: it is the point toward which Jesus moves throughout the Gospel. It becomes the focus from which the preaching of the Gospel goes out to the entire world (Lk 24:27; Ac 1:8). And then it "is transformed into the messianic symbol, the heavenly Jerusalem which is the end of the pilgrimage of the Christian (Heb 12:22) and the throne of the Lamb (Rv 14:1)" (J. L. McKenzie, op. cit. 431). And at the end of the world "the new Jerusalem comes down out of heaven!"

Comes down where? To the site of "Old Jerusalem." Why not? Old Jerusalem was the city over which the Redeemer wept. In it was the Temple that Jesus visited as a child of 12 and where He so often taught in His public life. If the "New Jerusalem" has more than symbolic reality, why should it not have it in the "Holy Land"? Why should it not throughout eternity be where "Old Jerusalem" was, where our Redeemer taught, suffered, died that we might live a life of glory and happiness throughout the endless reaches of eternity? Should not the 'new creation,' the transfigured cosmos, have a religious center, where God will be with His people in a very special and eternal way, where there will be no man-made temple but a temple that "is the Lord God the Almighty and the Lamb" (Rv 21:22)? What better site could there be for this eternal cosmic religious center than Old Jerusalem?

Three heavens we have thus envisioned for those who love God at the end of the world, or, if you prefer, one heaven with two extensions. There is the heaven of God where God's supreme glory and presence will be manifest. There is the heaven of the transfigured universe, the "new heavens and the new earth," where God will be specially present to the glorified men because wherever they go in this universe it will no longer be opaque to the presence of God but transparent to the glory and radiance of God so that the countenance of the triune God will shine everywhere. There is the heaven of the New Jerusalem, the center of religion and worship for the entire material cosmos, where there will be no man-made temple but a temple that "is the Lord God the Almighty and the Lamb" and where they can enjoy the "Temple-Presence and Glory of God" for all eternity.

We have said a great deal about the final state of the blessed, of those who have died "in Christ" and in the love of God, of those who have made in death their final fundamental eternal option for God and for Christ. We must still say a few words about the others, if there are such at the end of the world, and it seems that there will be. About those who loved themselves more than God, who made a final, fundamental, irrevocable decision against God and Christ, who chose eternal separation from God rather than eternal communion with God, and so condemned themselves to hell. What must we say about the final state of these?

A dogmatic Creed and a General Council declared that at the Second Coming of Christ the wicked arise with their own bodies and go into everlasting fire, to receive perpetual punishment. In our study of hell we noted that hell was much more the creation of unrepentant souls than of God. It does not issue from an arbitrary decision of God but is the logical working out of a man's own will to sin, of his own final and definitive rejection of God, of the everlasting opposition to God in which a man fixes himself in death. Such a man damns himself. We noted, too, that the essence of hell and damnation is the sinner's eternal separation from God, his eternal deprivation of the beatific vision, while the pain of sense today is regularly viewed not as a pain of "fire" in some literal sense of the word but rather a pain of conflict and hostility from a hostile universe.

Where will these damned human beings be? Throughout eternity they will be in hell. They will be somewhere, not nowhere. They will be some place where they are alive, conscious, think, will, suffer and are punished by separation from God and by conflict with a hostile world. They are not in the heaven of God, they are not in the heaven of the blessed. They are somewhere in the universe.

Are they in the transfigured universe? They must be, for there is no other "place" for them to be. But obviously they are not in the transfigured universe where the blessed are nor in the way in which the blessed are in the transfigured universe. For to the blessed the transfigured universe is a place of unending joy and happiness. It will not be that to the damned. To the blessed the transfigured universe will reflect the countenance of the Trinity and particularly the countenance of the Son, and the splendor of God's glory will blaze over it. It will not do that to the damned. They have chosen definitively to separate themselves from God and so they will be separated from the radiance of His glory also. And for them the universe will not be a place of joy and beauty and happiness. It will not be a friendly place. It will somehow be hostile to them, for in being out of harmony with God, they will be out of harmony with the universe that He transfigured for those who love Him and are united to Him. Where are they? They are in the universe, but in some mysterious dimension of it. They are in the universe but, according to A. Winklhofer, they are in "a place set apart, 'a prison' (Rv 20:7), bounded not by walls but by the incapability of the damned to apprehend other parts of the cosmos." And so "the whole vast creation may well be, for the damned it torments, far smaller and more restricted than it is for the blessed" (op. cit. 96).

The damned will be the same persons they were in their pilgrim and interim states and yet different. With the same minds and wills and souls they had in these states and yet different. For now they are embodied in "risen" bodies. Bodies that are in some sense material bodies and bodies of flesh and blood and bones, but yet very different from their pilgrim bodies. The damned will be able to see and hear and taste and touch and feel, to walk and run and talk. They will not be subject to time and space limits as they were as pilgrims. They will be men and women, human beings, but human beings with 'risen' bodies. They will have not only 'normal' psychic powers but also 'paranormal' psychic powers, for these seem to pertain to human nature as such. But most likely the separation of the damned from God and their disharmony with the transfigured universe will entail great limitations on the use of these paranormal powers. For the damned the universe will not be a transfigured universe, a thing of beauty and joy forever. Rather it will be alien and hostile. They will not see the Trinity shining through it for they have rejected God. For them the universe will be opaque to God, not transparent.

The risen bodies of the damned will not have the four qualities that are granted to the blessed. For these qualities derive from the indwelling Spirit and the wicked are not indwelt by the Spirit. So their bodies will not have the impassibility, the splendour, the subtility, the agility that the blessed will enjoy throughout all eternity. The wicked will not be immune to pain and suffering. But they will be immortal and incorruptible for these qualities pertain to the final state. And if their immortality and incorruptibility involve a non-necessity of eating, drinking, sleeping, they will not need to eat, drink, sleep, even though they have material bodies of flesh and blood which are fitted to their final state. Their risen bodies will not be glorious nor things of beauty. And it seems likely that the damned will have a very limited ability to move from place to place, a very limited access to the wide expanse of the universe. In our view they will be very lonely creatures, sharing the loneliness of Satan, the Great Prince of Loneliness. Just what they will be in their own view, in their own minds, we do not know. We can only wonder and wish they had chosen God.

And so our study of Everlasting Life After Death has come to an end, on a wishful note, with a wish that everyone will choose God in his pilgrim life. So that everyone will have everlasting life after death with God and with the entire family of God in the heaven of God, in the new heavens and the new earth, in the New Jerusalem. Many will not agree with our views of life after death. That is their right and privilege. But if our study draws them and others to a greater interest in and appreciation of life after death, we will be glad.

Notes for Chapter 13

1. The Phenomenon of Man, (English trans., 1964), p. 275.
2. W. M. Smith, The Biblical Doctrine of Heaven, (Chicago, Moody Press, 1968), p. 85.
3. C. J. Peifer, New Testament Reading Guide on Corinthians, (Collegeville, Liturgical Press), p. 56.

BIBLIOGRAPHY

Abbott, W. M., *The Documents of Vatican II*, New York, America Press, 1966.

Abbedananda, S. *Reincarnation*, Calcutta, 1951.

Addison, J. T., *Life Beyond Death in the Beliefs of Mankind*, New York, Houghton Mifflin Co., 1932. *1942*

Ahern, B. M., "The Concept of Union with Christ After Death In Early Christian Thought," Proceedings of the 16th Annual Convention of The Catholic Theological Society of America, June 19-22, 1961. "The Epistles to the Galatians and to the Romans," *New Testament Reading Guide*, Collegeville, The Liturgical Press, 1960.

Alberigo, J. et al., *Conciliorum Oecumenicorum Decreta, ed. altera.* Friburgi, Herder, 1962.

Aldwinckle, R., *Death In The Secular City*, Grand Rapids, W. B. Eerdmans Pub. Co., 1974.

Aquinas, Thomas, St., *Summa Theologica*, Pars Prima, 76.

Arendzen, J. P., *Purgatory and Heaven*, New York, Sheed & Ward, 1960.

Audet, L., "What. is the Risen 'Spiritual Body'?", *Theology Digest*, Spring, 1973.

Baillie, J., *And the Life Everlasting*, London, Oxford Univ. Press, 1934.

Barbanelle, M., *Spiritualism Today*, London, Jenkins, 1969.

Barr, J., *Old and New in Interpretation*, London, SCM Press, 1966.

Barth, K., *Church Dogmatics, III*, Edinburgh, T. & T. Clark, 1956.

Bartmann, B., *Purgatory*, London, Burns Oates & Washbourne, LTD, 1936.

Bastian, R. J., "Purgatory," *New Catholic Encyclopedia, XI*, 1966.

Baum, G., "Eschatology," *Chicago Studies*, v. 12, n. 3, Fall, 1973.

Becque, M. and L., *Life After Death*, New York, Hawthorne Books, 1960.

Beer, P. J., "Trent's Temporal Punishment," *Theological Studies*, Sept. 1974.·

Bender, H., "Parapsychology," *Sacramentum Mundi*, 5, 153ff.

Benoit, P., "Resurrection At the End of Time or Immediately After Death," *Immortality and Resurrection, New Concilium*, New York, Herder & Herder, 1970.

Benoit, P. and Murphy, R., *Immortality and Resurrection*, Billingshurst, Herder and Herder, 1970.

Berkouwer, G. D., *The Return of Christ*, Grand Rapids, W. B. Eerdmans, 1972.

Bernstein, M., *The Search for Bridey Murphy*, New York, Doubleday, Inc.

Berry, A., *The Next Ten Thousand Years, A Vision of Man's Future in the Universe*, New York, Sat. Rev. Press, E. P. Dutton & Co., Inc., 1974.

Berry, T., *Religions of India*, Milwaukee, Bruce Pub. Co., 1971.

Bobik, J., "Human Soul, Philosophical Analysis," *New Catholic Encyclopedia*, XIII.

Boettner, L., *The Millennium*, Philadelphia, The Presbyt. & Reformed Pub. Co., 1958.

Borgia, A., *Life In the World Unseen*, London, 1958.

Boros, L., "Death: A Theological Reflection," *The Mystery of Suffering and Death*, New York, Alba House, 1973.

————. *Living In Hope*, Garden City, Doubleday & Co., Image Book, 1973.

————. *The Mystery of Death*, New York, Herder and Herder, 1965.

————. *We Are Future*, Garden City, Doubleday, 1973.

Boyer, C., *Cursus Philosophiae*, II, Paris, Desclee de Brouwer, 1936.

Brady, I. C., "Immortality of Human Soul," *New Catholic Encyclopedia*, XIII.

Brandon, S .G. F., *The Judgment of the Dead*, London, Weidenfeld & Nicolson, 1967.

Broglie, V. de., *De Fine Ultimo*, Paris, Beauchesne et Ses Fils, 1948.

Brown, R. E., "How Much Did Jesus Know?", *Theology Digest*, Spring, 169, 44ff.

Buis, H., *The Doctrine of Eternal Punishment*, Philadelphia, The Presbyterian and Reformed Pub. Co., 1957.

Bulst, W., "Resurrection," *Sacramentum Mundi*, 5, 1969.

Bultmann, R., *History and Eschatology*, Edinburgh, 1957.

————. *Theology of the New Testament*, London, SCM Press, 1952.

Calvin, J., *Instit. chret.*, III, 21, Opera t. IV, p. 454, 374.

Campbell, R. J., *The Life of the World to Come*, London, Longmans, Green & Co., 1948.

Catechism, A New, New York, Herder and Herder, 1967.

Catherine of Genoa, St., *Treatise on Purgatory*, London, Sheed and Ward, 1946.

Catholic Commentary on Holy Scripture, Toronto, New York, Edinburgh, Thomas Nelson & Sons, 1953. The revised edition was not at hand when this book was in preparation.

Cayre, F., *Manual of Patrology*, Tournai, Desclee & Co., 1936.

Cerminara, G., *The World Within*, New York, W. Sloane Associates, 1957.

Ceroke, C. P., "Parousia in the Bible," *New Catholic Encyclopedia*, X.

Chardin, T. de., *The Phenomenon of Man*, London, Collins, 1959.

Charles, R. H., *Eschatology: Hebrew, Jewish and Christian Eschatology*, London, Adam and Charles Black, 1913.

Chicago Studies, v. 12, n. 3, Fall, 1973, Mundelein, Civitas Dei Foundation.

Clarkson, J. F. et al., *The Church Teaches*, St. Louis, B. Herder Book Co., 1955.

Congar, Y. M-J. "Salvation and the Non-Catholic," Blackfriars, July-August, 1957.

Cooney, C., *Understanding the New Theology*, Milwaukee, Bruce, 1969.

Cooper, I. S., *Reincarnation The Hope of the World*, Wheaton, 1951.

Cornelis, H., "Afterlife," *Sacramentum Mundi*, 1, 13ff.

————. "The Resurrection of the Body and Primitive Conceptions of The Last Things," *The Resurrection of the Body*. Notre Dame, Fides, 1964.

Corbishley, T., "The Resurrection of the Body," *A Catholic Commentary on Holy Scripture,* 720.

Cullmann, O., *Immortality of the Soul or Resurrection of the Dead*, New York, The Macmillan Co., 1958.

Darlap, A., "Demons," *Sacramentum Mundi* 2, 71.

Davis, C., "The Resurrection of the Body," *Theology Digest*, Spring, 1960.

Denzinger-Schönmetzer., *Enchiridion Symbolorum, Definitionum et Declarationum*, Freiburg i. B. Herder, 1963, (DS= its abbreviation).

Dictionary of Biblical Theology, New York, Desclee Co., 1967.

Dictionary of the Bible, Milwaukee, Bruce, 1965.

Ducasse, C. J., *The Belief in a Life After Death*, Springfield, Charles C. Thomas, Publisher, 1961.

Duffy, S. J., "Parousia in Theology," *New Catholic Encyclopedia*, 1966, 1037ff.

Durand, A., *Word of Salvation*, Milwaukee, Bruce, 1957.

Dyer, G., "Creation and Fall," *Chicago Studies*, Fall, 1973, 272ff.

————. "Limbo, A Theological Evaluation," *Theological Studies*, 19, (1958).

————. *Limbo, Unsettled Question*, New York, Sheed and Ward, 1964.

Evert, H., "Die Krise des Osterglaubens," Hochland, 60, (1968).

Evans, C. F., *Resurrection and the New Testament*, London, SCM Press, 1970.

Fannon, P., "And After Death," *Catholic Mind*, April, 1974.

————. *The Changing Face of Theology*, Milwaukee, Bruce, 1968.

Flanagan, N. M., *The Acts of the Apostles, New Testament Reading Guide*, 1960.

Fleming, D. L., "Pilgrim of the Future," *America*, April 12, 1975.

Flew, A., *Body, Mind and Death*, London, Collier-Macmillan, 1964.

Fodor, N., *Encyclopedia of Psychic Science*, New York, University Books.

Ford, A., *Unknown But Known*, New York, Harper & Row, 1968.

Fransen, P., "The Doctrine of Purgatory," *Eastern Churches Quarterly*, 13, (1959), 106.

Fritsch, A., "The Second Coming," *Theology of Earth*.

Fuller, J. G., "Is He Charlatan or Miracle Worker?," *Reader's Digest*, Sept. 1975.

Glasson, F. G., *The Second Advent*, London, 1963.

Glasson, T. F., *Greek Influence in Jewish Eschatology*, London, 1961.

Gleason, R., *The World to Come*, New York, Sheed and Ward, 1958.

Glorieux, P., "Endurcissement final et graces dernieres," *Nouvelle Revue Theologique*, LIX, 1932. "Moment of Death," *Theology Digest*, 10, 1962, 94-5.

Gorman, M., "Human Soul, Modern & Contemporary Thought," *New Catholic Encyclopedia*, XIII.

Guardini, R., *The Last Things*, New York, Pantheon, 1954.

Guibert, J. de, *The Theology of the Spiritual Life*, New York, Sheed & Ward, 1953.

Gumple, P., "Limbo," *Sacramentum Mundi*, 3, 317ff.

Guy, H. A., *The New Testament Doctrine of the 'Last Things'*, London, Oxford University Press, 1948.

Hansel, C. E. M., *ESP: A Scientific Evaluation*, New York, Charles Scribner's Sons, 1966.

Harlow, S. R., *A Life After Death*, New York, Doubleday & Co., 1961.

Head, J. and Cranston, S. L., *Reincarnation: An East-West Anthology*, Wheaton, 1968.

Hervé, J. M., *Manuale Theologiae Dogmaticae*, I, III, IV, Paris, Apud Berche & Pagis, 1957.

Holzer, H., *Life After Death*, London, Sidgwick & Jackson, 1971.

Hus, A., *Greek and Roman Religion*, New York, Hawthorne Books, 1962.

Jacobson, N. O., M.D., *Life Without Death*, New York, Dell Pub. Co., 1974.

Jerome Biblical Commentary, Englewood Cliffs, Prentice-Hall, Inc., 1968 (=JBC).

Jones, A., "Discourse on 'The End,' " *A Catholic Commentary on Holy Scriptures*, 893.

Kaufman, G., *Systematic Theology, A Historical Perspective*, New York, Scribner, 1968.

Kelly, J. N. D., *Early Christian Doctrines*, London, Adam and Charles Black, 1965.

Klinger, E., "Soul," *Sacramentum Mundi* 6, 139ff.
Kübler-Ross, E., "Life After Death," *Our Sunday Visitor*, Sept. 14, 1975. *The Chicago Tribune*, Oct. 16, 1975.
Küng, H., "The Origin of resurrection belief," *Theology Digest*, Summer, 1975.
Lamont, C., *The Illusions of Immortality*, New York, The Philosophical Library, 1950.
Langley, N., *Edgar Cayce on Reincarnation*, New York, Castle Books, 1967.
Laurenge, M., "Esquisse d'une etude sur le sort des enfants morts sans bapteme," *L'Annee Theologique, Augustiniennse*, XIII, 1952.
Leonard, W., *A Catholic Commentary on Holy Scripture*, "Judgment," 1164.
Leon-Dufour, X., *Dictionary of Biblical Theology*, New York, Desclee Co., 1967.
Lepp, I., *Death and its Mysteries*, New York, Macmillan Co., 1968.
Lewis, H. D., *The Elusive Mind*, London, George Allen & Unwin LTD, 1969.
Liljencrants, J., *Spiritism and Religion*, New York, Devin-Adair Co., 1918.
Litvag, I., *Singer In The Shadows*, New York, The Macmillan Co., 1972.
Long, H. S., "Transmigration," *New Catholic Encyclopedia*, XIV.
Lubac, H. De, *The Religion of Teilhard de Chardin*, London, Collins, 1967.
Lussier, E., "Universal Conflagration of the Parousia," *Catholic Biblical Quarterly*, 12, (1950), 243ff.
MacMaster, R. K., "Theosophy," *New Catholic Encyclopedia*, XIV.
Marcus, J. T., *Heaven, Hell and History: A Survey*, New York, Macmillan, 1967.
Martin, J. P., *The Last Judgment in Protestant Theology from Orthodoxy to Ritschl*, Edinburgh, Oliver & Boyd, 1963.
Marty, M. E., and Peerman, D. G., *New Theology*, no. 5, New York, Macmillan, 1971.
McKenzie, J. L., *Dictionary of the Bible*, Milwaukee, Bruce, 1965.

Michel, A., *The Last Things*, St. Louis, B. Herder Book Co., 1929.

Michl, J. "Hell," *Sacramentum Verbi*, I, New York, Herder and Herder.

Moltmann, J., *The Future of Hope*, Herder and Herder, 1970.

—————. *Theology of Hope*, London, SCM Press, 1965.

Monroe, R. A., *Journeys Out of the Body*, Garden City, 1971.

Montefiore, H., *Can Man Survive?*, London, Collins Fontana, 1969.

Murphy, G., *Challenge of Psychical Research*, New York, Harper & Bros., 1961.

Myers, F. W. H., *Human Personality and Its Survival of Bodily Death*, London, 1903.

New Catholic Encyclopedia, New York, McGraw Hill Book Co., 1966.

New Testament Reading Guide, Collegeville, The Liturgical Press, 1960.

Nicoll, W. R., *Reunion in Eternity*, New York, 1919.

Nolan, B. M., "The Meaning of the Parousia Today," *Theology Digest*, v. 18, n. 2, 1970.

Nowell, R., *What a Modern Catholic Believes about Death*, Chicago, The Thomas More Press, 1972.

Oakley, F., "Historical Problems with papal infallibility," *Theology Digest*, Summer, 1972.

Ogden, S., *The Reality of God and Other Essays*, London, SCM Press, 1967.

Orchard, Dom B., "The Character of the Antichrist," *A Catholic Commentary on Holy Scripture*, 1141.

Ostrander, S., and Schroeder, L., *Psychic Discoveries Behind the Iron Curtain*, Englewood Cliffs, Prentice Hall, Bantam Books, Inc., 1971.

Pannenberg, W., *Jesus: God and Man*, London, SCM Press, 1968.

Panneton, G., *Heaven or Hell*, Westminster, The Newman Press, 1965.

Pax, E., "Parousia," *Sacramentum Verbi*, New York, Herder and Herder.

Peifer, C. J., *First and Second Corinthians, New Testament Reading Guide*.

Pendergast, R., *America*, March 30, 1974.

Penelhum, T., *Survival and Disembodied Existence*, New York, Humanities Press, 1970.

Phillips, D. L., *Death and Immortality*, New York, St. Martin's Press, 1970.

Pieper, J., *Death and Immortality*, New York, Herder and Herder, 1969.

Pittenger, N., *God in Process*, London, SCM Press, 1967.

Plastaras, J., "Heaven in the Bible," *New Catholic Encyclopedia*, VI, 968ff.

Pousset, E., "La Resurrection," *Nouvelle Rev. Theologique*, 91, 10, 1969.

Puharich, A., *Beyond Telepathy*, Garden City, Doubleday, Anchor Press, 1973.

Rahner, K., "Hell," *Sacramentum Mundi*, 3, 7-9.

————. "Last Things," *Sacramentum Mundi*, 3, 274-276.

————. *On The Theology of Death*, New York, Herder and Herder, 1961.

————. "Parousia, Theological Doctrine," *Sacramentum Mundi*, 4, 345ff.

————. "Person," *Sacramentum Mundi*, 4, 415-419.

————. "Remarks on the Theology of Indulgences," *Theological Investigations*, IV, 347ff.

————. "Resurrection, Theology," *Sacramentum Mundi*, 5, 331ff.

————. "The Hermeneutics of Eschatological Assertions," *Theological Investigations*, IV, 1966.

————. "The Life of the Dead," *Theological Investigations*, IV, 347ff.

Ratzinger, J., *Introduction to Christianity*, New York, Herder and Herder, 1970.

Rayan, S., "The Eschatological Hope of Hinduism," *The Problem of Echatology*, *Concilium*, v. 41, New York, Herder and Herder.

Rees, W., *1 and 2 Corinthians, A Catholic Commentary on Holy Scripture*.

Rhine, J. B., *New World of the Mind*, New York, William Sloane Associates, 1953.

Rhine, J. B. & Brier, R., *Parapsychology Today*, New York, The Citadel Press, 1968.

Robinson, H. W., *The Christian Doctrine of Man*, Edinburgh, T. & T. Clark, 1911.
Robinson, J. A. T., *In the End, God*, London, Collins Fontana, 1968.
Rogers, L. W., *Elementary Theosophy*, Wheaton, 1956.
Royce, J. E., "Soul, Human, Immortality," *New Catholic Encyclopedia*, XIII.
Sacramentum Mundi, New York, Herder and Herder, 1969.
Santos, A., "Infancia y Bautismo," *Estudios Ecclesiasticos*, XXXI, 1957.
Schep, J. A., *The Nature of the Resurrection Body*, Grand Rapids, W. B. Eerdmans Pub. Co., 1964.
Schleiermacher, F., *The Christian Faith*, Edinburgh, T. & T. Clark, 1928.
Schlette, H. R., *Kirche Unterwegs*, Freiburg, Olten, 1966.
Schlier, H., "The End of Time," *Theology Digest*, Fall, 1969.
Schmid, J., "Resurrection of the Body, Biblical," *Sacramentum Mundi*, 5.
Schmitt, J., "Resurrection," *Sacramentum Mundi*, 5.
Schnackenburg, R., *God's Rule and Kingdom*, New York, Herder and Herder.
Shaw, J. M., *Christian Doctrine*, New York, Philosophical Library, 1954.
————. *Life After Death*, Toronto, The Ryerson Press, 1945.
Shea, J., *What a Modern Catholic Believes about Heaven and Hell*, Chicago, Thomas More Press, 1972.
Simon, U., *Heaven in the Christian Tradition*, New York, Harper & Bros., 1958.
————. *The End Is Not Yet: A Study of Christian Eschatology*, Digswell Place, England, 1964.
Siwek, P., *Experimental Psychology*, New York, Jos. Wagner, Inc., 1958.
Smith, A. J., *Immortality*, New York, Prentice-Hall, Inc., 1954.
Smith, C. R., *The Bible Doctrine of the Hereafter*, London, Epworth Press, 1958.
Smith, J. J., "Resurrection Faith Today," *Theological Studies*, Sept. 1969.
Smith, W. M., *The Biblical Doctrine of Heaven*, Chicago, Moody Press, 1968.

Splett, J., "Body" & "Immortality," *Sacramentum Mundi*, I, 233ff., 3, 108ff.

Spragget, A., *The Unexplained*, New York, New American Library, Inc., 1967.

Stanley, D. M., *The Gospel of St. Matthew, New Testament Reading Guide*.

Stevenson, I., M.D., *Twenty Cases Suggestive of Reincarnation*, New York, American Society for Psychical Research, 1966.

Strawson, W., *Jesus and the Future Life*, London, Epworth Press, 1970.

Theissen, A., "The Longing of Irrational Nature," *A Catholic Commentary on Holy Scripture*, 1065.

Theology Digest, St. Louis, Mo.

Theological Investigations, Baltimore, Helicon Press, 1963ff.

Theological Studies, Baltimore, Theological Studies, Inc.

Thielicke, H., *Death and Life*, Philadelphia, Fortress Press, 1970.

Thompson, C. H., *Theology of the Kerygma*, Englewood Cliffs, Prentice-Hall, 1962.

Tierney, B., "Historical Problems with papal infallibility," *Theology Digest*, Summer, 1972.

Tremel, Y. B., "Man Between Death and Resurrection," *Theology Digest*, 5, (1957).

Troisfontaines, R., *I Do Not Die*, New York, Desclee Co., 1963.

Trooster, S., *Evolution and the Doctrine of Original Sin*, Glen Rock, Newman, 1968.

Vawter, B., *1 and 2 Thessalonians, New Testament Reading Guide*.

Walker, D. P., *The Decline of Hell*, Chicago, Univ. of Chicago Press, 1964.

Ward, W. B., *After Death, What?*, Richmond, John Knox Press, 1967.

Weisengoff, J. P., "Death and Immortality in the Book of Wisdom," *Catholic Biblical Quarterly*, 3, 1941, 104ff.

Whately, R., *A Future State*, Philadelphia, 1857.

Wiesinger, A., *Occult Phenomena: In the Light of Theology*, Westminster, The Newman Press, 1957.

Wilkins, V., *From Limbo to Heaven*, New York, Sheed and Ward, 1961.

Williams, M. E., "End of the World," *New Catholic Encyclopedia*, V.

Winklhofer, A., *The Coming of His Kingdom*, New York, Herder and Herder, 1963.

Woods, R., *The Occult Revolution*, New York, Herder and Herder, 1968.

Wright, J. H., "Judgment," *The New Catholic Encyclopedia*, VIII, 30ff.